When Dr. Alan Streett writes a boo[...] [...] the way he reveals biblical truth in such a practical and applicable manner. In a day when world events lead believers to focus so much on Christ's second coming that they forget to appropriate all the first coming provides, *Heaven on Earth* is a welcome addition. Streett reminds us that we do not have to wait for our Lord's millennial reign to be blessed. Christ is ruling already from the Father's right hand. This reminder should move every believer to get this book…read it and reap!

O.S. Hawkins
president and CEO, GuideStone Financial Resources

Good biblical scholarship always needs clearheaded and careful writers who can help the church grasp the core essentials of the gospel of the kingdom. Alan Streett has written a rare book, combining good scholarship with a compelling and clear style that allows him to speak powerfully to a wide audience. There is gold in this hill—search and find. I am quite sure your efforts will be rewarded.

John H. Armstrong
president, ACT 3 Network

Alan Streett has written a very readable theology of the kingdom of God for everyman (to borrow from N.T. Wright's series). But it is more than a theology, for it is the grand narrative of God's relationship to the world and humanity told in a fascinating manner without any mincing of words when it comes to bringing out its practical implications. It is at a length and in a style that all can read (with notes for scholars), so I can only hope that as many as can get their hands on it will indeed "take up and read." At the end of the work one wants to stand and sing the "Hallelujah Chorus."

Peter Davids
visiting professor of Christianity
Houston Baptist University

Since Jesus spoke so often of the kingdom, shouldn't we? I heartily commend Alan's contribution to this important conversation about one of the Bible's often overlooked themes, the kingdom of God. Read it and be challenged.

Ed Stetzer
president, LifeWay Research
author of *Subversive Kingdom*

Alan Streett has come upon a discovery that is revolutionizing his understanding of the Bible, the gospel, and the Christian life. You feel his exhilaration in every chapter as he grapples deeply with Jesus' core message—not simply about how to get your soul to heaven when you die, but how God's dreams for planet earth can come true, beginning with you, and catching all of us up in God's transforming mission. This is a courageous work that will stimulate needed conversations about the Bible and the gospel, especially in Baptist and Evangelical circles. Highly recommended.

Brian D. McLaren
author and speaker

HEAVEN
on
EARTH

R. ALAN STREETT

HARVEST HOUSE PUBLISHERS
EUGENE, OREGON

Cover by Dugan Design Group, Bloomington, Minnesota

Cover photo © Peter Zelei / Vetta / Getty Images

Backcover author photo by Domus Aurea—Photography by Renée

HEAVEN ON EARTH

Copyright © 2013 by R. Alan Streett
Published by Harvest House Publishers
Eugene, Oregon 97402
www.harvesthousepublishers.com

Library of Congress Cataloging-in-Publication Data

Streett, R. Alan (Richard Alan)
  Heaven on earth / R. Alan Streett.
      p. cm.
ISBN 978-0-7369-4914-9 (pbk.)
ISBN 978-0-7369-4915-6 (eBook)

1. Kingdom of God. I. Title.
  BT94.S88 2013
  231.7'2--dc23
                          2012041345

Printed in the United States of America

13 14 15 16 17 18 19 20 21 / LB-JH / 10 9 8 7 6 5 4 3 2 1

To the members of
The Presidents' Class
Dallas, Texas

Acknowledgments

A few of the people who have helped me write this book deserve special mention.

Bob Hawkins, president of Harvest House Publishers, and I are kindred spirits. We like to talk about our sons, discuss theology, think outside the box, and drink coffee. When Bob has business in Dallas, we sometimes get together at Starbucks. On one such occasion, after an animated conversation on the present reign of Christ, Bob invited me to put my thoughts into print. Thanks, Bob, for your encouragement and for the opportunity to share my ideas with a wider audience.

I also wish to extend my appreciation to my editor, Gene Skinner, who saw the book to completion once it left my hands. Gene and his team did a great job getting the manuscript ready for publication.

A special thanks to the students of Criswell College (Dallas, Texas) who have signed up for my classes on the kingdom of God over the years. As I presented my ideas and theories in the classroom and received their feedback, my understanding of the kingdom developed more fully.

Finally, and most of all, I wish to recognize the extraordinary effort of my wife, Lynn Fenby Streett, who proofread, edited, and offered suggestions on how I could communicate my ideas more clearly to a lay audience. She kept this book from being a dry academic treatise.

Contents

1

Discovering the Kingdom

Repent, for the kingdom of heaven is at hand!
MATTHEW 3:2

The concept of the kingdom of God is elusive. From the beginning of Christianity, the greatest minds have been baffled by it. Theologians have equated it variously with heaven, the church, Israel, Christendom, democracy, socialism, communism, an ethical ideal, an inward spiritual experience, Christ's millennial reign, and the eternal state. No wonder there is so much confusion!

In more recent times, New Testament scholars have taken a renewed interest in the kingdom of God. Their inquiries have advanced our knowledge of the subject, but we have many more avenues to explore and questions to ask and answer.

For more than a decade, learning about the kingdom of God has been my all-consuming passion. In the course of my study, I have spent an inordinate amount of time reading the major scholarly and popular books and journal articles about it. I have enjoyed countless discussions and debates about the kingdom, and I've written about it, lectured on it, and taught courses about it. In my opinion, nothing is of more importance than correctly understanding the kingdom. It is the overarching theme of the entire Bible, a thread that runs throughout it, and the great umbrella under which all other subjects are subsumed.

My goal is to introduce you to the kingdom of God in the hope that you too will become captivated by it. If I succeed, you will never be the same. Are you ready to embark on the adventure of a lifetime?

The journey begins in a garden (Genesis 1–2) and ends in paradise (Revelation 21–22). Along the way, we will meet many interesting characters and discover great treasures. Be forewarned, however—the trip is not for the faint of heart. We will encounter various obstacles, but the road signs are plentiful, and our maps are reliable. If we take our time to navigate carefully, we can reach our destination. If we succeed, our knowledge of the kingdom of God will be crisp and clear. Best of all, we will discover how to tap into the kingdom's riches and enjoy them here and now.

Why Understanding the Kingdom Is Important

The gospel is essential to Christianity. The apostle Paul called it "the power of God to salvation" (Romans 1:16). But what is the gospel? We know the word means "good news," but good news about what? And what about the phrase "to salvation"—what does it connote? Does it refer to going to heaven? Escaping hell? Having our sins forgiven? Gaining eternal life? Being declared righteous by faith? Inviting Jesus into our hearts?

These familiar and popular answers do not adequately define either "good news" or "salvation." They are peripheral at best. At its core, the gospel is about the kingdom of God. The Gospel of Mark opens, "The beginning of the gospel of Jesus Christ." A few verses later, it is described as "the gospel of the *kingdom of God*" (verse 14). There are not two gospels. There is only one. The good news of Jesus Christ and the good news of the kingdom are the same. Unfortunately, Jesus is often preached without reference to the kingdom. But apart from the kingdom, there is no gospel, and there is no salvation.

"Wait a second," you might protest. "When I got saved, I never heard anything about the kingdom of God. I simply asked Jesus to be my Savior!"

I understand your concern. I had a similar experience, but like so many others, I was misguided. During my senior year at the University of Baltimore, a psychology professor shared his testimony with our class, concluding with the words, "You're a sinner. You need to be saved. Pray and invite Jesus into your heart."

That night as my head lay on the pillow, I heeded the advice. I said, "Jesus, forgive me of my sins and come into my heart." I don't know what I expected—heavenly choirs, shafts of moonbeams, great floods of emotion and tears—but whatever it was, it did not happen. The next night, I repeated the process. During the next three years, I prayed more than a thousand times but with no tangible results. I eventually entered seminary, hoping to find answers to my spiritual unrest. Despite the new environment, I continued following my destructive patterns of life without any ability to change.

I was not angry with God, but I was disappointed and disillusioned. Why had God not answered my prayers? Why did salvation seem to elude me?

I know I am not alone. Maybe you have been there and done that, and you haven't noticed a significant change either. Possibly you took the four steps found in many salvation booklets, traced the Roman Road to salvation, or repeated the sinner's prayer but without assurance of salvation or evidence of spiritual growth. Untold thousands have prayed the prayer, walked the aisle, or responded in some way to a gospel invitation without effectual results. Life goes on as before.

In my case, salvation didn't take hold because my professor, although well intentioned, had a defective grasp of the gospel. He presented a truncated gospel that had little resemblance to the good news that Jesus and the apostles preached. Therefore it lacked the power to save. No wonder I was confused!

A faulty understanding of the gospel is the first pothole that stands in the way of our quest for the kingdom. To overcome this obstacle, let's turn to the Scriptures for a correct definition of the gospel.

A New Paradigm

As a professor of evangelism, I must provide my students with a clear and precise definition of the gospel. Unless we comprehend the true nature of the gospel, how can we expect to communicate it effectively?

If the goal of the gospel is simply to get people into heaven, as many believe, what is its relevance to daily life? Most people who hear the gospel will not die for years, so they will have little incentive to respond immediately. If the gospel has little or no relevance for the here and now, the logic for evangelism is weakened. It would be like me trying to sell you a front-row seat to a New York Yankees game for a date yet to be determined by the ball club sometime between now and 2080! You would not be likely to purchase a ticket. It may be a good deal, but where's the urgency? Waiting would seem to be more prudent.

Professor William Abraham explains that there must be a logic for evangelism.[1] The gospel must have relevance for the present and not only for the distant future. According to New Testament accounts, the imminent arrival of God's kingdom (and not the promise of going to heaven) was the thrust of Jesus's gospel sermons. It provided the rationale for evangelism. The words "gospel" and "kingdom" are so interconnected that the New Testament writers use the umbrella terms "kingdom of God" or "kingdom of heaven" 20 times to describe the good news of salvation.

When the message that Jesus and the apostles preached is compared to most contemporary gospel messages, the difference is like night and day. In many ways, the messages are complete opposites of each other. One emphasizes a future salvation, but the other invites people to enter the kingdom of God now. According to one, you have to wait to experience the blessings of the kingdom, but according to the other, the benefits of the kingdom are available for you to enjoy this moment while you are alive and well on planet earth.

A discovery of the kingdom of God and its relevance for today will revolutionize your life! Join me for a short jaunt through the New Testament. Get ready to be surprised by what lies ahead—the kingdom of God will leap off each page. By the end of this chapter, you are likely to be asking yourself, "How have I missed this all these years?"

John the Baptist and the Kingdom

According to the four Gospel writers, Jesus's public ministry began with the appearance of John the Baptist, who called the Jews to turn away from their self-centered ways and toward the God of their forefathers. John's message was simple and direct: "Repent, for the kingdom of heaven is at hand!" (Matthew 3:2).

I have long been able to quote this verse from memory, but I had not pondered its meaning until just a few years ago. Have you ever considered what this verse meant to John's first-century audience?

First, John called on his audience to do something—"Repent!" They were to obey this command then and there without delay. The message was relevant for them.

Second, John gave them a reason for this action—"for the kingdom of heaven is at hand." He did not say, "The kingdom is 2000 years away," or "The kingdom is being delayed indefinitely." Yet many popular Bible teachers and commentaries hold that the kingdom is entirely in the future. If that were the case, John missed the mark by a country mile, and his message had no application for his audience.

What do you think? Was John correct about the kingdom, or was he misguided? I will stick with the first option. John called the people on the banks of the Jordan to repent in order to prepare for the kingdom's soon arrival.

Third, John saw no need to explain the phrase "kingdom of heaven" because Palestinian Jews of his day were already familiar with the term. They had long anticipated and eagerly awaited the appearance of a deliverer sent by God to defeat Israel's enemies and usher in a golden age of universal peace, over which God would rule. Although the Jews had countless theories about how this would occur, they all understood the general scheme. In whatever manner it happened, John's hearers needed to ready themselves lest they miss out on the kingdom.

Fourth, the words "at hand" mean the kingdom was near in time and in space. Both ideas are important. Many Jews believed in the imminent arrival of the kingdom (time) and that its advent would occur in their homeland (space). Even our English word "kingdom" conveys these two concepts. A kingdom consists of a king and a domain. The people of God understood John to mean that God's rule was "at hand" in both senses.

Jesus and the Kingdom

When John the Baptist was arrested and killed, "Jesus came to Galilee, preaching the gospel of the kingdom of God, and saying, 'The time is fulfilled, and the kingdom of God is at hand'" (Mark 1:14-15). Immediately we notice that John and Jesus proclaimed the same message—the good news of the kingdom. But Jesus added a new twist by announcing, "The time is fulfilled." The kingdom was no longer merely close by. Time was up. This intensified the kingdom message.

We might compare John's and Jesus's messages of the kingdom to an announcement of a pregnancy. A woman desires a child but seems unable to get pregnant. One day, she receives word that her life is about to change—she is expecting! This news brings great joy and expectation. Still, she must wait nine months for the baby's arrival. In the meantime, she prepares herself in anticipation of the blessed event.

Then one day, she suddenly feels a twinge of pain. Labor begins— the time is *at hand.* As everyone waits with baited breath, the hour arrives and the baby is born—the time is *fulfilled.* A new day has dawned for everyone. The married couple become parents, and their parents become grandparents.

In like manner, the Old Testament prophets spoke of the arrival of the kingdom. Israel was pregnant with expectation. As the countdown begins, the years and months turn into weeks and days. Measured expectation is transformed into anxious anticipation. With the onset of labor, John the Baptist declares, "The kingdom of heaven is at hand." His message foreshadows Jesus's announcement—"The time is fulfilled." The kingdom is birthed in the person and ministry of Jesus.

In Luke's version, Jesus makes this announcement in a synagogue in Capernaum, near his hometown of Nazareth. After reading from the scroll of Isaiah, which speaks of the promised kingdom, Jesus concludes by saying, "Today this Scripture is fulfilled in your hearing" (Luke 4:21). This verse offers more clues as to the manner of the kingdom's arrival.

We first notice the words, "This Scripture is fulfilled." Jesus is referring to the inspired words of Isaiah's prophecy about the kingdom coming to earth.

Second, we are given the specific time of its fulfillment—today, not tomorrow or next year or in two millennia!

Finally, we are given a geographic indicator of the kingdom's start—"in your hearing." Right there in the midst of the synagogue crowd.

When we put the pieces together, we see that the kingdom arrived with Jesus as he launched his public ministry. The kingdom of God was no longer a future hope, but a present reality. As missionary strategist Lesslie Newbigin so insightfully remarked, "It now had a name and a face—the name and face of the man from Nazareth."[2] The waiting period was over, and God was in a climactic way initiating his work of salvation on earth.[3]

Luke tells us that Jesus went on to perform many miracles (which pointed to the inbreaking of the kingdom). But when the crowds requested that he remain among them, he declined by saying, "I must preach the *kingdom of God* to the other cities also, because for this purpose I have been sent" (Luke 4:40-43). Jesus had a singular message. He was a herald of the kingdom. This is evidenced by Luke's further comment that Jesus went throughout all of Galilee, "preaching and bringing the glad tidings of the *kingdom of God*" (Luke 8:1).

Jesus advised the apostles not to follow their faithless neighbors who worried about life's daily needs, but instead to "seek the kingdom of God, and all these things shall be added to you…for it is your Father's good pleasure to give you the kingdom" (Luke 12:22-32).

Jesus preached the gospel of the kingdom far and wide to every kind of person, including Nicodemus (John 3:3-5), a rich young ruler (Luke 18:24-25), a wise scribe (Mark 12:34), and a convicted thief (Luke 23:42-43). He used parables (Matthew 13), beatitudes (Matthew 5), and object lessons (Mark 14:25) to teach about the kingdom.

The First Disciples and the Kingdom

As an itinerant teacher, Jesus traveled with a group of disciples who assisted in his mission. He often sent them out on preaching assignments of their own, instructing them to "preach the *kingdom of God*"

(Luke 9:2). The narrative reveals that they followed orders: "So they departed and went through the towns, preaching the *gospel* and healing everywhere" (verse 6). Luke equates preaching the kingdom with preaching the gospel. The kingdom is the essence of the gospel message.

In Mark's account of the same event, we learn that the apostles also "preached that people should repent" (Mark 6:12), which is the same response Jesus expected from his hearers. The disciples called on their listeners to reorient their lives toward God and his kingdom. The good news of the kingdom was relevant, germane, and applicable to their first-century audience.

Jesus invited some who responded positively to the gospel to join his preaching band, and he encouraged others to minister in their own communities. To an unnamed disciple in the latter category, Jesus commands, "You go and preach the kingdom of God" (Luke 9:57-60). This shows that Jesus had only one message he wished to get across.

As his fame spread and his ministry grew, Jesus sent out 70 more followers to cities, instructing them, "Heal the sick there, and say to them, 'The kingdom of God has come near to you.'" He also told them that if their message was rejected they should say to the townspeople, "The very dust of your city which clings to us we wipe off against you. Nevertheless know this, that the kingdom of God has come near you" (Luke 10:1,9-11). Judgment was to be pronounced because the people scorned the good news of the kingdom's arrival. They refused to repent, so they will perish.

On another occasion, when Jesus's accusers charge him with using black arts and magic to perform exorcisms, he counters, "If I cast out demons with the finger of God, surely the kingdom of God has come upon you" (Luke 11:20).

Do you see a pattern emerging? Every preacher mentioned in the four Gospels focused on the kingdom. It is the one constant, the central theme of the gospel message.

Prior to the ministry of John the Baptist, the kingdom existed only as a hope. John turned it into a living expectation. This can be seen in Jesus's words to the Pharisees: "The law and the prophets were until John. Since that time the kingdom of God has been preached" (Luke 16:16).

The coming of John the Baptist brought a paradigm shift. The Old Testament law and prophets provided God's people with a moral guide. When the nation continually failed to abide by these ethical standards, God announced the coming of a future deliverer who would usher in the reign of God and invite penitents to come under his rule. The Baptist was the first to preach the nearness of the kingdom and to identify Jesus as this promised messianic ruler. But John was not the last. Others picked up the torch.

The Early Church and the Kingdom

Our journey continues as we step out of the four Gospels and into the book of Acts. In this exciting book, which spans the period between AD 30 and AD 64, Luke describes the early believers, apostles and lay people alike, spreading the kingdom message to the ends of the Roman Empire. He mentions that after Jesus was crucified and resurrected but before he ascended to heaven, he spent 40 days with his apostles, "speaking of the things pertaining to the kingdom of God" (Acts 1:3). Stop and think about that for a moment. Jesus could have spoken about anything, but he chose to speak about one thing only—the kingdom. Thus, he ended his earthly ministry the same way he began it—declaring the gospel of the kingdom!

Have you ever wondered what Jesus actually said about the kingdom of God during those six weeks? To find out, you can read about his postresurrection appearances. Check out the Great Commission, for instance, and you will find Jesus saying, "All authority has been given to Me in heaven and on earth. Go therefore and make disciples of all the nations, baptizing them in the name of the Father and of the Son and of the Holy Spirit, teaching them to observe all things that I have commanded you; and lo, I am with you always, even to the end of the age" (Matthew 28:18-20). This is one example of Jesus "speaking of the things pertaining to the kingdom of God." How so?

First, Jesus claims to possess authority over the entire creation. As Abraham Kuyper (1837–1920), theologian and prime minister of the Netherlands, famously said, "There is not one square inch of the entire creation about which Jesus does not cry out: 'This is mine!'" Second,

his reach extends beyond heaven to earth. This means Jesus has authority over Caesar and client kings, so he is the King over all other kings.
Those claiming to be kings are obligated to bow before him. Third,
authority is given to him. He rules on God's behalf.

Fourth, he calls upon his followers to make disciples of all the
nations. The significance of this command must not be understated.
For the early Christians, obedience to the Great Commission involved
nothing less than going to nations that Rome had conquered and
claimed as its own and calling on the people to switch their allegiance
from Caesar to Christ. Such an effort was considered treasonous. The
kingdoms of Christ and Caesar were on a collision course. The new
disciples were required to pledge their loyalty to a foreign King in a
public baptism in the name of a God who was foreign to Rome. This
could mean the death penalty, especially if the new converts were
Roman citizens or served in a governmental capacity.

So this is what it means for Jesus to speak of "the things pertaining to the kingdom of God" (Acts 1:3). When you read other postresurrection accounts, ask yourself what else Jesus had to say about the
kingdom.

As Jesus stood on the mount before his ascension to heaven, he
promised his followers that he would one day return to earth. But
until then they should be his witnesses (Acts 1:8). The book of Acts is
the account of their heroic efforts to complete that commission. We
should not be surprised, therefore, to find them preaching about the
kingdom. From start to finish, the book of Acts chronicles their evangelistic exploits. For instance, we find Peter on the Day of Pentecost
declaring that God raised up and exalted Jesus "to sit on his throne," a
kingly position of authority (2:30-32). We later follow Philip, the lay
evangelist, as he travels to Samaria and preaches "the things concerning
the kingdom of God and the name of Jesus Christ" (8:12).

At Thessalonica, the apostle Paul and his team are charged with
sedition for teaching and acting "contrary to the decrees of Caesar, saying there is another king—Jesus" (17:7). Two chapters later Paul moves
into Asia Minor and speaks boldly in the synagogues "concerning the
things of the kingdom of God" (Acts 19:8). In his farewell address to

the Ephesian elders, he reminds them that he had spent three full years in their city testifying "to the gospel of the grace of God," which he describes as "preaching the kingdom of God" (Acts 20:24-25).

From there Paul goes to Jerusalem, where he is arrested for preaching the gospel. He is eventually taken to Rome, where he is placed under house arrest, awaiting trial. Although fettered to a soldier, he uses his visitation privileges as opportunities to proclaim the gospel. "Many came to him at his lodging, to whom he explained and solemnly testified of the kingdom of God" (Acts 28:23). A few verses later, the book of Acts closes with these words of summary: "Then Paul dwelt two whole years in his own rented house, and received all who came to him, preaching the kingdom of God and teaching the things which concern the Lord Jesus Christ with all confidence, no one forbidding him" (Acts 28:30-31). Thus, the book of Acts closes in the same way it opens. The kingdom of God serves as bookends.

In Paul's magnum opus on the nature of salvation, he asks the believers in Rome several questions:

> How then shall they call on Him in whom they have not believed? And how shall they believe in Him of whom they have not heard? And how shall they hear without a preacher? And how shall they preach unless they are sent? As it is written: "How beautiful are the feet of those who preach the gospel of peace, who bring glad tidings of good things!" (Romans 10:14-15).

The quote about preaching the gospel and bringing glad tidings comes from the book of Isaiah, where the content of the gospel is revealed as "Your God reigns!" (Isaiah 52:7). For the apostle Paul, *the gospel is about the reign of God* and particularly about his reign over earth through Jesus Christ.

Look at the Record

Without a doubt, the good news of the kingdom is the central theme of all first-century evangelistic preaching. The list of preachers includes John the Baptist, Jesus, the 12 apostles, an unnamed disciple, 70 disciples, Peter, Philip, and Paul.

When we consider the amount of time the founding church leaders spent teaching and preaching about the kingdom, shouldn't we expect the same from our evangelists and pastors? Where is the gospel of the kingdom being preached today? I am not referring to the future reign of Christ, as important as that is, but the kingdom of God as a present reality. If Jesus and the apostles walked the earth today, would they even recognize the gospel message heralded from most pulpits?

Gospel Counterfeits

Product counterfeiting is illegal. Dishonest manufacturers and distributors cheat people out of tens of billions of dollars a year. Every day unsuspecting customers buy electronics, athletic clothes, watches, and a myriad of other items that carry the brand or logo of a reputable company, only to discover later the disappointing merchandise was a knockoff. A counterfeit Rolex might look like the real McCoy at first glance, but it doesn't work like a Rolex. I know!

A group of my students gave me one when I left my job as a professor to become a pastor. They said they wanted to demonstrate how much they loved and appreciated me. When I opened the box to see a beautiful gold Rolex, I was overwhelmed. As I began to thank them profusely, they nodded, smiled sheepishly, and said they hoped I would remember them whenever I checked the time of day. The fake Rolex stopped working in less than 24 hours! P.T. Barnum would have said I was the victim of humbug.

But counterfeiting the gospel is not a laughing matter. It is so serious, in fact, that the apostle Paul excoriates the Galatians for "turning away...to a different gospel." He then pronounces judgment on those perverting the gospel: "If we, or an angel from heaven, preach any other gospel to you than what we have preached to you, let him be accursed" (Galatians 1:6-8). We might expect a cult to endorse a false gospel, but we should not expect our churches and trusted parachurch organizations to distort the gospel.

Christians rarely set out to twist the gospel. But they often preach a gospel that is shaped more by tradition and culture than by the Scriptures.

I must add a caveat. This book is not intended to be a diatribe against any Christian group or minister. I have nothing but the highest regard for all who answer God's call to ministry and sacrificially devote their time and energy to the cause of Christ. Rather, I am demonstrating that the gospel is about the kingdom as defined by Jesus. Because it is good news in the fullest sense of the term, it has relevance for us here and now on earth. Salvation, as we shall see in the next few chapters, is less about heaven and more about wholeness of life. From start to finish the good news is about how God's people of every generation can enjoy kingdom benefits and blessing while they are still alive, not only after they die and go to heaven.

If Jesus came to bring abundant life (John 10:10), why don't we experience it? I hope you will know the answer by the end of the book. More importantly, you will know how to apply the principles of the kingdom to your daily life and tap into a wealth of divine resources.

2

In the Beginning Was the Kingdom

Fill the earth and subdue it; and have dominion…over
every living thing that moves upon the earth.

GENESIS 1:28

We first learn of the kingdom of God in Genesis, the book of beginnings. There we discover the foundation for all theology, including kingdom theology.

The foundation is the most important part of any building. Without a firm and level foundation, a building will be off kilter and weak, and it won't stand the test of time. I live in north Texas, where the soil is known as black gumbo. It shifts, expands, and contracts depending on ground moisture. For years, builders constructed houses on highly reliable pier-and-beam foundations that were raised above ground level. In more recent times, they have switched to less expensive slab foundations that lay directly on the ground, often with disastrous results. When the earth shifts under a house, it has the same effect as a localized miniature earthquake. It may not be felt, but it causes damage. Walls crack, doors stick, and the integrity of the building is called into question. My home is built on a slab foundation, so I must water the foundation regularly to maintain soil consistency.

In similar fashion, many popular Bible teachers lack a solid foundation for their beliefs about the kingdom of God. They build their

kingdom theology on popular theories, faulty assumptions, preconceived ideas, selected New Testament texts, or the traditions of their
denominations or theological circles.

We will try to avoid these pitfalls. Genesis opens with the words,
"In the beginning...God created the heavens and the earth." Recognizing God as the Creator is the basis or starting point for understanding
kingdom theology. Craig Bartholomew and Michael Goheen observe,
"By causing the creation to come into existence by his word of power,
God establishes it as his own vast kingdom. He thus establishes himself as the great King over all creation, without limits of any kind, and
worthy to receive all glory, honor, and power in the worship of what
he has created."[1]

As Creator of the universe, God is its rightful ruler. Genesis speaks
occasionally about the heavenly bodies, but its main focus is planet
earth.

Human Engineering

In Genesis, God creates the first human out of the earth. Unlike
most other things, Adam is not created *ex nihilo*, or out of nothing.
Rather, God forms him out of something else—the dust of the ground.
Adam's newly created body lay dormant in an inanimate state until
God "breathed into his nostrils the breath of life" and Adam "became
a living being" (Genesis 2:7). God imparts something of himself to
man!

From this account we learn that Adam has both an earthly and a
godly component. One might say he possesses a human and divine
nature. Adam is created out of the earth, but he is infused with the
breath of God. God then creates a woman from Adam's side (2:21-
23). Together they live in an earthly garden paradise. The first man
and woman are not created as angels to live in heaven, nor are they
given wings to travel between heaven and earth. Rather, they are created entirely *out of* the earth and *for* the earth. This is their sole sphere
of existence.

The Breath of God

Breath is essential to life. In fact, it is the animating force of life. Adam was a motionless and lifeless lump of clay until God breathed into him the "breath of life." Everyone reading this book took a first breath (inspiration). We'll all take a last breath (expiration). When we do, we die.

The Hebrew (Old Testament) word *ru'ach* can variously be translated breath, spirit, and wind. The meaning is determined by the context in which it is used, causing confusion at times. The Greek (New Testament) word *pneuma* can be translated in similar fashion. Both Matthew and Luke speak of Jesus giving up his spirit and dying (Matthew 27:50; Luke 23:46).

The Bible also speaks of breath in relation to the kingdom of God. Just as God breathed his breath into Adam's nostrils, he speaks through Ezekiel the prophet of a day when he will revive dead Israel by breathing life into it (Ezekiel 37:5). Jesus later breathes on his disciples, who are representative of Israel. Through this act, Israel is being restored to life (John 20:22).

The Exaltation of Man

In Genesis 1:27-29, we find an overview of man's creation. The more detailed account is in Genesis 2.

> Let Us make man in Our image, according to Our likeness; let them have dominion over the fish of the sea, over the birds of the air, and over the cattle, over all the earth and over every creeping thing that creeps on the earth. So God created man in His own image; in the image of God He created him; male and female he created them (Genesis 1:26-27 NKJV).

Three things stand out in this passage. First, humans are like God. Of all God's creatures, they alone are made in his image. Humans are God's highest form of creation.

Second, God gives them authority or dominion to rule over the earth. The text possibly holds a clue to the meaning of being created in God's image. "Image" and "dominion" are in proximity to each other in the text, so the image of God likely includes the capacity to rule. Having derived their authority from him, they will rule under God and for God, representing him to the human race as it grows numerically and expands geographically beyond the cradle of civilization. They will serve on God's behalf as his vice-regents on the earth. As such, they are stewards of God's assets and accountable to him for the way they govern.

Third, Adam and Eve are given equal responsibility to rule because both are made in God's image. The text gives no indication that God intended women to be subservient to men.

Eden as God's Temple

Genesis reveals that God is actively involved with his creation. He walks with Adam and Eve in the garden and communicates with them. Later in the Old Testament we will see that God takes up residence on earth in the tabernacle and then in the temple. In a real sense, then, the garden of Eden serves as God's first temple. Here he dwells with his people on earth.[2]

God blesses the first couple and calls on them to reproduce: "Be fruitful and multiply, and fill the earth and subdue it; and have dominion…over every living thing that moves upon the earth" (Genesis 1:28). As procreators, Adam and Eve become creators themselves. All subsequent human life will come directly or indirectly from their loins. Thus, creation is not a single event only, but an ongoing one; it includes a human as well as a divine dimension. Obviously, fulfilling the mandate to replenish the entire earth will require multiple generations and take them far beyond the garden. As God's vice-regents, Adam and Eve will govern a territory that will eventually spread throughout the earth.

That God assigns such awesome responsibility to this fledgling couple reveals that his kingdom plan involves trust and risk. This tells us something about God. The establishment of the kingdom of God on earth is a joint effort between the Creator and humankind. God is willing to risk success and failure so that humans might learn to rule responsibly.

Next, we read that God provides for the couple's physical needs. "See, I have given you every herb that yields seed which is on the face of all the earth, and every tree whose fruit yields seed; to you it shall be for food" (Genesis 1:29 NKJV). This food will sustain them in their mission.

Let's summarize what we have learned so far. God creates humans *out of* the earth, *for* the earth, to *fill* the earth, to *rule* over the earth, and to be *sustained* by the earth.

Where did we get the idea that we are meant for heaven? Or that salvation is an escape from earth? We certainly don't get it from Genesis, the foundational book for all theology.

A Serpentine Plot

Next, God issues a warning: "Of every tree of the garden you may freely eat; but of the tree of the knowledge of good and evil you shall not eat, for in the day that you eat of it you shall surely die" (Genesis 2:16-17 NKJV). God sets limitations on what is best for Adam and Eve. And Adam and Eve are not immortal beings. They need to eat or they will die.[3]

Shortly, after God pronounces that all he has made is good, a slithering creature leads a serpentine rebellion against God's kingdom plans.

> Did God say, "You shall not eat from any tree in the garden?"
> The woman said to the serpent, "We may eat of the fruit of
> the trees in the garden; but God said, 'You shall not eat of
> the fruit of the tree that is in the middle of the garden, nor
> shall you touch it, or you shall die.'" But the serpent said
> to the woman, "You will not die; for God knows that when
> you eat of it your eyes will be opened, and you will be like
> God, knowing good and evil" (Genesis 3:1-5).

This is no ordinary snake—at least not like any we have encountered. It has intelligence and communicates clearly with the couple. It claims that God is holding back something beneficial to Adam and Eve, "for God knows" something they don't. He has an ulterior motive. He doesn't want them to know what he knows. They now have to decide whom to trust—God or the serpent. They need to determine whether God has their best interests at heart when he forbids them to eat from the tree.[4]

Rather than obey the voice of their Creator, they ironically obey the voice of a seductive creature over which they have been given rule and dominion. In doing so, they relinquish their authority to him. He gets the upper hand. The apostle John will later identify the serpent as the dragon, Satan, the devil, and the deceiver who opposes God and his Christ (Revelation 12:7-9; 20:2).

By default, a kingdom emerges in the garden paradise that rivals God's own. From this time forward, another voice will challenge God's authority over people's lives. Humankind will become divided—some will comply with God's voice, and others will submit to the voice of the enemy. Two kingdoms exist simultaneously side by side—God's and Satan's—each one bidding for the allegiance of God's people.

Exile and Promise

For Adam and Eve, the consequences of heeding the serpent's voice are immediate. First, they become self-conscious and experience shame because of their nakedness. Second, they become fearful of God and hide from him (Genesis 3:7-10).

But before God addresses the man and woman, he speaks to the serpent: "I will put enmity between you and the woman, and between your seed and her Seed; He shall bruise your head, and you shall bruise His heel" (verse 15 NKJV). Two opposing categories of people will emerge—those designated as Eve's offspring, who will follow God's voice, and those identified as the serpent's offspring, who will obey the voice of their diabolical master. Interestingly, thousands of years later, Jesus will place people into these same two camps (John 8:44).

God then declares in cryptic form that one of the woman's seed will decisively defeat the satanic seed, although he will be injured in the process. This defeat will be the turning point in restoring God's kingdom to his people. Known as the *protoeuangelion*, this is the first promise that speaks of the demise of satanic forces on earth.

Adam and Eve's sin will have detrimental effects on birth, death, and everything in between. When Adam and Eve emerge from hiding, God says this to Eve:

> I will greatly increase your pangs in childbearing;
>   in pain you shall bring forth children,
> yet your desire shall be for your husband,
>   and he shall rule over you (Genesis 3:16).

Here we get the first hint that things will grow progressively more difficult for humankind in its attempt to subdue and take dominion over the earth. The mother of all future generations will suffer discomfort as she brings children into the world, and she will be subservient to her husband. God originally designated her to be coruler over the earth, but he now declares that her husband will rule over her. This is a major paradigm shift!

God then turns to Adam.

> Cursed is the ground because of you;
>   in toil you shall eat of it all the days of your life;
> thorns and thistles it shall bring forth for you;
>   and you shall eat the plants of the field (Genesis 3:17-18).

The command to subdue the earth is never rescinded, but Adam will have a more difficult time fulfilling his mission. He now must toil to harvest the earth's resources that will sustain his life. Additionally, God announces that Adam's days will be numbered. This is implied by the phrase "all the days of your life." God then adds this:

> By the sweat of your face
>   you shall eat bread
> *until you return to the ground,*
>   for out of it you were taken;
> you are dust,
>   and *to dust you shall return* (verse 19).

Adam is not only made *from* the earth and *for* the earth, but he will now return *to* the earth. From this picture we discover that death by sin refers to physical death. The breath of God that animates man's body will depart, and he will die. This is a fulfillment of God's original warning, "You will surely die."

Finally and most importantly, the first two humans are expelled from their garden paradise, which means they will no longer have access to the source of life.

> Then the LORD God said, "See, the man has become like one of us, knowing good and evil; and now, he might reach out his hand and take also from the tree of life, and eat, and live forever"—therefore the LORD God sent him forth from the garden of Eden, to till the ground from which he was taken. He drove out the man; and at the east of the garden of Eden he placed the cherubim, and a sword flaming and turning to guard the way to the tree of life (verses 22-24).

Despite their exile from the garden, Adam and Eve remain under orders to multiply and to replenish and rule over the earth. But their task will not be an easy one. The earth will no longer be a pristine and friendly environment. With no access to the tree of life, Adam and Eve will grow old and die and relinquish their rule to others. The pattern will be repeated for generations to come.

We know from the New Testament that at the end of the age, God will personally intervene to reestablish the earthly garden to its original condition. Paradise lost will become paradise restored! Until then, humans are under orders to rule an imperfect earth on behalf of God. We face many obstacles as we attempt to bring creation under the reign of the Creator, but God promises to guide us in our mission.

Life Outside the Garden

Cain and Abel follow in their parents' footsteps. Cain subdues the land (he's a farmer), and Abel takes dominion over the animals (he's a shepherd). Although they live east of Eden without access to the tree of life, God does not abandon them. Rather, he continues to speak with them. He desires to have a relationship with humans. The brothers can still respond to the Voice (Genesis 4). But they and all future generations after them will come to realize that God is not the only one speaking to them. Other voices now seek to influence them and move them away from serving God and fulfilling his mandate to rule the world under his auspices.

When Cain murders Abel in a jealous rage, God curses the ground so that it will not yield enough resources to sustain his life (Genesis 4:11-12). Cain departs from God's presence and builds a city, which he names Enoch (verses 16-17). There is little evidence from this point onward that Cain or his descendants ever again hear God's voice or seek to know him.

After Abel's untimely death, Adam and Eve have another son, Seth, who begins a godly progeny. As civilization grows and advances, two distinct lines spring from the one family. The first rules its affairs without divine assistance, but the other calls on the name of the Lord (Genesis 4:25-26). Humankind is thus divided between those who rebel against God's voice and those who obey.

The Great Deluge and a New Beginning

As the decades pass into centuries, chaos and ungodliness gain the upper hand until evil fills the world. God's kingdom plan for humans to rule as his vice-regents seems to be a dismal failure. God decides to take action.

> The Lord saw that the wickedness of humankind was great in the earth, and that every inclination of the thoughts of their hearts was only evil continually. And the Lord was sorry that he had made humankind on the earth, and it grieved him to his heart. So the Lord said, "I will blot out from the earth the human beings I have created—people together with animals and creeping things and birds of the air, for I am sorry that I have made them." But Noah found favor in the sight of the Lord (Genesis 6:5-8).

A destructive flood rids the earth of wickedness. In an act of compassion God spares Noah's family, the last from the godly line of Seth, along with a small remnant of animals. As he did with Adam, God commissions Noah, a "new Adam," made in God's image (Genesis 9:6), to "be fruitful and multiply, abound on the earth and multiply in it" (verse 7). Noah's family becomes the fountainhead of a new humanity, but they fail miserably in this role. Noah plants a vineyard, gets drunk, and lies unclothed in his tent. When he discovers that Ham, his youngest son, has gazed on his nakedness, he places a curse on Ham's offspring but blesses the other brothers (verses 25-27).

In a sense, history repeats itself. A division takes place within the ruling family, separating the brothers.

Instead of obeying God's mandate to multiply and spread across the face of the world, humans settle in one location. They build a city and a tall tower and determine to make a name for themselves, lest they be "scattered abroad upon the face of the whole earth" (Genesis 11:4). This action, which is exactly the opposite of what God wants, is humankind's prideful attempt to create its "own kingdom independently of God."[5] In the midst of the people's disobedience, God takes the initiative to scatter them throughout the earth, forcing them to abandon their construction plans. "Therefore it was called Babel, because there the LORD confused the language of all the earth; and from there the LORD scattered them abroad over the face of all the earth" (verse 9).

As kindred tongues geographically band together, they naturally conduct commerce, barter with their neighbors, protect themselves from internal and external dangers, settle boundary disputes, and so forth. Such interactions involve friendly cooperation at the start, but eventually the people need to form governmental structures. At first, perhaps they need only a sheriff or a judge. But in time, the population increases, and problems associated with numerical growth result. The people must enact laws, collect taxes, and develop infrastructures. Apart from the guiding voice of God, these societies take many forms, including democratic, communistic, socialistic, dictatorial, capitalistic, and communal.

The people also form religions around gods or elemental spirits (demons?). They believe these spirits speak to them through priests and enable them to survive in an intimidating and chaotic world. Eventually, hostilities arise, and nations fight wars, conquer lands, take prisoners, sign peace treaties, develop military budgets, ad infinitum. Internal strife takes place within national borders, including exploitation of the weak, corruption, riots, civil wars, and the like. Throughout history, the story remains constant; only the names and faces change.

The Calling of Abram

With the world in a state of rebellion against its rightful King, God's utopian plan for humankind seems to have failed once again. The mandate for humans to rule earth on God's behalf and according to his will has yet to be carried out successfully. Undaunted by these human failures, God chooses one solitary man, Abram, to do his bidding. To this descendant of Terah of the ancient line of godly Seth, now living in Ur of the Chaldeans, God communicates a command and a promise.

> Go from your country and your kindred and your father's house to the land that I will show you. I will make of you a great nation, and I will bless you, and make your name great, so that you will be a blessing. I will bless those who bless you, and the one who curses you I will curse; and in you all the families of the earth shall be blessed (Genesis 12:1-3).

God calls Abram to leave his homeland, describing his destination simply as "the land that I will show you." All Abram has to go on is a promise. By responding positively to God's voice, he begins a journey of faith, leaving behind allegiance to the gods of Ur. Abram will eventually see the land and purchase a cemetery plot, but he will never actually settle there. This will be left to his descendants.

The people of Babel had vowed, "Let us make a name for ourselves" (Genesis 11:4), but now God pledges that he will make Abram's name great. The fragmented and scattered nations live autonomous of God's rule, but God promises to make of Abram a great nation. His purpose for choosing Abram is that "all the families of the earth shall be blessed," that is, that they shall experience God's merciful love. Families make up nations. As goes the family, so goes the nation. In the end, those who side with Abram and his seed will prosper, and those who seek to harm them will be cursed.

God has not forgotten or abandoned his kingdom plan for the world. He will now use Abram to fulfill the divine mandate, which is essentially a political agenda. A great nation will emerge from Abram's family that will serve as an alternative society to the rebellious nations that operate according to self-will. In the midst of a world in chaos, they will reflect God's will and character. The blessings should lead other nations to seek similar blessings under the banner of God's benevolent reign.

Salvation, therefore, is much more than spiritual deliverance from personal sin. It includes rescue from political forces and structures that have aligned with Satan. Adam and Eve are liberated from a dangerous garden, Noah is saved from an evil world, and Abraham is delivered from an idolatrous nation. On the positive side, God enjoins them to multiply and form a new society that rules in accordance with his ethical guidelines.

God's Royal Contract with Abraham

In Genesis 15 and 17 God reestablishes his covenant with Abram and reiterates his promises, explaining them in greater detail. For instance, God gives the geographical dimensions of the promised land, which Abram's offspring will inherit.

> On that day the LORD made a covenant with Abram, saying, "To your descendants I give this land, from the river of Egypt to the great river, the river Euphrates, the land of the Kenites, the Kenizzites, the Kadmonites, the Hittites, the Perizzites, the Rephaim, the Amorites, the Canaanites, the Girgashites, and the Jebusites" (Genesis 15:18-21).

Two chapters later, God charges Abram, "Walk before me, and be blameless" (17:1). He then changes Abram's name to Abraham and adds, "I will make you exceedingly fruitful; and I will make nations of you, and kings shall come from you" (verses 5-6).

God's call of Abraham to be the father of multitudes constitutes a third creation story of sorts. Adam and Eve, Noah, and now Abraham were each given a fresh start to produce a new humanity. In a sense, they each become God's new creation.[6]

Genesis 17 also reveals that God has not given up on the idea of godly kings who rule in his name. They will come from Abraham's (and therefore Eve's) descendants. These "Abrahamic" kings, unlike the kings of the other countries, are to represent God and obey his voice. God goes on to explain that his covenant is not only with Abraham but also with his offspring "throughout their generations" (verse 7).

Next, God informs Abraham, "As for Sarai your wife, you shall not call her Sarai, but Sarah shall be her name. I will bless her, and moreover I will give you a son by her. I will bless her, and she shall give rise to nations; kings of peoples shall come from her" (Genesis 17:15-16).

This, then, is God's plan throughout human history—one that originated in the garden of Eden but got sidetracked—to have all nations, all kings, and all people living in covenant faithfulness to him. These goals will not be fulfilled immediately but will be reached progressively as history moves toward God's universal reign over earth through his human representatives.

3

The Kingdom in the Old Testament Era

*The scepter shall not depart from Judah, nor
the ruler's staff from between his feet.*

GENESIS 49:10

Abraham and Sarah indeed conceive in their old age and have the son of promise. From Isaac comes Jacob, whose name is changed to Israel. He, in turn, has 12 sons, who become heads of 12 tribes. God reconfirms with Isaac and Jacob the covenant he made with Abraham.

Joseph: From Pit to Prince

Joseph, one of Jacob's 12 sons, enrages his brothers by telling them of a dream in which they bow before him. In a jealous reaction, they bind him, throw him into a pit, and then sell him to slave traders, who in turn carry him off to Egypt. Over the years, through many twists and turns, Joseph rises to a position of authority, second only to Pharaoh. When famine strikes the entire Mesopotamian region, Egypt alone is spared because God in a dream forewarns Joseph to stockpile a seven-year supply of grain.

"All the world came to Joseph in Egypt to buy grain" (Genesis 41:57). Among those seeking help are his brothers, representing the family of Jacob. They are brought before Joseph, whom they fail to recognize. When he reveals his identity, they fear for their lives, bow before him, and ask for his mercy, thus fulfilling his prophetic dream. Joseph explains that their evil act of selling him as a slave years ago was used by God to save lives (Genesis 45:3-5; 50:20).

Joseph then moves his brothers and their families to Egypt and gives them safe haven. The Hebrew people are an industrious lot who find favor with the Egyptians. Despite being surrounded by false gods and pagan idolatry, they faithfully worship God, submit to his voice, and maintain their witness to the God of Abraham, Isaac, and Jacob before the Egyptian people.

As Genesis moves toward a conclusion, we encounter the aged Jacob (that is, Israel) at death's door (Genesis 48:1-2,10). Calling his sons to his side, he prophesies over each. This is what he announces to Judah:

> Judah, your brothers shall praise you;
>> your hand shall be on the neck of your enemies;
>> your father's sons shall bow down before you…
> The scepter shall not depart from Judah,
>> nor the ruler's staff from between his feet,
> until tribute comes to him ["until Shiloh comes" NKJV];
>> and the obedience of the peoples is his (Genesis 49:8,10).

With these words we gain further insight into how God's kingdom on earth will be established. God's designated or authorized ruler will come from the tribe of Judah alone. The rule will continue "until tribute [or Shiloh] comes," which New Testament scholars interpret to be a cryptic reference to the Messiah, God's final and ultimate King.

Jacob's inspired prophecy will not happen anytime soon. It lies in the distant future and will be revealed in God's time.

Just as God promised, his people increase exponentially. With the passing of generations, a new Pharaoh comes on the scene who fears that the Hebrews might soon outnumber his own people and seize the land, so he orders all Jews enslaved and their firstborn sons slaughtered (Exodus 1:8-11,15-16,22). This is a turning point in the story. A paradigm shift takes place when an antagonistic new Pharaoh succeeds a line of Pharaohs who have shown favor to the Jewish people.

Ironically, in the midst of the slaughter, Pharaoh's own daughter rescues and adopts one of the Hebrew boys. She names him Moses and, unbeknownst to her, chooses his biological mother to serve as his nursemaid and nanny. As Pharaoh's newly adopted grandson, Moses is given all the privileges of royalty, and by the age of 40 he reaches the penultimate position in the government.

After discovering his true ethnicity, Moses attempts to free some Hebrew slaves from the cruelty of a local Egyptian taskmaster but commits a murder in the process and must flee for his own life. For the next 40 years he resides in a foreign land, marries, and settles down to the life of a shepherd before having an encounter with Yahweh, who instructs him from a burning bush to go back to Egypt and lead the Jews out of Egyptian captivity. He reluctantly obeys the Voice.

The Exodus

When Moses confronts Pharaoh for the first time, the tyrant defiantly responds, "Who is the LORD, that I should heed him and let Israel go? I do not know the LORD, and I will not let Israel go" (Exodus 5:2). He soon discovers the answer to his own question. God sends ten plagues, proving himself to be far more powerful than Egypt's maniacal monarch or its gods. In the Exodus story, God's people escape from Egypt and are formed into an independent nation under God's rule. Israel will become God's kingdom.

To protect the Hebrews from the tenth plague and to prepare them for their liberation, God instructs each family to kill a lamb, smear its blood on the doorpost of their house, and prepare and eat a Passover meal. After passing over the Jewish homes where the blood is applied, the angel of death moves on to the unprotected Egyptian homes and takes the lives of all Egyptian firstborn, both humans and beasts. This horrid plague motivates Pharaoh to finally let God's people go free.

Thus, salvation is once again political. As the throngs of liberated slaves cross the Red Sea and reach a place of safety, they sing in unison the Song of Moses (Exodus 15:1-18), which concludes with the words, "The LORD will reign forever and ever." In singing this canticle by the sea, Israel acknowledges Yahweh to be the true King, whose dominion is everlasting and far superior to the world's most powerful Pharaoh.

The women join in "with tambourines and with dancing" as Miriam directs them, "Sing to the Lord, for he has triumphed gloriously; horse and rider he has thrown into the sea" (verses 20-21). The people sing jubilantly, and their dance and actions portray their new political, economic, and social position as free people.

The Birth of a Nation

The Exodus is the pivotal point in Israel's history, marking its birth as a free people. It paves the way for the Mosaic covenant, which forms the Hebrew people into a new society. At Mount Sinai God enters into a covenant with Israel and gives Moses this instruction:

> Thus you shall say to the house of Jacob, and tell the Israelites: You have seen what I did to the Egyptians, and how I bore you on eagles' wings and brought you to myself. Now therefore, if you obey my voice and keep my covenant, you shall be my treasured possession out of all the peoples. Indeed, the whole earth is mine, but you shall be for me a priestly kingdom and a holy nation. These are the words that you shall speak to the Israelites (Exodus 19:3-6).

The late Methodist theologian Georgia Harkness denotes, "The concept of the covenant between God and his chosen people…underlies [the] concept of kingdom."[1] When Israel enters the covenant, the people pledge their allegiance to God and his kingdom. Yahweh is the rightful ruler over the creation, but most nations refuse to acknowledge his sovereignty. Only God's people recognize God as their King. According to God's promise to Abraham (Genesis 18:18), his people will constitute a holy nation. Israel will serve as an alternative to the surrounding nations by conducting its affairs according to the divine principles of justice, servitude, and mercy. The blessings it will receive from living under the benevolent reign of Yahweh will be in sharp contrast to the nations living under the domination of tyrannical rulers, where exploitation and enslavement are the norm.

Israel will additionally serve as a priestly kingdom representing Yahweh to the surrounding nations, who will see what it is like to live under the reign of God and enjoy the blessings of his provision.

God's Provisions to Help Israel Keep Its Pledge

When Moses presents God's covenant requirements to the people, they respond, "Everything that the LORD has spoken we will do" (Exodus 19:8). In answering the call to be God's special people, Israel affirms that holiness will be its trademark (Leviticus 26:1-13; also see Leviticus 11:44). If Israel is faithful to the covenant, God will be its defender and provider. As a result, the wayward nations will witness Israel's blessings, flock into its borders, and serve its God.

Passover

To assist Israel in its mission, God makes three provisions. First, he instructs his people to eat an annual Passover meal, commemorating the meal they ate on the night of their escape from Egypt, which anticipated and effectuated their release. In doing so, he asks them to participate in a liturgical act of memory. Liturgy involves remembrance and performance. In some sense it is a ritualistic and dramatic reenactment of the past through the use of storytelling and symbols.

Passover was to be a yearly opportunity for the Israelites to praise God for their liberation from domination and their new political reality as a nation. As a nation of free people, Israel is not to oppress others. Rather it is to be an advocate for justice and a champion of the downtrodden. The Passover meal is intended to help Israel remember its past and serve as a reminder of its obligations. If the people apply the lessons of the past to the present, they will find favor with God and humankind.

The Law

Second, Yahweh provides Israel with the law to guide the people in accordance with his sociopolitical principles (Exodus 20). The first commandment prohibits the worship of other gods and recognizes Yahweh's superiority over them all. The psalmist will later connect Yahweh's power over the pagan gods with his office as king: "For the LORD is a great God, and a great King above all gods" (Psalm 95:3). The Old Testament laws were designed to regulate the affairs of God's people and to assure that justice prevails.

The King

Third, God supplies Israel with guidelines for choosing a king who is qualified to rule the nation under him.

> When you have come into the land that the LORD your God is giving you, and have taken possession of it and settled in it, and you say, "I will set a king over me, like all the nations that are around me," you may indeed set over you a king whom the LORD your God will choose. One of your own community you may set as king over you; you are not permitted to put a foreigner over you, who is not of your own community. Even so, he must not acquire many horses for himself, or return the people to Egypt in order to acquire more horses, since the LORD has said to you, "You must never return that way again." And he must not acquire many wives for himself, or else his heart will turn away; also silver and gold he must not acquire in great quantity for himself. When he has taken the throne of his kingdom, he shall have a copy of this law written for him in the presence of the levitical priests. It shall remain with him and he shall read in it all the days of his life, so that he may learn to fear the LORD his God, diligently observing all the words of this law and these statutes, neither exalting himself above other members of the community nor turning aside from the commandment, either to the right or to the left, so that he and his descendants may reign long over his kingdom in Israel (Deuteronomy 17:14-20).

From this passage we see that God intends for Israel to have a king. He gives clear instructions about the kind of ruler he wants the people to choose. According to the divine stipulations, Israel's king must not be like the rulers of the surrounding nations.

1. He must be a king of God's choosing (verse 15).

2. He must be a native Jew and not a foreigner (verse 15).

3. He must be a man of simple tastes (verse 16). He must not accumulate a corral of horses for himself and financially

oppress his people. In today's parlance, we might say he must not buy a fleet of luxury automobiles while his people take public transportation.[2]

4. He must not have dealings with tyrannical Egypt in order to make personal gains for himself (verse 16).

5. He must not enter into multiple marriages (verse 17). This is probably a reference to political marriages with daughters from other kingdoms, who would move his heart away from trusting in Yahweh.

6. He must live modestly and not use his office to accumulate wealth (verse 17).

7. He must be a person who keeps and reads a personal and accurate copy of God's Word (verse 18). The purpose for this requirement is fourfold:

    1. that he may fear God (verse 19)

    2. that he may learn to live in accord with its precepts (verse 19)

    3. that he may live humbly before the people as their equal and not above them, for he is not above the law (verse 20)

    4. that his dynasty may prosper for many generations (verse 20)

From the beginning of creation, God planned for his people to be ruled by a divinely sanctioned leader who listens to and obeys God's voice. Through this process of faithful rule and unwavering obedience, the knowledge of God will spread throughout the world.

The Wayward Trek Across the Wilderness

Barely into the journey of freedom, Israel forsakes her covenant with God and is tempted to return to the ways of Egypt. The journey to Canaan, which should have taken less than a month, turns into a 40-year trek across the wilderness and is characterized by disobedience and death. Only a few people of the original Exodus crowd reach the promised land. The others die in the desert.

The book of Deuteronomy tells of God's dealings with the second generation of Israelites as they prepare to enter Canaan. Chapter 28 contains blessings and curses. It opens with Moses admonishing the people, "If you will only obey the Lord your God, by diligently observing all his commandments that I am commanding you today, the Lord your God will set you high above all the nations of the earth; all these blessings shall come upon you and overtake you, if you obey the Lord your God" (verses 1-2). The blessings, which hearken back to God's first promise to Abraham, are enumerated in verses 3-14 and include fruitful childbearing, plentiful harvests and food supplies, security from invasions and the defeat of enemies, and economic prosperity with enough left over to lend to other nations.

Moses then states the purpose of God's covenant with Israel. "The Lord will establish you as his holy people, as he has sworn to you, if you keep the commandments of the Lord your God and walk in his ways. All the peoples of the earth shall see that you are called by the name of the Lord, and they shall be afraid of you" (verse 9-10).

God has chosen Israel to be a light to the surrounding heathen nations. If Israel remains true to its covenant with God, the Gentile nations will come to fear God and his people and will see the wisdom of coming under his reign.

On the other hand, if Israel turns away from God through disobedience and idolatry, he will send calamity on the nation. Instead of being a light to the nations, Israel will become a laughingstock (verses 15-68). The nations will view Yahweh with scorn and disdain, believing that their gods are more powerful than the God of Israel. Moses warns, "The Lord will scatter you among all peoples, from one end of the earth to the other…Among those nations you shall find no ease, no resting place for the sole of your foot. There the Lord will give you a trembling heart, failing eyes, and a languishing spirit" (verses 64-65).

Before his death, Moses again blesses the tribal leaders and reminds them that God is king over Israel (Deuteronomy 33:5). The nation must forever remember that Yahweh is King. Even Balaam, the erratic prophet, declares to Balak, "The LORD their God is with them, acclaimed as a king among them" (Numbers 23:21).

Settling in the Promised Land

With the death of Moses, the responsibility of leading God's people into Canaan and establishing Israel as a nation falls to young Joshua. The task is never an easy one. Throughout his tenure as leader, Joshua struggles to keep the nation faithful to God. Despite some good years, Israel is always dangerously close to forsaking its call and becoming like the surrounding nations.

In his farewell speech, Joshua exhorts the people to keep the law and warns them not to follow the ways of the heathen nations and not to intermarry with their children, lest they fall into a snare. If that happens, Joshua says, "the LORD your God will not continue to drive out these nations before you; but they shall be a snare and a trap for you... until you perish from this good land that the LORD your God has given you" (Joshua 23:13).

Unfortunately, with the passing of Joshua, the nation slides back into a pattern of unbelief and idolatry. Instead of being a positive influence on its neighbors, Israel succumbs to their sins.

Where, Oh Where, Is My King?

A long series of military rulers, or judges, leads Israel on a roller-coaster ride of moral ups and downs, typified by the words, "In those days there was no king in Israel; all the people did what was right in their own eyes" (Judges 21:25). The judges are accountable to God for assuring justice throughout the land, but they mostly fail in this task, leading to chaos. After being settled in the land for 400 years, the people finally call on the prophet Samuel to anoint a king to rule over them (1 Samuel 8:5).

But instead of choosing a king who meets God's qualifications (Deuteronomy 17:14-20), they want one of a different sort. The leaders explain to Samuel, "We are determined to have a king over us, so that we also may be like other nations, and that our king may govern us and go out before us and fight our battles" (1 Samuel 8:19-20). In other words, the people want a king who will be their protector, just like the kings of the other nations. This shows a lack of trust in God to be their provider and protector.

In conveying his displeasure to Samuel, God says, "They have rejected me from being king over them...from the day I brought them up out of Egypt to this day, forsaking me and serving other gods" (verses 7-8). God charges Samuel with the task of warning the people what will happen if they choose an ungodly king.

Like many Christians today, the Israelites want to have things both ways. On one hand, they want to identify with Yahweh. That's one reason they ask Samuel to be the one who appoints the king. On the other hand, they want to abandon their divine obligation to be a distinctive society. They desire to serve God in word and ritual but continue to live like their pagan neighbors. Their worship of God will become perfunctory and meaningless. By abandoning their call to be an alternative society (socially, economically, politically, and religiously), the people embrace an ideology of oppression.

Practically speaking, when Israel and the pagan nations are placed side by side, there is little difference. The Israelites might tip their hat to Yahweh, but their lifestyle does not reflect godliness.

The Monarchy

King Saul

God grants Israel's request and tells Samuel to anoint Saul to be ruler over his people (1 Samuel 9:16-17). The monarchy begins with Saul (1020–1000 BC), who is an impressive figure by all physical standards. But his moral lapses and paranoia undermine his divine mission and will ultimately lead to his demise (1 Samuel 13:14). He flaunts his power, embraces multiple wives and their gods, and unwisely leads Israel into war. When God refuses to answer Saul's prayers, Saul seeks advice from a witch. Samuel pronounces God's judgment on Saul: "Rebellion is no less a sin than divination, and stubbornness is like iniquity and idolatry. Because you have rejected the word of the Lord, he has also rejected you from being king" (1 Samuel 15:23). Eventually, rather than face the disgrace of defeat, Saul in an act of ultimate cowardice falls on his own sword.

King David

The crown passes to David (1000–962 BC), God's choice to be ruler over Israel (1 Samuel 16:12-13), who establishes Jerusalem as his new capital city and moves the ark of the covenant there. Jerusalem becomes the city of God, where God's presence dwells among his people. Despite moral lapses, David is a model king. He seeks to do God's will for the nation.

Because of David's faithfulness, God establishes a covenant with him in which he promises to build a Davidic dynasty through his son Solomon (2 Samuel 7:8-17). God vows, "When your days are fulfilled and you lie down with your ancestors, I will raise up your offspring after you, who shall come forth from your body, and I will establish his kingdom…Your house and your kingdom shall be made sure forever before me; your throne shall be established forever" (verses 12,16).

The covenants that God ratifies with Abraham and David are similar in several ways.

1. Both are established through night visions.

2. Both look into the distant future.

3. Both alter the trajectory of history.

4. God promises Abraham an everlasting posterity, and he promises David an endless dynasty.

5. God promises to raise up kings from Abraham's descendants (Genesis 17:6), and they show up in the Davidic line.

6. Both are linked by the phrase "from your body." That phrase is used in Genesis 15:4 NKJV and 2 Samuel 7:12 but nowhere in between.

We might say that rather than being two separate covenants, the covenant established with the patriarchs is renewed and fulfilled in David. This assurance of God's everlasting and universal rule through the house of David will later become the basis for the messianic hope. Until that day, God uses his kingly envoys to move redemptive history toward his desired goal. Each king was considered God's anointed agent, mediating his rule on earth. David understood this principle:

> Why do the nations conspire,
>   and the peoples plot in vain?
> The kings of the earth set themselves,
>   and the rulers take counsel together,
>   against the LORD and his anointed, saying,
> "Let us burst their bonds asunder,
>   and cast their cords from us" (Psalm 2:1-3).

Later in the same passage David describes himself not only as king but also as God's son:

> I will tell of the decree of the LORD:
> He said to me, "You are my son;
>   today I have begotten you.
> Ask of me, and I will make the nations your heritage,
>   and the ends of the earth your possession.
> You shall break them with a rod of iron,
>   and dash them in pieces like a potter's vessel" (verses 7-9).

As God's anointed son, the king is God's authorized representative to rule on God's behalf. Because of his unique relationship with Yahweh, who is the real power behind his throne, the king's authority extends over the entire earth.

In Psalm 45:1,6-7 the king himself is actually addressed as God. This means he stands in God's stead as his anointed ambassador.

> My heart overflows with a goodly theme;
>   I address my verses *to the king*;
>   my tongue is like the pen of a ready scribe…
> Your throne, O *God* [the king], endures forever and ever.
>   Your royal scepter is a scepter of equity;
>   you love righteousness and hate wickedness.
> Therefore God, your God, has anointed you
>   with the oil of gladness beyond your companions.

The word "God" is used three times in this passage. Its first use applies to King David. The psalmist calls him God because he rules on earth for God. The second and third use refers to the eternal God in heaven, who is the King of the king.

Centuries later, New Testament writers will interpret this psalm and others from a Christological perspective, identifying Jesus as the son of David (Matthew 1:1), the king of the Jews (2:2), and the ruler and shepherd of Israel (2:6). Likewise, the angel Gabriel will tell Mary, "You will name him Jesus. He will be great, and will be called the Son of the Most High, and the Lord God will give to him the throne of his ancestor David. He will reign over the house of Jacob forever, and of his kingdom there will be no end" (Luke 1:31-33). Jesus is variously called Messiah [or Christ], the Lord (Luke 2:11), and the anointed one (Acts 10:38). In identifying Jesus as God's final envoy, Hebrews 1:6-8 quotes Psalm 45. There is little debate that the New Testament authors saw Jesus as David's successor, through whom God establishes his eschatological (end-time) rule over earth. God's promises to set up his kingdom over the nations through the seed of Abraham and David will find their fulfillment in Jesus of Nazareth.

King Solomon

Solomon (962–922 BC) follows his father, David, to the throne and rules brilliantly and wisely at first (1 Kings 1–11). The pledge that God made to the patriarchs and to Moses, Joshua, and David seems to be coming to pass (Genesis 15:18; 1 Kings 4:21-34; 8:56). Israel is the envy of the surrounding nations, and Solomon completes his father's visionary project of building a temple—a permanent house for the ark of the covenant. God's abiding presence between the wings of the cherubim and among his people is a sure sign of his covenant blessings.

Unfortunately, Solomon's godly traits begin to wane. In the course of time, according to the biblical narrative, Solomon becomes the most powerful leader in the Mediterranean. He enters into political alliances with foreign kings by marrying their daughters. He may have been a genius of political strategy, but he willfully violates God's instructions for kings (Deuteronomy 17:14-17). His greed and his many wives turn him away from exclusive Yahweh worship and to idol worship.

Solomon's failure to submit to God's rule marks the beginning of the end for Israel as a united kingdom. Solomon forms a centralized government, accumulates wealth, and expands Israel's borders. In doing so, Israel slowly becomes more like other nations. It adopts a governmental system that dominates and oppresses the masses—the exact opposite of what God intended for Israel.

After Solomon's death, moral conditions in Israel deteriorate even further, resulting in a divided kingdom (1 Kings 11:31-35).

The Divided Kingdom

Rehoboam follows his father Solomon to the throne. His poor leadership skills and oppressive policies lead the nation to the verge of civil war. Ten tribes in the north break away and make Jeroboam their king. Only the tribes of Judah and Benjamin in the south remain loyal to Rehoboam.

Because Israel has forsaken its covenant pledge to God (Exodus 19:6-8) by rejecting his rule and embracing idol worship, he allows the northern and southern portions of the kingdom to separate from each other (1 Kings 11:31-35). The north will take the name Israel, and the south will go by the name Judah. Except for sporadic instances in the south, both kingdoms choose to serve their interests rather than God's. The divided and weakened nation becomes prey to invasions from surrounding nations. Both Israel and Judah find themselves making moral compromises and entering into political alliances with their heathen neighbors in order to survive.

Everything the people hated about living in Egypt, they experience under their own rulers. Cruelty, tyranny, oppression, injustice, high interest rates, heavy taxation, and even enslavement become their lot under the failing monarchy and divided kingdom. There are few if any distinguishable differences between God's kingdom and the peoples of the world. The nation has failed dismally at its mission of being an alternative society that lives obediently under the reign of God in contrast to the other nations.

Undaunted by circumstances, Yahweh commissions prophets to call on the national leaders to repent lest they cause judgment to fall on the people. The prophets denounce a host of defiant acts, including unholy political alliances, bribery, halfhearted worship, the charging of usury, and the oppression and affliction of the poor, disenfranchised, aliens, orphans, and widows.[3]

The Fall of Israel and Judah

The Assyrian Invasion of the Northern Kingdom (Israel)

Instead of heeding the prophetic warnings, the rulers choose to persecute and kill the prophets. Therefore, true to his word, God sends judgment by using Assyria to attack the recalcitrant northern kingdom. Assyria conquers Israel in 722 BC, takes the spoils of battle, and scatters the people abroad.

Yet God does not leave Israel without hope. As early as 750 BC, Amos envisions a day when God will restore Israel.

> I will raise up the booth of David that is fallen, and repair its breaches, and raise up its ruins, and rebuild it as in the days of old; in order that they may possess...all the nations who are called by my name...The mountains shall drip sweet wine, and all the hills shall flow with it. I will restore the fortunes of my people Israel, and they shall rebuild the ruined cities and inhabit them; they shall plant vineyards and drink their wine, and shall make gardens and eat their fruit. I will plant them upon their land, and they shall never again be plucked up out of the land I have given them, says the LORD your God (Amos 9:11-15).

Isaiah sees God receiving glory and praise from the ends of the earth (24:14-16) and Israel being transformed into a utopian kingdom, where "the LORD of hosts will make for all peoples a feast of rich food, a feast of well-aged wines" (Isaiah 25:6). The fulfillment lay in Israel's distant future, but a spark of hope has been ignited in the hearts of God's rebellious people.

The Babylonian Invasion of the South (Judah)

Because the kings of Judah (the southern kingdom) carry on the Davidic rule, they are given more opportunities and time to repent. For two more centuries, Isaiah, Micah, Zephaniah, Jeremiah, Ezekiel, and other prophets call on its leaders to turn back to God lest they face judgment. Jeremiah (626–587 BC), for example, charges the priestly authorities with transforming God's temple into "a den of robbers" (Jeremiah 7:8-11) and declares judgment on God's wayward people (Jeremiah 9:1-11; 22:13-19; 23:1-4). When God's warnings are ignored, his anger is kindled. God moves mighty Babylon, the new world power that has conquered Assyria, to invade Judah in 586 BC, burn the capital city, and lead its people into captivity.

With the southern kingdom decimated, God's prophets begin offering a glimmer of hope beyond judgment. Jeremiah reveals that after 70 years, God will turn the tables on Babylon, send a strong nation to destroy the evil empire, and free the Jews to return to their homeland (Jeremiah 25:11-14; 27:22; 29:10; 33:7-10).

The Medo-Persian Empire

First and Second Chronicles, which are combined into one book and placed last in the original Hebrew Scriptures, detail the downfall of the monarchy, the exile in Babylon, and the return of a Jewish remnant to Judah. In the final verses, King Cyrus, the ruler of Persia, stoutly defeats the Babylonians and takes the spoils of battle, including the masses of Jewish captives. The chronicler then writes about an interesting turn of events:

> In the first year of King Cyrus of Persia, in fulfillment of the word of the LORD spoken by Jeremiah, the LORD stirred up the spirit of King Cyrus of Persia so that he sent a herald throughout all his kingdom and also declared in a written edict: "Thus says King Cyrus of Persia: The LORD, the God of heaven, has given me all the kingdoms of the earth, and he has charged me to build him a house at Jerusalem, which is in Judah. Whoever is among you of all his people, may the LORD his God be with him! Let him go up" (2 Chronicles 36:22-23).

The Jews return in three waves under Nehemiah, Ezra, and Zerubbabel. They rebuild the city wall, restore the temple, and pledge to obey the Lord—all while also pledging allegiance to the Persian king. These events are discussed in the books of Ezra and Nehemiah.

Messianic Hopes

Some of Jeremiah's prophecies speak of events that take place beyond this initial return of the Jews to Palestine. He tells of a golden age to come when God will establish a new king of his choosing who will represent him on the earth.

> The days are surely coming, says the LORD, when I will raise up for David a righteous Branch, and *he shall reign as king* and deal wisely, and shall execute justice and righteousness in the land...

> Therefore, the days are surely coming, says the LORD, when it shall no longer be said, "As the LORD lives who brought the people of Israel up out of the land of Egypt," but "As the LORD lives who brought out and led the offspring of the house of Israel out of the land of the north and out of all the lands where he had driven them." Then they shall live in their own land (Jeremiah 23:5,7-8).

Israel's focus will no longer be on past deliverance from Egypt but on a future deliverance and the reuniting of north and south under a new covenant (Jeremiah 31:31-34). Hundreds of years later, both Jesus (Luke 22:20) and Paul (1 Corinthians 11:25) will make reference to this prophetic vision.

Similarly, Ezekiel pronounces judgment for Israel's disobedience (Ezekiel 1–24) and offers hope for a new Exodus and a restored nation (Ezekiel 36:22-28). He speaks of God raising up a new king to rule his people (37:21-22), and describes these future events in eschatological terms: "My servant *David shall be king over them*; and they shall all have one shepherd...and my servant *David shall be their prince* forever" (verses 24-25). King David died centuries before this prophecy, so the reference is to a new King, one who will ultimately fulfill the Abrahamic and Davidic covenants and usher in the kingdom of God.

Isaiah had also prophetically announced good news of a future restoration and economic favor for all people under the coming reign of God (Isaiah 61:1-2). He characterized the future kingdom as a continuous Jubilee, when everyone would experience social justice and freedom from want.

The Jews who returned to Judah with Nehemiah may have believed their homecoming marked the beginning of God's kingdom restoration. If so, time proved them wrong. The reconstruction of the temple opened the way for the establishment of "a ruling priestly aristocracy that owed their position to the [Persian] imperial regime, and it set up a temple administration to secure revenues for the imperial court as well as itself."[4]

But God continues speaking through even more prophets. Micah, Haggai, Zechariah, Malachi, and others call on the nation to repent, and they reiterate God's plan to gather his people from the four winds and unite them in peace under his reign (Haggai 2:6-9; Zechariah 9:9-10). A small remnant of covenant-keeping Jews hangs on to this hope and passes it down from one generation to the next. The vast majority, however, turn their backs on the will of God. They offer God lip service and go through the motions of serving God, but in reality, they serve their own interests. Through the prophets, God's voice can still be heard, but his words are ignored.

Greece

The Medo-Persian Empire eventually gives way to the rise of the Greek city-states and the ascendancy of Alexander the Great of Macedon, who conquers Palestine in 333 BC. Jewish life is altered once again as Hellenization sweeps the civilized world. Greek troops and teachers crisscross the empire, conquering and spreading their language and culture. Jerusalem Jews suddenly find themselves living under another regime, no longer as free as they were under Persian self-rule. The elite temple priesthood remains unhampered, however, as it embraces Greek culture and serves as the surrogate for the new empire, collecting taxes for the state and tithes for their own coffers. As a result, an ever-widening gap develops between common Jews and their priestly leaders.

Having been dominated by one Gentile kingdom or another since their days in Egypt, and ruled by their own tyrannical kings, the Jews look to God to free them from political oppression and to restore his kingdom to Israel under a new Davidic ruler. They also begin interpreting the prophetic Scriptures from a messianic perspective.

Resistance to Seleucid Rule

With the death of Alexander the Great in 323 BC, many vie for power over the kingdom. By the third century BC, Judea comes under control of the Egyptian Ptolemies and then the heavy hand of the Syrian Seleucids, who eventually inherit Alexander's kingdom. Circumstances reach a critical point when the Seleucid strong man Antiochus IV (175–164 BC) recruits willing Jewish collaborators to help him rule the Jewish homeland (1 Maccabees 1:20-64). But he faces mounting resistance when he proclaims himself to be "Epiphanes"— god manifest. He also plunders the Jerusalem temple of its treasury, collects excessive taxes, builds a gymnasium for the training of prospective young leaders, and encourages Jewish men to participate in athletic games that are played in the nude (1 Maccabees 1:13). When young men, embarrassed by the physical sign of their Jewishness, seek to "remove the marks of circumcision" and abandon the holy covenant (1 Maccabees 1:15), it becomes apparent that they are losing their identity as Jews.

In 167 BC, with sociopolitical pressures increasing, a remnant of Jews launches a resistance movement. Judas Maccabeus, the son of a priestly family, rises to a position of leadership. At the same time, a body of anonymous, apocalyptic literature surfaces that claims to contain revelations about the end of time. The Epistle of Enoch, the Assumption of Moses, the Animal Apocalypse, and others foretell God's divine imminent intervention, culminating with the arrival of God's universal kingdom on earth. Gleaning inspiration from these apocalypses, Jewish freedom fighters fight for national liberation.

Waging full-scale guerilla warfare against Antiochus and his troops involves prolonged and fearless combat, but the Jewish resisters win their freedom in 164 BC and oust their Greek oppressors. They ritually cleanse the sanctuary and begin a period of self-rule that lasts until

63 BC (1 Maccabees 4:36-59). Once again, many people may have
thought this was the start of God's long-awaited kingdom as foretold
by the prophets. If so, their hopes were short-lived.

The Maccabean Era

When Simon Maccabeus, Judas's brother, has himself named high
priest and leader of the nation, the Jewish masses find themselves living
under a new tyrant, only this time, he is one of their own. The priestly
Maccabean-Hasmonean family forms a dynasty that expands the borders of the new Jewish state and compels their Idumaean neighbors in
the south and the numerous foreign tribes in and around Galilee to
accept them as their rulers and adopt Judaism as their religion.[5] For
foreign males, this includes submission to circumcision. Like many
rulers before them, the Maccabees personally amass great power and
wealth and exploit their own people on the home front.

What should be a century of freedom for God's people is turned
into an era of subjugation for the demoralized masses. As a result, a
majority of Palestinian Jews again starts to yearn for deliverance, but
this time from their own oppressive rulers. To their dismay, a new
enemy rises—Rome—and they find themselves under the control of
occupation troops. They must have wondered, "Will the kingdom
ever come?"

4

Rome: The Final Empire

We found this fellow perverting the nation...
saying that He Himself is Christ, a King.

LUKE 23:2

Soon after Israel wins its own freedom from Antiochus Epiphanes, the Roman republic to the west begins flexing its military muscles. After defeating Carthage in North Africa (146 BC), Rome conquers one stronghold after another until the once mighty Greek Empire finally collapses in 88 BC.

In 64 BC, Pompey, hailed as the greatest military genius of his day, marches into northern Syria and defeats Antiochus XIII, claiming the Seleucid territory for Rome. He then sends a representative southward into Judea to negotiate a settlement with the Jews. When he arrives he finds them in armed conflict with each other over which of two brothers will serve as high priest and kingly ruler.

When it becomes apparent the Jews are unable to settle their own disputes and enter into an agreement with Pompey, he orders his troops to lay siege to Jerusalem and the temple. Pompey appoints his own high priest among the Jews but gives him no royal title. The Jewish state is officially dissolved and comes under the authority of Rome.

When the Roman senate names Julius Caesar ruler for life in 44 BC, power is transferred to one man, and the old republic takes its last breath and dies. This new political system is met with immediate internal opposition from Roman elites and ends in Caesar's assassination. A struggle for power ensues, and in time, Octavian (Caesar's grand-nephew and adopted son) emerges victorious over General Lepidus and Mark Antony, his two major competitors.

When Octavian officially succeeds his uncle (27 BC), Rome enters a new phase known as "empire." He and his successors will take the title *princeps*, or emperor. Jesus is born under the reign of Augustus (27 BC–AD 14) and begins his public ministry under Tiberius Caesar (AD 14–37), so it is important for us to know something about the Roman Empire during this era.

Roman Empire as a Domination System

A domination system is a social structure in which a small minority of elites or aristocrats exercises control over the vast majority of people through social and governmental structures.

Rome used several means, including military might, economic deprivation (such as high taxes and confiscation of lands), social stratification, an elaborate patron-client system, and the imperial cult of the emperor to dominate the masses. Each served to keep people in their place and in a state of passive submission. It was very effective.

We will look at some ways Rome kept people in tow and how Jesus and his movement challenged these oppressive methods and called people to reorient their lives toward God's kingdom.

Manifest Destiny

Augustus Caesar claimed to have a manifest destiny to rule the world given to him by the gods. He was to rule on their behalf and spread their will throughout the earth. This divine calling set Rome's agenda for the future. To accomplish this supposedly noble goal, Rome sent its military on expeditions to expand its territorial holdings throughout the Mediterranean region.

Rome was neither the first nor last to claim a manifest destiny. In his commission to Abram (in about 2000 BC), Yahweh said that through Abram's seed the nations of the world will be blessed (Genesis 12:1-3). Likewise, the founding fathers of the United States made similar claims to acquire land—through force, if necessary—and spread democracy. Whenever a people assert a divine right to expand their domain to other parts of the world, they develop a sense of destiny. Such was the case with Rome. But to those on the other end of the sword, whose land was seized and people enslaved, the mandate looked more demonic than divine.

Pax Romana

Historians consider *Pax Romana* ("Roman Peace") to be Augustus's greatest contribution to humankind. Through this effort Caesar sought to establish universal peace among people of different national and ethnic backgrounds under the Empire's banner of "peace and safety" (see 1 Thessalonians 5:3).

Augustus Caesar ordered his generals to take this message, which he termed "good news," to the nations beyond the regions of the Empire. On behalf of the emperor they offered a guarantee of peace and safety to any nation that submitted to Rome's rule, promising to protect it from invasion and to maintain law and order. If the nation rejected the emperor's peace plan, the Roman legions summarily invaded, conquered, and occupied its land. In such a case, rather than becoming subjects of Rome, the people became its slaves.

In many ways, Rome used Mafia-like tactics to accomplish its peace mission. The Mafia comes to your place of business and demands a monthly fee for protection. If you refuse to pay it, they bomb your store. The real protection you are purchasing is from the Mafia itself. Coercion works when you have the muscle to back up your threats. Rome did!

In this context of military power, an angel appears at night and delivers a birth announcement to some shepherds. "I am bringing you *good news* of great joy for all the people: to you is born this day in the city of David a Savior, who is the Messiah, the Lord." This announcement is followed with "a multitude of the heavenly host, praising God and saying, 'Glory to God in the highest heaven, and on earth *peace*

among those whom he favors!'" (Luke 2:10-14 NRSV). If God is bringing peace to earth, *Pax Romana* is insufficient and must be replaced.
If Jesus is the Prince of Peace (Isaiah 9:6), where does this leave the
emperor and the Jewish elites who work for him?

The apostle Paul's common greeting, "Grace to you and peace from
God our Father and the Lord Jesus Christ," is more of a political statement than a spiritual one. Paul is challenging Rome's claim that peace
comes from the god Jupiter or from Caesar, the son of god. When Paul
preached the "gospel of peace" (Ephesians 6:15), he stood opposed to
Rome's alleged "good news."

Thus the preaching of the gospel was as much a political act as a
spiritual one.

Emperor Worship

Religion was an integral part of everyone's life in the Empire and
was another way Rome controlled its subjects. Unlike modern democ-
racies that practice separation of church and state, in ancient societies,
politics and religion went hand in hand. Rome was an empire under
the gods. Temples devoted to Jupiter, Apollo, and Artemis were erected
on the highest elevations in major cities throughout the Empire and
served both religious and political purposes.

When the senate gave Octavian the divine title of Augustus, the cult
of the emperor was born, and it gained widespread popularity among
the masses. In times past, Rome honored its rulers posthumously. For
instance, in 42 BC, the senate honored the recently deceased Julius
Caesar by giving him the title *Divus Iulious* ("Divine Julius"). Not to
be outdone, Octavian claimed for himself the title *Divi filius* ("Son
of God") while he was still among the living! Some people in his day
took this to mean that Augustus was the human embodiment of a god,
while others viewed him as the gods' earthly representative, who did
their bidding. In 9 BC, the provincial assembly in Asia decreed Augustus to be divine, "equal to the Beginning of all things" and "sent...as
a Savior." His birthday marked "the beginning of good news" for the
entire world. He was given and accepted the titles Lord and Savior.

A temple to Augustus was built in Pergamum, and another one was constructed in Smyrna for Tiberius Caesar, his successor, who also carried the divine title until his death in AD 37. Gaius Caesar, also known as Caligula (AD 37–41), claimed godhood for himself and dressed in special-colored clothing associated with a variety of gods whenever appearing in public. Temples were built in Ephesus for Emperor Vespasian (AD 69–79) and his two sons, who reigned after him. Likewise, Nero (AD 54–68), who ruled during the days of the apostle Paul, and Domitian (AD 81–96), who reigned during the latter days of the apostle John, followed their predecessors in accepting divine accolades. Domitian wanted to be addressed as *Dominus et Deus noster* ("my Lord and my God"). Do these titles sound familiar?

The emperor cult served as the civil religion of the Empire. Citizens showed their patriotic loyalty to the emperor and the Empire by their participation in religious activities. All sectors of society—social, intellectual, political, economic, spiritual, and ethical—were touched and shaped by the imperial cult.

Public events and special days became opportunities to pay homage to the emperor. The emperor's birthday, which marked the Roman New Year, was such an occasion. Others included anniversaries of great victories and celebrations to remember deceased rulers, heroes, or significant historical events. People expressed piety and devotion and renewed their commitment to the emperor and the Empire at sporting events, national feast days, and even ordinary meals eaten in the name of Caesar.

It takes little imagination to see how Jesus and his movement were a thorn in the side of the Empire and the Jewish establishment, which supported it.

From his birth to his death, Jesus challenged the political stability of the Empire in Palestine. When Christ's followers confessed him to be Lord and Savior, they got everyone's attention—from local Roman officials to their Jewish surrogates. To challenge Caesar's exclusive right to these titles was an act of treason. If Jesus is Lord, Caesar is not! That's blasphemy! The New Testament is clear that Caesar has a vastly superior competitor.

Augustus and each of his successors was called Father of the

Fatherland (*Pater Patriae*) or Father of the Country, implying that the Empire was a big family over which the emperor stood as a father to protect, discipline, and bless his family members. He thus functioned as benefactor, making certain that everyone's needs were met. The title also spoke of the emperor's divine right to rule the earth on behalf of Jupiter and carry out his divine will.

When Jesus admonishes his disciples, "Call no one your father on earth, for you have one Father—the one in heaven" (Matthew 23:9 NRSV), he invites them to look to God for their welfare and not Caesar. Paul carries on this tradition when he writes, "Yet for us there is one God, the Father, from whom are all things and for whom we exist" (1 Corinthians 8:6 NRSV). If such bold statements were verbalized and overheard by the authorities, they would be deemed politically subversive and incur the wrath of Rome.

Additionally, the emperor accepted the title "king of kings"—that is, king over all lesser client kings, such as Herod. By contrast, the book of Revelation identifies Jesus as "the ruler of the kings of the earth" (Revelation 1:5 NRSV) and likens the emperor to a harlot who commits fornication with the kings of earth (Revelation 17:2,5,7), kings who together "make war with the Lamb...for He is Lord of lords and King of kings" (verse 14). It proclaims that the Lamb will prevail against the armies of the world, using a sword that proceeds from his mouth (authoritative words) rather than one he wields with his hand (violence). He is again declared to be "King of kings and Lord of lords" (Revelation 19:16).

This counter-imperial message, which the church circulated throughout Asia Minor, pitted the Jesus communities against their imperial dominators. When the Jews brought Jesus to Pilate, they charged, "We found this fellow perverting the nation...saying that He Himself is Christ, a King" (Luke 23:2). In the fourth Gospel, the Jews threaten Pilate by saying, "If you release this man, you are no friend of the emperor. Everyone who claims to be a king sets himself against the emperor" (John 19:12 NRSV).

The early church continued to proclaim that Jesus was King. At Thessalonica, a mob rushed into the home of Jason, looking for Paul and his missionary team, who were his houseguests. When they did not find them, they dragged Jason to the rulers of the city, crying out, "These who have turned the world upside down have come here too. Jason has harbored them, and these are all acting contrary to the decrees of Caesar, saying there is another king—Jesus" (Acts 17:6-7). The message remains the same over time: Jesus is King! He alone deserves our highest allegiance—not the president of the United States or the Queen of England.

The gospel has real-life ramifications for us on earth here and now, just as it did for Jesus's followers in the first century. Christ demands absolute allegiance. He wants no opposing loyalties to stand between you and him.

Social Stratification

Another means of Roman domination was social stratification—a multilevel social hierarchy that one might liken to a pyramid. The great majority of people, consisting of dirt-poor peasants and a smattering of hardworking artisans, were at the bottom of the pyramid. Most Jews were in this category. They worked seven days a week from sunlight to sunset, often as day laborers or tenant farmers, to earn enough to put food on the table but little else. In the event of inclement weather, when workers could not go into the fields, they did not get paid. In the case of drought or harvest failure, they nearly starved or had to borrow money at high interest rates. If they owned a house or land, it was often confiscated when a loan remained unpaid. Thus the rich got richer and the poor got poorer.

Many people became slaves when their nation was conquered or when their debt became too large to pay off in a reasonable amount of time. Throughout the Empire, slaves accounted for as much as 20 percent of the total population.

At the top of the social pyramid sat Caesar, the son of god, along with his family members. The ruling elites, an aristocratic noble class, assisted Caesar in running the Empire. They were all Roman citizens and extremely rich, and they usually belonged to families with notable pedigree. They consisted of senators, governors, ambassadors, councilors, generals, landowners, and merchants. The next-wealthiest class

was known as the equestrians because they were allowed to purchase
horses with funds out of the public treasury. Pontius Pilate was likely a
member of this class. Decurions, the final group of Roman elites, represented Caesar at the citywide level and included proconsuls, such as
Gallio (Acts 18:12-17).

Assisting the Roman ruling class were native elites—rulers and busi-
nessmen from the annexed nations who aligned themselves with Rome
and helped keep the populace in place. In Palestine, these included client kings, such as the Herods, and temple priests, including Caiaphas
and Annas. These and their assistants maintained civility among the
masses, promoted law and order, supported the goals of the Empire,
and collected taxes.

The Herodian kings and the priestly aristocracy were the representatives of Rome throughout Galilee and Judea. It was in their best interest to keep things on an even keel. For their loyalty to Rome above all
other allegiances, the native retainers gained great wealth, lands, and
power. No wonder most Jews opposed their native leaders and viewed
them to be political hacks who compromised with Israel's oppressors.
As a result, the common people occasionally took to the streets in protest. If things got out of hand, the native elites called on the Roman
troops to restore order.

Roman elites made up approximately 2 percent of the Empire's
entire population; the native elites, another 6 percent or so. The peasants constituted the remaining 92 percent. The typical peasant lived
from hand to mouth.

The wealthy lived in sprawling villas, but the poor resided in one-
room apartments without any conveniences or furniture. They slept
on mats and used their outer cloaks as blankets or pillows. The poorest of the poor might live in makeshift lean-tos next to outer walls of
buildings or even in caves.

It was in Rome's interest to keep the poor in their place. The Empire
worked to maintain a perpetual class system. It you were born poor,
you most likely would die poor.

Such oppression was extremely difficult for the Jewish masses
because they knew God had created Israel to be a free nation with

equality for all. When Jesus came on the scene preaching the gospel of the kingdom, he called on God's people, and especially their leaders, to abandon allegiance to Rome and reorient their lives toward God's ethical standards. They were to stop oppressing people, taking their land, and charging interest. Instead, they were to practice egalitarianism, care for widows and orphans, and return property. They must trust God to care for them.

Taxation

Taxation was another successful means of oppression. Nations were required to show their loyalty and submission to Rome. The Empire levied heavy taxes on its subjects, allegedly in order to provide social services. However, taxes were used mainly to increase the net worth of Caesar and the other noblemen. Rome levied four kinds of taxes on conquered nations: a land tax, a head tax based on a census (this is why Joseph and Mary went to Bethlehem), a toll tax for using Roman roads, and a shipping tax. The ruling elites never worked themselves; they got rich off the backs of the poor and taxes.

The Gospel of Luke links Jesus's birth in Bethlehem historically to a census ordered by Augustus (Luke 2:1-7). In complying with the edict, Mary and Joseph traveled from their home in Nazareth to be registered and assessed their share of the tax burden. The registration was an instrument used to keep tabs on all subjects to make sure they did not escape paying the head taxes. Jesus and his family were part of a nation that was dominated by the strong hand of Rome, and therefore, they were expected to comply with the oppressive economic policies of the Empire.

King Herod levied additional taxes on his own people in Judea to upgrade public works, build new cities and temples dedicated to the Caesars, acquire land, construct royal palaces for himself, and complete the massive Jewish temple in Jerusalem. When he placed a golden Roman eagle, the symbol of Rome's power, over the main gate of the temple, the Jews protested, and upon his death they tore down the icon. Under the corrupt leadership of its Rome-appointed priests, the temple became an instrument of economic and political oppression. The priests not only made sacrifices to God on behalf of the Jews but also offered daily sacrifices honoring Caesar. They also collected taxes on behalf of Rome and used the temple complex as a storehouse for the taxes.

For many Jews, paying taxes and tribute to Caesar was an extreme hardship, and they revolted on numerous occasions. When this happened, the native retainers sought to calm them and stabilize the situation. If unsuccessful, the military stepped in to quell the protest decisively and brutally.

Patronage

Patronage was another tool the Empire used to maintain political and economic control over its people. It was observed universally and extended up and down the hierarchical ladder. Caesar, at the top of the social pyramid, was the ultimate patron, caring for those under him and providing political favors and offices, property, titles, and so on. In turn, the recipients did the same for others below them in social rank.

In exchange for his benevolence, Caesar's clients pledged him their faith (*fides* in Latin and *pistis* in Greek). They built monuments to him, dedicated buildings in his name, sponsored feast days, and the like.

In the outer provinces, the poor, having been forced off their land, often depended on patronage for survival. Many sought to link themselves to a patron who could provide them food, advice, influence, or a small weekly allowance in exchange for their loyalty and honor. This might include clearing a pathway for him to walk, promoting his candidacy for office, and generally assisting when and wherever needed. Services were exchanged for benefits. As such the beneficiary (the client) was beholden to the benefactor (the patron). No one wanted to lose the goose who laid the golden egg, so all toed the line. Thus patronage became an instrument of coercion and control with underlings doing the bidding of their superiors. Patronage served a positive economic function, but it also kept people in their place.

When Jesus called on God's people to stop looking to Caesar and start looking to God to meet their needs, he was attempting to set them free from oppression. He offered an alternative when he challenged,

"Seek first the kingdom of God and His righteousness, and all these things shall be added to you" (Matthew 6:33).

Land Acquisition and Eminent Domain

Unlike the economy of our technologically advanced twenty-first century, the first-century economy was driven by agricultural output. Therefore, Rome sought to increase its landholdings by invading other nations. Never truer was the adage "To the victor go the spoils." The emperor spread the lands gained through battle among his family, friends, and nobles, who in turn passed down their landholdings from one generation to the next. The conquered peoples who lost their lands were forced to work as sharecroppers on property they once owned. They were allowed to keep only 30 percent of the harvest to feed their families. On top of this, they had to pay taxes to Rome and rents to their landlords. The new landowners kept the remaining 70 percent of the crops and sold it in the marketplace for profit.

Some peasant landowners, whose property had been confiscated through war, were forced to work as hired hands without any claim on the crops. As a result, they had to purchase from the *agora* the very food they grew or else starve. The peasants had no recourse but to go along with the oppressive system. If they publicly protested or conducted a work stoppage, the army beat them into submission, or they lost their employment and their only source of income. To navigate the economy, peasants resorted to deception, often hiding crops or lying to tax collectors about their production output.

Voluntary Associations

Voluntary associations, known as *collegia*, offered opportunities for people to gather regularly with others of like mind and common interests. There were all kinds of associations. Some focused on a particular occupation or trade. Others were philosophical and provided a venue for intellectual debate. Still others were comprised of members with common national and ethnic roots. Many were entirely religious and were dedicated to the study and worship of a Roman deity.

Nearly everyone living in the Empire, even the poorest of the poor, belonged to one or more voluntary associations, which ranged in membership from less than a dozen to ten times that amount. Depending on the size and financial worth of the association or the sponsoring patron, meetings were held either in homes, rented quarters, local temples, or buildings that the associations owned. Usually the members met on a monthly basis. Some people belonged to more than one association.

Rome required two things of all associations: They must honor the emperor with a libation at their meals, and they must not participate in any action against the state. Therefore, associations were a means to dominate people and keep them in line with the political agenda of the Empire.

Regardless of the precise nature of an association, all had one thing in common—they were "supper clubs." They held regular reclining banquets, usually monthly.

The reclining banquet served an important social function in the Roman Empire. The core values of the Empire were acknowledged and honored, and social identity and boundary markers were observed by those living in a stratified society. The format and seating arrangements of the banquet served this end.

Banquet Format

A typical Roman banquet lasted three or four hours but could go long into the night. It was divided into two sections—the full-course meal, called a *deipnon*, followed by a *symposion* (Latin, *convivium*, or "second table"), a prolonged period of leisurely drinking that included entertainment or discussion. The two segments were joined together by a ceremonial libation—a drink offering of mixed wine that was sacrificed in honor of the emperor or a deity associated with the household, guild, or ethnicity. Libations were followed by the singing of a hymn to the deities and occasionally patriotic songs in remembrance of some great battle. There was no such thing as a nonreligious or secular banquet.

Banquet Seating

Everyone had his particular place in the pecking order at the banquet table, which was determined and affirmed by where he reclined.

Each table had an ascribed ranking. Guests were arranged according to social rank, which fluctuated according to the rank of the other guests. The sponsoring patron or association president determined the seating order and the menu. Guests of higher rank might be given larger portions or better fare than those of lesser status.

A person's status in society determined which banquet he attended and where he reclined. There was rarely a mixing of social classes at the banquet table. Elites ate with elites and peasants with peasants, so the banquet reflected the social fabric of the Empire. The banquet was consequently another instrument Rome used to dominate the masses and keep them in their place.

The End of the Domination System

Jewish leaders conveniently supported the domination system, but the vast majority of God's people reluctantly complied, were punished, or starved. As a nation, Israel had been either in captivity or occupied by foreign powers for most of its existence. When would this come to an end?

At the time of John the Baptist and Jesus, messianic expectations were on the minds of the Jews. They based their hopes on many of the eschatological and apocalyptic writings of the Old Testament prophets who spoke of God's intervention in human affairs and restoration of the kingdom to Israel. They longed for a political salvation or deliverance, a liberation from human enslavement rather than from personal sin.

Daniel 2

One of the sources that sparked hope in the hearts of God's people was the prophecy of Daniel, a vibrant and intelligent Jewish youth who was captured during Babylon's invasion of Judah in 605 BC. In time he rose to prominence in Babylon because he successfully interpreted King Nebuchadnezzar's troubling and mysterious dreams about a giant statue with a head of gold, body and arms of silver, a torso and thighs of bronze, and legs and feet of iron mixed with clay. Daniel, claiming insight from the God of Israel, said the mammoth monument represented four powerful kingdoms of the world that would be pulverized by a rock not cut with human hands. The rock would grow into a mountain and cover the whole earth, representing the kingdom of God, which shall stand forever (Daniel 2:20-45).

The first three kingdoms are clearly identified in the book of Daniel as Babylon, Medo-Persia, and Greece (8:20-21). The identity of the fourth is debatable. Most first-century Jews, including the historian Josephus, believed it to be Rome. I personally believe the fourth symbolic kingdom is left unnamed because it represents not only Rome but also all other ungodly kingdoms that would rise and fall "in the latter days" (2:28). Regardless, each succeeding empire is more powerful than its predecessor (verses 32-33) and conquers it. But more important, the rock destroys each kingdom.

When the final kingdom is crushed, the kingdom of God—presumably a Jewish kingdom—remains standing. It is instituted by God, but it is not otherworldly. It is a real, earthly, political kingdom that never ends.

This account in Daniel 2 gave the first-century Jews hope for deliverance. They eagerly waited for the God-sent Rock to destroy Rome and set them free.

Daniel 7

On another occasion Daniel has a night vision of his own with multiple scenes about four great beasts that come out of the sea (Daniel 7:2-3), representing the same four kingdoms depicted in Nebuchadnezzar's dream. Pictured as ferocious beasts, these kingdoms dominate weaker nations and claim prey for themselves. History supports Daniel's vision. These beastly kingdoms are symbolized by a winged lion (Babylon), a bloodthirsty bear (Medo-Persia), a swift-footed leopard (Greece), and a strong, ten-horned, iron-toothed, "dreadful and terrible" monster (Rome), respectively. In the end, they are all toppled, although not by a rock but by a person (verses 7-12).

After seeing a heavenly court scene in which justice is meted out to the beasts, Daniel witnesses the coronation of a king.

> I was watching in the night visions,
> And behold, One like the Son of Man,
> Coming with the clouds of heaven!

He came to the Ancient of Days,
And they brought Him near before Him.
Then to Him was given dominion and glory and a kingdom,
That all peoples, nations, and languages should serve Him.
His dominion is an everlasting dominion,
Which shall not pass away,
And His kingdom the one
Which shall not be destroyed (Daniel 7:13-14).

These verses provide Jesus with his understanding of the kingdom. He sees himself as the Son of Man who receives a kingdom from God. Is it any wonder the disciples and others expect Jesus to overthrow Rome and usher in God's kingdom? To their minds, Israel's liberation is at hand under the conquering Messiah. Their expectations are quickly dashed when Jesus is crucified.

However, if they had read Daniel's prophecy with understanding, they might not have been disappointed. The Son of Man does not come *down* to earth; he goes *up* to heaven and into the presence of God. The fulfillment of this prophecy is found in the book of Acts when Jesus is taken up in the clouds to heaven. As his disciples watch him ascend, two angels appear and ask, "Men of Galilee, why do you stand gazing up into heaven? This same Jesus, who was taken up from you into heaven, will so come in like manner as you saw Him go into heaven" (Acts 1:10-11).

Daniel's prophetic vision continues, "To Him was given dominion and glory and a kingdom" (7:14). His reign takes place in heaven, but it is over the earth. Daniel then reveals the purpose for him receiving dominion, glory, and a kingdom: "that all peoples, nations, and languages should serve Him." Notice that the people who serve him are on earth, and they include others than Jews. They are Gentiles living in all nations and speaking all languages. But Jesus himself is in heaven.

Daniel's vision also speaks to the perpetuity of the kingdom. The one on the throne will rule forever. All other kingdoms will pass away, but the one ruled by the Son of Man will never topple.

The God-given dominion that Adam lost will be transferred to the Son of Man. This perpetual kingdom on earth will not be Israel's alone but will encompass all nations. Divided humanity will be united as one under the banner of the Son of Man.

"Son of Man" is Jesus's favorite title for himself (it appears 32 times in Matthew alone), so he likely views his kingdom mission in light of Daniel's vision. This means he never intended to overthrow Rome in the way the people imagined. Rather, he called on the Jews to come under the present reign of God while still living in Rome. A few heed the appeal, but most find his message a curiosity or an annoyance. Jesus knows his kingdom will start out small, but in time it grows until it touches millions around the world.

Rome and all the other nations with leaders who listen to the voice of the enemy eventually fall, but the final judgment does not occur until the Lord returns to earth to establish his ultimate kingdom.

Summary

God's people were living under the oppressive hand of the Roman Empire. They yearned for a deliverer to lead them in another exodus. From the book of Daniel, they learn of a Son of Man who fits the profile, triumphs over enemy nations, and revives God's kingdom.

In our next chapter we will see how the people's emotions are stirred when they hear John the Baptist and Jesus preach, "The kingdom of God is at hand."

5

God's Appointed and Anointed King

Where is He who has been born King of the Jews?

MATTHEW 2:2

Matthew's genealogy and birth narrative identifies Jesus as the promised Christ, or Messiah (Matthew 1:16-18). He is the long-awaited and divinely sent ruler who frees God's people from human bondage. After years of silence, the Voice speaks once more. Through an angelic representative, God informs Joseph that Mary's conception is "of the Holy Spirit" and that "she will bring forth a Son, and you shall call his name JESUS" (verses 20-21). This child is the promised one foretold by Isaiah the prophet, and his birth signifies that God dwells once again among his people (verses 22-23). God has not forsaken them. He is Immanuel and remains faithful to his covenant. The name Jesus—or more literally, Joshua—means "Jehovah saves." Thus Jesus's birth is a sign of God's presence and points to redemption for Israel.

By the way, did you notice that Joseph and Mary learn the gender of their unborn baby long before invention of the sonogram? The Voice reveals it to them!

Herod must blanch when the Magi inquire of him, "Where is He who has been born King of the Jews?" After all, *Herod* has been Israel's king for more than 30 years! Caesar Augustus appointed Herod to rule Israel on Rome's behalf in 40 BC. The Roman senate quickly confirmed him as king of the Jews. Because their Gentile captors had appointed Herod, most Jews refused to recognize him as Israel's legitimate king. They considered him to be a Roman puppet and compromiser whose loyalties were to Caesar and not to God.

After his appointment, Herod took three years to gain control over the region. The unruly Jews resisted him at every turn. In the end, Herod succeeded in subduing the masses but not without slaughtering hundreds of Jewish resisters in the process. For instance, Herod ordered his troops to make three successive expeditions into Galilee to end Jewish protest against him. The brutal attacks left the town of Sepphoris, Nazareth's western neighbor, in ruins. Galilee remained a center of unrest as people sought freedom from foreign rule. As a result, Galileans were quick to follow anyone—whether a charismatic prophet or a guerilla leader—who sought the downfall of Herod the usurper.

By opening his Gospel with the birth narrative of Christ, Matthew contrasts Jesus and Herod. One is appointed by God to be King of the Jews. The other is appointed by Caesar to the same office. The first is God's legitimate king; the second is a counterfeit.

Herod inquires of his counselors where the Christ was to be born, and they quote the prophet Micah.

In Bethlehem of Judea, for thus it is written by the prophet:

"But you, Bethlehem, in the land of Judah,
Are not the least among the rulers of Judah;
For out of you shall come a *Ruler*
Who will shepherd My people Israel" (Matthew 2:5-6).

Herod knows that if word gets out of a newly born king of the Jews, the people will riot in the streets and seek Herod's ouster—the first-century equivalent of an Arab Spring!

Herod is not about to let this happen, nor will he abdicate his throne, so he asks the magi to find the infant and report back to him so he can visit and acknowledge the new King. In reality Herod plans to kill Jesus!

After being warned in angelic visions, the magi take a circuitous route home to avoid the scheming Herod. Joseph and his family likewise obey the Voice and leave for Egypt. Ironically, the first Jews under Moses did just the opposite. They left Egypt and marched toward the promised land to escape Pharaoh. Mary, Joseph, and Jesus now exit the Holy Land and trek toward Egypt to escape Herod (Matthew 2:13-15). In a sense, Israel has become what Egypt was long ago—a place of oppression (Revelation 11:7-8). And Herod is a tyrant like Pharaoh—out to kill newborns (Matthew 2:16-18). Eventually, Jesus and his parents will move north to Nazareth and set up residence.

Jesus is born to be God's King, but he has not ascended to his throne.

The Baptism of God's King

Matthew's next scene takes place 30 years later with John the Baptist, a wilderness prophet who calls out to the Jewish masses, "Repent, for the kingdom of heaven is at hand!" (Matthew 3:1-2).[1] The Baptist's message focuses on a single theme—the kingdom—and includes both a command and an explanation.

The command to repent is a call for the hearers to change direction or reorient their lives. The word "for" signals the reason or explanation for the change: "For the kingdom of heaven is at hand." Everyone listening to the message would have understood John to mean that God's end-time rule as foretold by the Old Testament prophets was about to take place. Only those taking the necessary step of repentance, breaking with the past and giving God their full allegiance, would be ready for its arrival.

The phrase "at hand" is not an easy one to interpret. It may refer to timing or presence or both. If the former, then the kingdom is imminent; it is about to begin. If the latter, then the kingdom is immanent; God's presence is close at hand.

When describing John the Baptist, Matthew quotes from Isaiah 40:3.

This is he who was spoken of by the prophet Isaiah, saying:

> "The voice of one crying in the wilderness:
> 'Prepare the way of the Lord;
> Make His paths straight'" (Matthew 3:3).

This prophecy includes elements of both timing and presence. The time of the Lord's arrival is at hand. Israelites need to respond forthrightly and publicly. "Then Jerusalem, all Judea, and all the region around the Jordan went out to him and were baptized by him in the Jordan, confessing their sins" (verses 5-6). These words explain the initial steps of preparation. Repentance includes baptism and confession of sins. This is the response God still expects from all who hear the good news of the kingdom. Baptism was associated with the kingdom of God before it became part of church ritual.

When Jesus comes down from Nazareth to be baptized, John protests, saying that Jesus doesn't need to be baptized; if anything, John should be baptized by Jesus. "But Jesus answered and said to him, 'Permit it to be so now, for thus it is fitting for us to fulfill all righteousness.' Then he allowed Him" (verse 15).

Jesus knows his baptism is part of God's kingdom plan. It will bring John's ministry to a climax and will launch his own ministry. For Jesus's ministry to commence, he must be baptized. John's ministry is one of preparation, readying Israel for the arrival of the kingdom. God's people, including Jesus, must be prepared.

How does baptism prepare Jesus for the kingdom? Matthew writes, "Jesus came up immediately from the water; and behold, the heavens were opened to Him, and He saw the Spirit of God descending like a dove and alighting upon Him" (verse 16).

Through his birth, Jesus is *appointed* God's King. At his baptism, Jesus is *anointed* by the Spirit to be God's King.

The phrase "the heavens were opened" means something supernatural is happening. Eternity is breaking into time (Ezekiel 1:1; Revelation 4:1). God's Spirit or presence descends and comes on Jesus.

For Matthew's first-century readers, the description of the Holy Spirit descending on Jesus "in bodily form" as a dove (Luke 3:22) carries special meaning. It denotes that Jesus is divinely inaugurated as Israel's new King. Let me explain.

Rome chose nearly all its kings by observing the flight of birds, a form of divination known as augury. According to Cicero (106–46 BC), Romulus, the legendary founder and first king of Rome, was named to his royal post through this method. Augurs were trained to read avian signs and confirm whom the gods had chosen to be the next emperor. They watched to see upon whose shoulder a bird landed, and that man became the new emperor. Avian signs accompanied the selection and confirmation of all Roman rulers from Octavian to Domitian except one.[2]

When the senate confirmed Octavian as Rome's emperor in 27 BC, it bestowed upon him the title Augustus, which is linked etymologically to the word "augury," possibly because he was confirmed and consecrated through the art of augury. The term "augur" is found in our English word in*augur*ation, which refers to the coronation of a king. Roman kings were literally in*augur*ated.

To first-century believers, the descent of the Holy Spirit on Jesus "in bodily form" as a dove is a sign that Jesus is God's choice to be his earthly King, just as the Roman gods send birds to confirm their choice of the Roman emperor.

The Voice from heaven speaks once again and announces, "This is My beloved Son, in whom I am well pleased" (Matthew 3:17). The first part of this sentence is a quote from Psalm 2:7, an enthronement psalm that describes David's installation as king. Whenever a new king of Israel took the throne, he was anointed by a prophet and declared to be God's son, or his representative on earth (see 2 Samuel 7:12-16). In the Gospels, Jesus is portrayed as God's final King, the end-time Messiah. At Jesus's baptism, the Voice confirms that the future kingdom rests on Jesus's shoulders.

The last part of the declaration ("in whom I am well pleased") is a paraphrase of Isaiah 42:1-2: "Behold! My Servant, whom I uphold, My Elect One in whom my soul delights! I have put My Spirit upon Him."

The combination of Psalm 2:7 and Isaiah 42:1-2 gives us a composite picture of God's Messiah. He is both King and Servant. To Jewish as well as Roman minds, this duality is an oxymoron. A king doesn't serve—he is served. Yet this is how God describes his King. Likewise, Jesus himself will declare, "The Son of Man did not come to be served, but to serve, and to give His life a ransom for many" (Mark 10:45).

The descent of the dove upon Jesus gives a clue to what kind of King he will be. Roman kings ruled harshly with iron fists. They were confirmed to office by the flight of an eagle, the national symbol of Rome. The eagle, the strongest and most aggressive of the birds, dominated the skies. It could fly higher and swoop down faster than any other bird, picking off its prey with little or no resistance. It was a fitting symbol of Roman power. The dove, on the other hand, is associated with tranquility and peace. Unlike the eagle, which devours others and even destroys its own, the dove nurtures its own and doesn't harm other living things.

At his baptism, Jesus is inaugurated by God to be a new kind of ruler. Unlike Caesar, he will be a Servant-King. He is confirmed to office by two heavenly signs—the Voice and the dove.

At Jesus's birth, God appoints him to be King. At Jesus's baptism, God anoints him and announces him to be God's chosen King.

The Holy Spirit and the Kingdom of God

With the descent of the Holy Spirit at Jesus's baptism, the kingdom of God arrives. You may wonder, "But wasn't the Holy Spirit around in Old Testament times? Didn't Old Testament prophets, priests, and kings also possess the Holy Spirit?" The answer to both questions is yes, but the Spirit's descent on Jesus is different. The Old Testament prophets spoke of a special arrival of the end-time or eschatological Spirit at the start of the kingdom of God (Isaiah 32:15; 42:1-2; 61:1; Ezekiel 36:26-27; 37:14; Joel 2:28). Thus the kingdom age can be characterized as the age of the Spirit.

The prophet Isaiah writes this regarding the Messiah, who ushers in the kingdom:

> There shall come forth a Rod from the stem of Jesse,
> And a Branch shall grow out of his roots.

> The Spirit of the LORD shall rest upon Him,
> The Spirit of wisdom and understanding,
> The Spirit of counsel and might,
> The Spirit of knowledge and of the fear of the LORD (Isaiah 11:1-2).

Isaiah goes on to say the Spirit residing on the Messiah, here identified as the Rod and Branch, marks the start of the universal age of peace (verses 6-9). The giving of the end-time Spirit occurs at Jesus's baptism and launches his kingdom ministry. New Testament scholar James D.G. Dunn boldly proclaims that wherever the end-time Spirit is found, the kingdom of God is also found.[3] Jesus had been around for 30 years, but the kingdom was not inaugurated in his life until the heavenly dove came upon him.

In speaking later of the effects of his baptism, Jesus says, "The Spirit of the Lord is upon me." He explains he has been anointed to carry out his kingdom assignments (Luke 4:18-19). Apart from the Spirit, Jesus cannot fulfill his mission.

Therefore we conclude that the kingdom resides initially with Jesus, the man empowered by the end-time Spirit. He is prepared to do kingdom work and is sensitized to hear the Voice from heaven. In the power of the Spirit he will take on and conquer (through nonviolent means) the enemies of God, including the world rulers and the demonic forces behind the throne. So it is not surprising to find Jesus, immediately after his baptism with the Spirit, confronting the devil in his first battle.

The Temptation: Shortcut to the Throne

Jesus next encounters the devil in the desert: "Then Jesus was led up by the Spirit into the wilderness to be tempted by the devil" (Matthew 4:1). The same Spirit who anoints him for kingdom service now brings him to the door of temptation. In God's providence, Jesus must face his archenemy before he begins his kingdom ministry.

In a sense, Jesus symbolically follows the pattern of Israel's journey of old, passing through the water and emerging in the wilderness to be tested. There is one major difference. Israel, collectively called God's son (Exodus 4:21-22), fails the tests, but Jesus, God's royal Son and representative of Israel, passes the test.

We cannot know whether Jesus physically sees the devil or his encounter takes the form of a vision. In either case, it is real. The devil tempts him three times. We will deal only briefly with the first two temptations, giving most of our attention to the third. The reason will become apparent.

In the first two temptations the devil seeks to get Jesus to act presumptuously because of his special status as God's Son or King. In both cases, the devil says, "If [or since] you are the Son God..." (Matthew 4:3,6). This appeal tempts Jesus to abandon faith in his Father and to act in what appears to be his own self-interest. The devil entices Jesus, famished by 40 days of fasting, to turn stones to bread and then to throw himself down from the temple mount so God can display his special love for him by dispatching angels to the rescue.

If Jesus obeys this voice, which spoke so deceptively and persuasively millennia ago to Adam and Eve, he will forfeit his right to rule the world under God. Jesus, however, defeats the devil by responding, "It is written" (verses 4,7). God's voice is the only one he will obey.

The third temptation is our main focus. "Again, the devil took Him up on an exceedingly high mountain, and showed Him all the kingdoms of the world and their glory. And he said to Him, 'All these things I will give You if You will fall down and worship me'" (Matthew 4:8-9). The "kingdoms of the *oukemene*" should be understood to include all the kingdoms and nations under the auspices of the Roman Empire. Rome controlled the known world at that time. The phrase "and their glory" refers to the splendor, wealth, culture, and beauty that make them desirous.

Satan claims the prerogative to give these kingdoms to Jesus, and Jesus never challenges his claim. Satan is called the "god of this age" (2 Corinthians 4:4) and "the prince of the power of the air" (Ephesians 2:2). John writes in his first epistle that "the whole world lies under the sway of the wicked one" (1 John 5:19). Satan is a king maker. Satan is the power broker behind the world governments as leaders continue to obey his voice.

In a Faust-like bargain, the devil offers Jesus the rule of the entire world. There is only one stipulation: Jesus must fall down and worship

Satan (Matthew 4:9). Many books and movies are based on deals with the devil. It seems like such a no-brainer—get whatever your heart desires in exchange for bowing the knee to Satan. But the deal is not so simple. The cost is more than meets the eye. The contract includes hidden details and small print that must be read and understood. Jesus sees through the deceptive maze. Maybe that's why he would later ask two probing questions: "What profit is it to a man if he gains the whole world, and loses his own soul? Or what will a man give in exchange for his soul?" (Matthew 16:26).

How would you answer?

Jesus refuses to make a deal with the devil. Instead, Jesus commands, "Away with you, Satan!" Then Jesus gives his reason for rejecting the deal: "For it is written, 'You shall worship the LORD your God, and Him only you shall serve'" (Matthew 4:10). This quote from Deuteronomy 6:13 exposes Satan's wiles. He has attempted to make worship a simple act of bowing the knee. Jesus says it involves much more—worship involves service. On another occasion Jesus explains that whoever you serve is your master (Matthew 6:24). To worship Satan is to serve him as master. To obey his voice is to do his bidding.

Had Jesus accepted the diabolical offer, he would have become a new Caesar over the entire earth. He likely would have led Israel to mount a rebellion against Rome and possibly through demonic means defeat the mightiest empire known to man. Jesus would have been crowned the new king. But at what cost, and to what end? He would have been the devil's king, not God's. In the end, he would have died and lost it all! Such a fleeting prize in exchange for his soul.

Satan's offer to Jesus is no different from God's. Both offer Jesus the kingdoms of the world, but Satan offers Jesus a shortcut. Jesus can be crowned without being crucified. Unlike Adam, who obeyed the voice of the serpent, Jesus raised his voice against the mortal enemy of his soul. "Then the devil left Him, and behold, angels came and ministered to Him" (Matthew 4:11). Years later, James writes, "Resist the devil and he will flee from you" (James 4:7). Having passed the test, Jesus is crowned as earth's King.

Jesus's initial triumph over the devil was no cakewalk. It was a stressful and traumatic encounter as Satan used his full arsenal to get Jesus to give in to temptation. Possibly this experience is the basis of Jesus's later instructions to pray, "Do not lead us into temptation, but deliver us from the evil one" (Matthew 6:13). Having experienced the full force of temptation, Jesus does not wish his disciples to go through a similar circumstance.

Jesus Commences Kingdom Ministry

The next major leg on Jesus's journey toward the kingdom involves a change of address. "When Jesus heard that John had been put in prison, He departed to Galilee" (Matthew 4:12). He leaves Judea and travels 80 miles northward, arriving in his hometown of Nazareth. But his stay is short-lived: "Leaving Nazareth, He came and dwelt in Capernaum, which is by the sea, in the regions of Zebulun and Naphtali" (verse 13). The word "dwelt" indicates a permanent residence. This means Jesus leaves his family behind. For the eldest son to leave his widowed mother to the care of others might not be seen as the most responsible thing to do.

Jesus is ready to launch his own full-time ministry, and Capernaum becomes his headquarters. This city of 15,000—half Jews and half Gentiles—is located near the Sea of Galilee. The reason for Jesus moving to Capernaum is now given:

> That it might be fulfilled which was spoken by Isaiah the prophet, saying:
>
> "The land of Zebulun and the land of Naphtali,
> By the way of the sea, beyond the Jordan,
> Galilee of the Gentiles:
> The people who sat in darkness have seen a great light,
> And upon those who sat in the region and shadow of death
> Light has dawned" (Matthew 4:14-16).

This quote from Isaiah 9:1-2 refers back to the days when the northern kingdom of Israel was held captive by evil Assyria, facing gloom and dark despair. Isaiah the prophet speaks of a great light at the end of the tunnel that offers hope of liberation and restoration for God's people. Matthew sees its fulfillment happening in the life of Jesus! With his arrival in Capernaum, a new day is dawning and the darkness is receding.

Matthew recalls, "From that time Jesus began to preach and to say, 'Repent, for the kingdom of heaven is at hand'" (4:17). If these words sound familiar, they are. Do you remember how Matthew 3 opens? "In those days John the Baptist came preaching in the wilderness of Judea, and saying, 'Repent, for the kingdom of heaven is at hand!'" (Matthew 3:1-2).

John and Jesus preach the same message: "The kingdom is at hand." Jesus picks up where John leaves off. Each proclaims that God is about to do something fantastic. His kingdom is about to arrive. Therefore the people need to get their lives in order; they need to rearrange their priorities lest they be unprepared.

All four Gospel writers agree that Jesus's ministry consists of teachings and actions. Through words he explains what the kingdom is like and how we should live as kingdom citizens in the midst of a world hostile to Christ. Through deeds, which include healings, exorcisms, and other miracles, Jesus demonstrates the power of the kingdom and his kingly authority over earth.

6

Exorcism: A Sign of the Kingdom's Arrival

*If I cast out demons by the Spirit of God, surely
the kingdom of God has come upon you.*

MATTHEW 12:28

From the start of his public ministry, Jesus performs acts of power, including exorcisms, which astonish the masses. According to the Gospel of Mark, Jesus's first exorcism takes place on a Sabbath at a synagogue in Capernaum. After he teaches the Word of God, his attention is drawn to a shriek from a man with an unclean spirit who cries out, "Let us alone! What have we to do with You, Jesus of Nazareth? Did You come to destroy us? I know who You are—the Holy One of God!" (Mark 1:24).

We can only imagine the disturbance this causes among the synagogue members. But Jesus acts quickly and decisively by rebuking and commanding the spirit, "Be quiet, and come out of him!" Despite a struggle to remain embedded, the demon leaves, but only after convulsing the man (verses 25-26).

Mark concludes his account with these words: "Then they were all amazed, so that they questioned among themselves, saying, 'What is this? What new doctrine is this? For with authority He commands even the unclean spirits, and they obey Him.' And immediately His fame spread throughout all the region around Galilee" (verses 27-28).

Exorcisms were not uncommon in the ancient world, even among the Jews. Most exorcists used incantations and secret formulas to expel evil spirits. Here, the crowd is shocked that Jesus doesn't use such ploys. He displays a unique authority over demons and does not rely on any recognizable method. His word alone causes demons to take flight. Authorized by his Father and anointed by the Spirit, he sets the captives free.

Jesus sees each exorcism as a victory over Satan himself. Entering enemy territory, Jesus plunders Satan's house, or kingdom. Each triumph is a sign that God's kingdom has arrived and that Satan is losing his grip over people's lives.

Binding the Strong Man

When defending the integrity of his exorcisms and speaking of their purpose, Jesus likens them to binding a strong man (Mark 3:27). This concept is significant because Jews believed the forces of evil would be bound at the end of time.

> It shall come to pass in that day
> That the LORD will punish on high the host of exalted ones,
> And on the earth the kings of the earth.
> They will be gathered together,
> As prisoners are gathered in the pit,
> And will be shut up in the prison;
> After many days they will be punished.
> Then the moon will be disgraced
> And the sun ashamed;
> For the LORD of hosts will reign
> On Mount Zion and in Jerusalem
> And before His elders, gloriously (Isaiah 24:21-23).

The noncanonical book of Enoch, which was popular among Jews in Jesus's day (and later quoted in the canonical book of Jude), describes the binding of God's enemies, particularly Azazel and his associates (1 Enoch 10:4-16). And the book of Revelation speaks of Satan being bound in a bottomless pit for 1000 years (Revelation 20:1-3).

When Jesus likened his exorcisms to the binding of a strong man, his listeners understood that the age to come had arrived. They must have been confused, however, when Jesus did not set up the kingdom as expected. We know in hindsight that the kingdom had already come but not yet in its fullness. Jesus began the kingdom. It will reach its consummation at his second coming. Each exorcism points to that day when all will submit to the reign of God, and Satan and his hordes are bound.

The Deliverance of the Gadarene Demoniac

Jesus's miracles and especially his exorcisms were more than individual acts of compassion. We should view them as enacted prophecies. In the Old Testament, God occasionally instructed prophets to act out their prophecies as graphic lessons to the people.

For instance, Jeremiah is told to tie a linen sash around his waist, go to the Euphrates River, and hide it in a rock. Then he is ordered to go back some days later and retrieve it. When he does, he notices the sash is soiled and ruined. God gives the explanation:

> Thus says the LORD: "In this manner I will ruin the pride of Judah and the great pride of Jerusalem. This evil people, who refuse to hear My words, who follow the dictates of their hearts, and walk after other gods to serve them and worship them, shall be just like this sash which is profitable for nothing" (Jeremiah 13:9-10).

You can find a few examples of the many other enacted prophecies in these chapters: Jeremiah 16, 19, and 27; Ezekiel 4 and 12; and Hosea 1-4.

The deliverance of the Gadarene demoniac (Matthew 8:28-34; Mark 5:1-19; Luke 8:26-39) has a dual function. First, Jesus sets the demoniac free. Second, Jesus dramatically enacts a prophecy of all Israel being set free.

When the man from the tombs meets Jesus on the seashore, the demon inside him cries out, "What have I to do with You, Jesus, Son of the Most High God? I implore You by God that You do not torment me" (Mark 5:7). These words are a response to Jesus's command. "For He said him, 'Come out of the man, unclean spirit!' Then He asked him, 'What is your name?'" (verses 8-9).

The first clue this passage should be read at two levels is found in the demon's response. "And he answered, saying, 'My name is Legion; for we are many'" (verse 9). On a literal plane, the demoniac's response means that he is possessed by a myriad of demons. To the readers of the Gospels, however, the word "Legion" had political connotations as well. It was commonly used to refer to a contingent of 6000 Roman foot soldiers. Jews rubbed shoulders every day with Roman occupation troops.

The second clue that this passage has a future political connotation as well as a literal one is found in the mention of pigs. After begging Jesus not to send them out of the country, the demons request that he send them into the swine. Jesus grants permission (verses 11-13). According to Josephus, a pig's or boar's head was the symbol of the Roman Tenth Legion (*Fretensis*), which besieged Jerusalem (*Jewish War* 5.71-97) and occupied the Mount of Olives in the Jewish War (AD 67–70).

The conclusion of the exorcism provides the final clue. "Then the unclean spirits went out and entered the swine (there were about two thousand); and the herd ran violently down the steep place into the sea, and drowned in the sea" (verses 13-14). Does this account jog your memory about another army drowning in a sea? The wording is nearly identical to that of the Exodus scene at the Red Sea (Exodus 15:1,10). God delivers Israel from Egyptian domination, but Pharaoh's army perishes in the sea.

The exorcism at Gadara points to something beyond one man's deliverance. The driving of the Legion into the sea can be viewed as an enacted prophecy, announcing Rome's ultimate defeat and the imminent coming of God's kingdom. A new Exodus has begun. God's people will be set free from social, economic, and political oppression, just as the demoniac was freed of his demons.

A House Divided Cannot Stand

On another occasion, Jesus heals a demon-possessed man who is both blind and mute (Matthew 12:22). The spectators marvel and ask, "Could this be the Son of David?" They are asking whether Jesus is the promised Messiah. As we have already noted, the masses were expecting a messianic figure who would set the captives free (Luke 4:18-21).

In contrast to the people's amazement, when the Pharisees get wind of the news, they charge, "This fellow does not cast out demons except by Beelzebub, the ruler of the demons" (Matthew 12:24). By accusing Jesus of being in league with the devil, these religious elites hope to defame his character and draw his disciples away.

Jesus forthrightly exposes the illogic of their charges. If he casts out demons by Satan's power and at the same time serves the prince of demons, Satan's kingdom is divided and cannot stand (verses 25-26). Their allegations don't make sense! Then he adds, "By whom do your sons cast them out?"

After silencing his critics, Jesus concludes, "But if I cast out demons by the Spirit of God, surely the kingdom of God has come upon you" (verse 28).

This is one of the key kingdom texts in the Gospels. Here we find Jesus making an unequivocal statement that the kingdom has arrived, evidenced by the fact that his exorcisms are done by the Spirit of God. This means that the kingdom has a present as well as a future aspect. When the kingdom comes to earth in its fullness, people will be free from all oppression because Satan will be bound. But the kingdom had its beginning at Jesus's baptism and was manifested through his ministry. His exorcisms by the Spirit of God were the evidence.

> Peter reminds the household of Cornelius, the Gentile centurion, "God anointed Jesus of Nazareth with the Holy Spirit and with power, who went about doing good and healing all who were oppressed by the devil, for God was with Him" (Acts 10:38).

Luke's account of this incident is nearly identical to Matthew's except for one revealing detail. In Luke's version, Jesus announces, "But if I cast out demons with the finger of God, surely the kingdom of God has come upon you" (Luke 11:20). This means the terms "finger of God" and "Spirit of God" are synonymous, and Jesus and the disciples use them interchangeably. Jesus's use of the term "finger of God" is an obvious allusion to Exodus 8:19, where Pharaoh's charlatan magicians admit that Moses performed his miracles by the finger of God. Just as Moses freed God's people from Egyptian bondage and led them to the edge of a kingdom, so Jesus does the same. His mission, however, is eschatological. He leads a new Exodus and offers a new kingdom.

Note that Luke 11 opens with the Lord's Prayer, in which Jesus teaches the disciples to pray, "Your kingdom come." In verse 20, he says, "The kingdom of God *has come* upon you." Their prayer in some sense is answered before the chapter comes to an end!

It is difficult to reconcile the tension between the "already" and "not yet" kingdom. The most satisfying way to understand the kingdom is to recognize that God's final reign manifested itself in the ministry of Jesus—especially through his miracles, healings, and exorcisms—but will not reach its fullness until the present evil age comes to an end at the return of Christ.

A Gentile Is Set Free

Our next case of exorcism offers new insights into Jesus's kingdom ministry. While traveling through the region of Tyre and Sidon (modern-day Lebanon) along the Mediterranean coastline, Jesus slips into a house to escape the press of the crowds. But he doesn't go unnoticed.

> A woman whose young daughter had an unclean spirit heard about Him, and she came and fell at His feet. The woman was a Greek, a Syro-Phoenician by birth, and she kept asking Him to cast the demon out of her daughter. But Jesus said to her, "Let the children be filled first, for it is not good to take the children's bread and throw it to the little dogs" (Mark 7:25-27).

We do not learn whose house Jesus enters, but likely he has a contact in the area. From Mark 3:8, however, we know that word of Jesus's miracles had spread far and wide, even to this predominately Gentile region. A contingent of curious people from the twin cities actually made a trek to witness the miracles for themselves. Most likely, some of these folk became Jesus's disciples, and now some months later Jesus comes to their town and stays in one of their homes.

When an uninvited Gentile woman enters the house, pleading for him to help her demon-possessed daughter, Jesus ignores her request and then insults her. For her to approach a Jewish holy man is scandalous. After all, she is under a double curse, being both a woman and a Gentile.

From these verses we learn two things about Jesus's kingdom mission. First, he gives priority to helping Jews ("the children"). God is obligated by covenant to free Israel from bondage. Second, he suggests that ministry to Gentiles ("little dogs") will take away from ministry to the Jews.

Jesus's disciples ask him to send her away (Matthew 15:23). But refusing to be muted, the desperate mother stops her begging and snaps back, "Yes, Lord, yet even the little dogs under the table eat from the children's crumbs" (Mark 7:28). In other words, who gets the leftovers?

What leads her to respond in this way? Most likely, she hangs on to one word in Jesus's initial response: "Let the children be filled *first.*" If there is a first, there must also be a second. She is not asking him to give priority to her child, but to give her the crumbs from the main meal that fall on the floor. She willingly accepts her assigned place. She is second, with no rightful claims on the God of Israel. She accepts her designation as a house pet that sits under the table and begs.

Touched by her persistence and humility, Jesus replies, "For this saying go your way; the demon has gone out of your daughter" (Mark 7:29). She doesn't retort, "But you need to come and exorcise the demon." Rather, she believes and obeys. Mark ends the narrative by adding, "And when she had come to her house, she found the demon gone out, and her daughter lying on the bed."

How's that for a crumb! If this is a crumb, can you imagine what a T-bone steak must be like? What a celebration the people of Tyre must have had that day!

If the exorcism of the Gadarene demoniac was an enacted prophecy, we might look at this narrative similarly and draw comparable conclusions. In this encounter Jesus accomplishes two goals. He delivers the girl of her literal demon, but this time from a distance. He foretells through his dramatic action that Gentiles as well as Jews will be delivered one day from the clutches of political, economic, and social oppression and from the demonic powers behind the throne.

To my knowledge, this is the only time Jesus travels beyond the geographical borders of Israel. In doing so, he makes a statement that God's plan of salvation includes Gentiles.

Being a Gentile, I receive great hope from the account of this exorcism. It provides assurance that though I am not included in God's original covenant with Israel, God's kingdom promises are for me as well. As we shall see in a later chapter, Gentiles are no longer second-class citizens, but joint heirs with believing Jews of an inheritance that is unspeakable and full of glory.

The Triumph of Faith

Sometime later, Jesus descended the Mount of Transfiguration to find crowds swelling and a debate taking place between the disciples and religious leaders (Mark 9:14-16). Before he can discern the topic of discussion, a frantic father approaches and says, "Teacher, I brought You my son, who has a mute spirit. And wherever it seizes him, it throws him down; he foams at the mouth, gnashes his teeth, and becomes rigid. So I spoke to Your disciples, that they should cast it out, but they could not."

This child's case would be a challenge even to modern medicine because his symptoms (he can't speak and has periodic seizures) are neither organic nor psychological. Medical treatment would be of no avail.

Upon hearing this report, Jesus answers, "O faithless generation, how long shall I be with you? How long shall I bear with you? Bring him to Me."

Jesus is likely addressing the apostles, but the problem is not theirs alone. The entire nation is faithless. Jesus's tone conveys a feeling of exasperation. His example, teachings, and powerful acts should have bolstered their faith by now. Yet they still have a "no can do" attitude.

How about us? What is our faith quotient? Most of us are like the ten spies who returned from the promised land and reported to Moses that the enemy could not be defeated. Maybe we need to get our eyes off the problem and get our eyes on the solution. Nothing is too difficult for Jesus to handle!

When the child is brought to Jesus, the demon suddenly throws the boy into a full-orbed seizure, and he falls to the ground, foaming at the mouth (Mark 9:20). I don't know about you, but I would be scared out of my wits. With the boy convulsing in front of him, Jesus calmly asks the dad, "How long has this been happening to him?"

If I were the father, I would say, "This is no time for small talk! My son needs help *now!*"

Remarkably, he simply answers the question: "From childhood. And often he has thrown him both into the fire and into the water to destroy him. But if You can do anything, have compassion on us and help us."

In other words, the seizures are potentially life threatening because they come at unexpected times.

This leads us to two of the most familiar and important verses in Mark's Gospel. Jesus says, "If you can believe, all things are possible to him who believes." Without hesitation the father cries out through his tears, "Lord, I believe; help my unbelief!"

The issue is not whether Jesus can heal, but whether we can believe. Compare verses 22 and 23. The father pleads, "If you can," and Jesus replies, "If *you* can." The father asks, "If you can do anything," and Jesus responds, "If you can *believe.*" Then he follows with "all things are possible." There is a big difference between the two men's statements. One conveys doubt about Jesus's limited ability to help. The other conveys doubt about the father's limited ability to believe—but if he is able, anything can be accomplished.

The key to unleashing God's power in this situation, according to Jesus, is the father's faith. This is an important lesson. God can heal regardless of whether we believe. But often he chooses not to intervene if we don't believe he will. The only time Jesus cannot perform mighty miracles occurs in Nazareth. The people's unbelief is the cause (Matthew 13:58). God responds to faith.

The father's answer, "Lord, I believe; help my unbelief!" is an admission that he believes God *can* heal, but he is uncertain that he *will*. Does that sound familiar? Are you confident God has the ability to intervene but uncertain that he will? If so, take the next step and follow this father's example. He asks Jesus to help his unbelief. Have you ever made that kind of request? Or do you simply tack on the words "if it be thy will" to the end of your prayers? We need to believe not only that God *can* heal but also that he *will*. If we have doubts about the latter, we need to ask him for help.

> When Jesus saw that the people came running together, He rebuked the unclean spirit, saying to it: "Deaf and dumb spirit, I command you, come out of him and enter him no more!" Then the spirit cried out, convulsed him greatly, and came out of him. And he became as one dead, so that many said, "He is dead." But Jesus took him by the hand and lifted him up, and he arose (Mark 9:25-27).

Luke adds, "Jesus…gave him back to his father. And they were all amazed at the majesty of God" (Luke 9:42-43).

What can we learn about the kingdom of God from this story? Both cases of child exorcisms—the daughter of the Syro-Phoenician woman and the son of the Jewish man—when viewed as enacted prophecies, show that children will have a place in God's future kingdom. In the ancient world, children had no rights, and along with peasant women, slaves, widows, and others, they were considered marginal figures in the Empire.

Accounts of children being possessed by demons illustrates the oppressive and dominating nature of the Roman Empire, which, under the guidance of Satan, sought to control people and keep them from rising above their circumstances.

But in God's kingdom, children have a significant place and equal status. In fact, Jesus likens the kingdom of God to children (Matthew 19:13-15; Mark 10:13-16; Luke 18:15-17).

Other Cases

Everywhere Jesus ministers, he confronts demon-possessed people. Some are mentioned by name and become his disciples and traveling companions.

> He went through every city and village, preaching and bringing the glad tidings of the kingdom of God. And the twelve were with Him, and certain women who had been healed of evil spirits and infirmities—Mary called Magdalene, out of whom had come seven demons, and Joanna the wife of Chuza, Herod's steward, and Susanna, and many others who provided for Him from their substance (Luke 8:1-3).

We can only imagine the reaction Jesus received when he entered a town with female disciples as well as males. We believe these same women were present at Jesus's crucifixion, burial, and resurrection (Luke 24:10).

Luke also mentions another occasion when Jesus frees "a woman who had a spirit of infirmity eighteen years" (Luke 13:11) and then uses the healing as an object lesson in two parables about the kingdom of God (verses 18-21).

Jesus Gives the Disciples Authority

After expending great energy and long hours preaching the gospel of the kingdom and ministering miracles to the masses, Jesus comes to the stark realization that he alone will not be able to help them all before his time runs out. "When He saw the multitudes, He was moved with compassion for them, because they were weary and scattered, like sheep having no shepherd" (Matthew 9:36).

Jesus is emotionally distraught by the sight. He senses that the masses are tired and beaten down, left to fend for themselves, and thus vulnerable to attack from wolves. Jesus is likely thinking of Ezekiel 34.

The word of the LORD came to me, saying, "Son of man,
prophesy against the shepherds of Israel, prophesy and say
to them, 'Thus says the Lord GOD to the shepherds: "Woe
to the shepherds of Israel who feed themselves! Should not
the shepherds feed the flocks? You eat the fat and clothe
yourselves with the wool; you slaughter the fatlings, but
you do not feed the flock. The weak you have not strength-
ened, nor have you healed those who were sick, nor bound
up the broken, nor brought back what was driven away,
nor sought what was lost; but with force and cruelty you
have ruled them. So they were scattered because there was
no shepherd; and they became food for all the beasts of the
field when they were scattered"'" (Ezekiel 34:1-5).

Israel's priests and elders are shepherds in the worst sense of the
word. Rather than protecting the sheep and meeting their daily needs,
the leaders look out for their own well-being. As a result, the sheep
wander off and become prey for the wild animals. God tells Ezekiel,
"I will seek what was lost and bring back what was driven away, bind
up the broken and strengthen what was sick; but I will destroy the fat
and the strong, and feed them in judgment…I will establish one shepherd over them, and he shall feed them—My servant David. He shall
feed them and be their shepherd. And I, the LORD, will be their God,
and My servant David a prince among them; I, the LORD, have spoken" (verses 16,23-24).

Jesus sees himself in the role of a new King David, who will restore
God's kingdom to Israel. But he needs help to gather in the sheep.
Speaking to his disciples, Jesus observes, "The harvest truly is plentiful,
but the laborers are few" (Matthew 9:37). He switches the metaphor
from animal husbandry to horticulture, but the lesson is the same. The
window of time is short. You either gather the harvest or lose it. Jesus
needs more workers to reach the throngs of people, lest they be lost.
There is so much work to do—preaching, healing, and exorcisms—and
so few to do it. So he calls on the disciples to pray that God will send
laborers into the harvest fields (verse 38).

The answer soon follows when Jesus chooses 12 from among his many disciples to go and minister to Israel. They are identified as apostles, or representatives, or ambassadors. "He gave them power over unclean spirits, to cast them out, and to heal all kinds of sickness and all kinds of disease" (Matthew 10:1). The word "power" (Greek, *exousia*) means power of authority or power to rule. We are all familiar with the phrase "power of attorney," which speaks of a transfer of power or authority to another person to serve as your agent or representative. Those with power of attorney have the right to speak and act on your behalf. This delegated authority is limited to certain areas. Jesus gives the 12 apostles authority "over unclean spirits, to cast them out."

Twelve is a significant number because it is clearly connected with the nation of Israel. He sends them with this instruction:

> Do not go into the way of the Gentiles, and do not enter a city of the Samaritans. But go rather to the lost sheep of the house of Israel. And as you go, preach, saying, "The kingdom of heaven is at hand." Heal the sick, cleanse the lepers, raise the dead, cast out demons. Freely you have received, freely give (verses 5-8).

Their mission is identical to Jesus's mission—to proclaim the imminent reign of God. Not some otherworldly and futuristic message, but a here-and-now kingdom in the midst of the people on earth.

Again we see the connection between exorcism and the kingdom of God. Proclamation and demonstration are Siamese twins (also see Luke 9:1-2).The healings and exorcisms are signs that the kingdom has arrived.

When Jesus sees the need to send out additional workers, he commissions 70 more and authorizes them in the same manner as the Twelve (Luke 10:1-11). Their message is also the same—the kingdom of God (verses 9,11). They return from their mission rejoicing: "Lord, even the demons are subject to us in Your name." Notice that they exercise the authority over demons on Jesus's behalf. Jesus rejoices with them, saying, "I saw Satan fall like lightning from heaven. Behold, *I give you the authority* to trample on serpents and scorpions, and *over all the power of the enemy*, and nothing shall by any means hurt you." By saying he witnessed Satan's fall as they cast out demons, Jesus implies that exorcisms are enacted parables of Satan's defeat and God's present reign.

As far as we know, these 70 disciples are not part of Jesus's inner circle. They are not given positions as elders in the church at Jerusalem after Jesus's death and resurrection. They are more like laypeople on a short-term mission trip. Yet Jesus gives them authority over demons, a sure sign that the kingdom has come.

Exorcism in the Early Church

The nascent church continued preaching the gospel of the kingdom, so we should not be surprised to find believers dealing with demon possession. Satan entices Ananias and Sapphira to lie to God and the church (Acts 5:3). When Philip, a layman, preaches Christ in Samaria, demons flee.

> The multitudes with one accord heeded the things spoken by Philip, hearing and seeing the miracles which he did. For unclean spirits, crying with a loud voice, came out of many who were possessed; and many who were paralyzed and lame were healed. And there was great joy in that city (Acts 8:6-8).

Luke identifies the content of Philip's message as "the things concerning the kingdom of God and the name of Jesus Christ" (verse 12).

Likewise the apostle Paul has several encounters with demonized people. On the isle of Paphos, he causes a supernatural blindness to come upon Elymas, a Jewish sorcerer and advisor to proconsul Sergius Paulus, enabling the proconsul to receive the gospel unhindered (Acts 13:6-12). At Philippi, Paul is arrested after casting a demon from a fortune-teller who seeks to impede his gospel preaching (Acts 16:16-24). Luke summarizes Paul's ministry in Ephesus this way: "Now God worked unusual miracles by the hands of Paul, so that even handkerchiefs or aprons were brought from his body to the sick, and the diseases left them and the evil spirits went out of them" (Acts 19:11-12). Paul's authority over demons was delegated by the exalted Lord Jesus.

After witnessing Paul's success at exorcism, his itinerant Jewish exorcists "took it upon themselves to call the name of the Lord Jesus over those who had evil spirits, saying, 'We exorcise you by the Jesus whom Paul preaches'" (verses 13-14).

Confronting the Devil in the Twenty-First Century

Exorcism is a sign of the kingdom's arrival, so we might ask, shouldn't we expect to see people delivered from demonic oppression today? After all, Satan and his demons haven't disappeared, have they? So where are all the demons? In Western society we rarely hear of exorcisms, but they seem to be more prevalent in some African, Indian, and Latin American cultures. Have all the demons migrated to Third World countries?

As children of the Enlightenment, Westerners are skeptical of supernatural phenomena. We have a tendency to delegitimize reports of demon possession, choosing to label bizarre behavior as simply a manifestation of mental illness. And in most cases, that may indeed be the correct diagnosis. But what about the others, whose problems cannot be traced to a medical or psychological source? Must they be left to face their demons alone without hope or comfort? Could some of these unfortunate souls, who are unresponsive to medical treatment or psychotherapy, be possessed? Some might even be confined to psychiatric wards for the criminally insane, where they will remain for life.

Both Jesus and the early church preached the gospel of the kingdom and successfully set captives free. Could our inability to cast out demons be linked somehow to our failure to preach the real gospel—the gospel of God's kingdom?

Satan Is Still Active on the Earth

- "We know that we are of God, and the whole world lies under the sway of the wicked one" (1 John 5:19).

- Satan is called "the god of this world" (2 Corinthians 4:4 NRSV).

- "Satan himself transforms himself into an angel of light" (2 Corinthians 11:14).

- The gift of discerning of spirits is needed for today (1 Corinthians 12:10).

- Paul refers to principalities and powers (Romans 8:38; Ephesians 1:21; 6:12; Colossians 1:16).

- Satan is called "the prince of the power of the air, the spirit who now works in the sons of disobedience" (Ephesians 2:2).

- Paul exhorts us to refrain from unwarranted anger lest we give place to the devil (Ephesians 4:27). He also says we "wrestle...against principalities, against powers, against the rulers of the darkness of this age, against spiritual hosts of wickedness in the heavenly places" (6:12). He warns his readers to be armed for battle with spiritual armor, including the shield of faith, with which they will be able to "quench all the fiery darts of the wicked one" (verse 16).

- "The coming of the lawless one is according to the working of Satan, with all power, signs, and lying wonders, and with all unrighteous deception among those who perish, because they did not receive the love of the truth, that they might be saved" (2 Thessalonians 2:9-10).

- Paul instructs Timothy to bring the rebellious to repentance "that they may come to their senses and escape the snare of the devil, having been taken captive by him to do his will" (2 Timothy 2:26).

- "Resist the devil and he will flee from you" (James 4:7).

- "Be sober, be vigilant; because your adversary the devil walks about like a roaring lion, seeking whom he may devour. Resist him" (1 Peter 5:8-9).

- "Beloved, do not believe every spirit, but test the spirits, whether they are of God" (1 John 4:1).

- "That serpent of old, called the Devil and Satan... deceives the whole world." He is "the accuser of our brethren" (Revelation 12:9-10).

7

Kingdom Healings and Miracles

He sent them to preach the kingdom of God and to heal the sick.

LUKE 9:2

As God's anointed King, Jesus calls others to join him in his mission (Matthew 4:18-22). With them by his side, he begins to minister in the power of the Holy Spirit. "Jesus went about all Galilee, teaching in their synagogues, preaching the gospel of the kingdom, and healing all kinds of sickness and all kinds of disease among the people" (verse 23). Teaching from the Hebrew Bible, preaching the reign of God, and healing people of physical ailments—Jesus not only *proclaims* the kingdom, he *demonstrates* it.

No longer is the kingdom "at hand" as he and John had previously exclaimed. It now has arrived in a manifestation of power. Remember Luke's account of Jesus standing in the synagogue and declaring, "The time is fulfilled"? He had said he was anointed from on high to perform miracles (Luke 4:18-19). There is no doubt, at least in Jesus's mind, that his miracles are evidence of the kingdom's arrival.

John the Baptist later sends two runners to ask of Jesus, "Are You the Coming One, or do we look for another?" (Matthew 11:3). Jesus answers abruptly:

> Go and tell John the things which you hear and see: The
> blind see and the lame walk; the lepers are cleansed and
> the deaf hear; the dead are raised up and the poor have
> the gospel preached to them. And blessed is he who is not
> offended because of Me (verses 4-6).

In his response, Jesus refers to Isaiah 35:5-6, a passage predicting that people will be miraculously healed when the kingdom comes to earth. Jesus understands his miracles to be fulfillments of these kingdom prophecies. The arrival of the kingdom and miracles go hand in hand.

Peter likewise preaches, "God anointed Jesus of Nazareth with the Holy Spirit and with power, who went about doing good and *healing all* who were oppressed by the devil, for God was with Him. And we are witnesses of all things which He did both in the land of the Jews and in Jerusalem" (Acts 10:38-39).

Matthew notes that Jesus's ministry was characterized by miracles from the beginning:

> His fame went throughout all Syria; and they brought to
> Him all sick people who were afflicted with various dis-
> eases and torments, and those who were demon-possessed,
> epileptics, and paralytics; and He healed them. Great mul-
> titudes followed Him—from Galilee, and from Decap-
> olis, Jerusalem, Judea, and beyond the Jordan (Matthew
> 4:24-25).

This overview, which lists a wide variety of sicknesses and afflictions, is Matthew's way of affirming that nothing is beyond Jesus's ability to heal or conquer. When word gets out that Jesus is a God-anointed miracle worker, the crowds flock to him.

Jesus's Miracles—Evidence the Kingdom Has Arrived

We will briefly review ten examples of Jesus using his kingdom power to perform miracles. Each demonstration confirms that the end-time kingdom has invaded the realm of humankind.

1. Healing a Leper (Matthew 8:2-4)

> A leper came and worshiped Him, saying, "Lord, if You are willing, You can make me clean." Then Jesus put out His hand and touched him, saying, "I am willing; be cleansed." Immediately his leprosy was cleansed (verses 2-3).

After showing deference to Jesus by bowing down before him, this leper cautiously springs his question. Approaching another person in public is a brazen and socially unacceptable move for a leper. Despite his boldness, his question reflects a reticence. He believes Jesus *can* heal, but *will* he? How thrilled and surprised he must be when Jesus throws all caution aside and touches his contagiously diseased body! Without a moment's hesitation Jesus replies, "I am willing; be cleansed."

I have searched the Gospels to find a single case of Jesus refusing a person's request for healing. I have yet to find one. This is no exception. The leprosy disappears instantly. In a moment's time, the man's life is totally changed. I can only imagine the reunion he has with his family—hugging his kids and kissing and caressing his wife. He can work, provide for his loved ones, and start tithing to the Lord.

Many theologians believe the Gospel writers include miracle stories in order to prove that Jesus is divine. But miracles are not proof of deity. Many Old Testament prophets heal people and even raise them from the dead, yet they are mere mortals.

Jesus's miracle ministry is a demonstration that the kingdom of God has arrived. The eschatological Spirit resides in Jesus and empowers him to do the impossible. Wherever God's authorized and anointed King travels, the kingdom of God is there. Jesus's miracles are signs of the kingdom's presence.

2. Healing the Centurion's Servant (Matthew 8:5-13)

Next Matthew tells of a Roman soldier who comes to Jesus in Capernaum, pleading on behalf of his trusted aide: "Lord, my servant is lying at home paralyzed, dreadfully tormented." Luke adds that the servant is at the point of death (Luke 7:2). Jesus responds immediately: "I will come and heal him."

I am not sure many of us living in the twenty-first century can appreciate this situation. This military officer has pledged his allegiance to Caesar alone as Lord, but now he addresses Jesus as Lord. This must cause more than a few eyebrows to rise. After all, onlookers might view his confession as an act of treason. Even more startling, at least from a Jewish point of view, is that Jesus, an itinerant rabbi, is willing to rub shoulders with an unclean Gentile!

Notice how the soldier reacts to Jesus's willing response.

> Lord, I am not worthy that You should come under my roof. But only speak a word, and my servant will be healed. For I also am a man under authority, having soldiers under me. And I say to this one, "Go," and he goes; and to another, "Come," and he comes; and to my servant, "Do this," and he does it (verses 8-9).

The centurion doesn't expect Jesus to make a personal visit to his home. A word will suffice. Jesus marvels at the soldier's reply and turns to the crowds that follow.

> Assuredly, I say to you, I have not found such great faith, not even in Israel! And I say to you that many will come from east and west, and sit down with Abraham, Isaac, and Jacob in the kingdom of heaven. But the sons of the kingdom will be cast out into outer darkness. There will be weeping and gnashing of teeth (verses 10-12).

This statement reveals much about God's ultimate kingdom plans. When the kingdom comes to earth in its fullness and believers throughout the ages recline at the messianic banquet, their number will include Gentiles. The tragedy is that many Jews ("the sons of the kingdom") to whom God originally gave the kingdom will not be part of the final kingdom. Admission into the kingdom is based on faith alone, not ancestry. You don't make it in merely because your parents were God-fearing people.

Then Jesus grants the centurion's request. "'Go your way; and as you have believed, so let it be done for you.' And his servant was healed that same hour."

We all know people suffering from debilitating and dreaded diseases. They walk into a doctor's office feeling a bit under the weather, and they emerge with a bad report or even a death sentence. We think, "If they had only lived in Jesus's day, he would have healed them." In truth, we still have access to Jesus's healing power. Distance is not a factor with him. He healed the centurion's servant from a distance with a word, and he can still do it today! When Jesus ascended to the Father, he didn't take the kingdom with him! He still reigns over the earth and continues to minister through his Spirit, which is given to the church.

3. Healing Peter's Mother-in-Law (Matthew 8:14-15)

After Jesus heals the centurion's servant, he and his disciples go to Peter's house for a meal and a relaxing evening. But on arrival, Jesus notices Peter's mother-in-law "lying sick with a fever." We have no idea how sick she is, but we know she is out of commission. "So He touched her hand, and the fever left her. And she arose and served them," which is a likely reference to cooking them a meal. The recipient of a kingdom miracle now ministers to God's anointed kingdom servants.

Of the three healings we have examined thus far, Jesus heals by touch on two occasions and by word alone on another. In each case, he exercises kingdom authority.

As word spreads, people start bringing their friends and relatives to Jesus, and he heals all who are sick (verse 16). None of them return home in the same condition in which they arrived.

A Theological Explanation (Matthew 8:17)

Before moving on to the next miracle story, Matthew highlights the significance of these healings, connecting them to an Old Testament prophecy: "that it might be fulfilled which was spoken by Isaiah the prophet, saying: 'He Himself took our infirmities and bore our sicknesses.'" This quote from Isaiah 53:4 describes a Messiah whose suffering brings physical healing to God's people.

Matthew writes his Gospel many years after Christ's death, so these insights are the result of prolonged reflection. Most of his readers, living sometime between AD 66 and 85, never met Jesus or witnessed his miracles firsthand. Therefore, they are dependent entirely on Matthew's Gospel for their knowledge. We too must rely on the Gospel writers for our information about the meaning of Jesus's ministry.

So often we think of Christ's death on the cross only as it relates to forgiveness of sins. But it involves more than spiritual health. The apostle Peter applies Isaiah 53:4 in this way (1 Peter 2:24), but Matthew links it to physical sickness. As a result of these two interpretations, a controversy exists regarding the benefits of the crucifixion.

The best explanation is that Christ's death secures salvation for the *whole* person—forgiveness for the soul and healing for the body. But neither sin nor sickness will be eliminated entirely from the earth until Christ returns to set up his ultimate kingdom. Between now and then we struggle with both. However, we can experience a foretaste of the kingdom to come. Both forgiveness and healing are available to us in the interim. This is one of the benefits of Christ's redemptive work.

Allow me to make another observation. Matthew links healing to Christ's suffering on the cross, yet all the healings in Matthew's Gospel take place *prior* to the crucifixion. This leaves us with a dilemma. How does Jesus heal in advance of the cross? The same way he forgives sin prior to the cross—the effects of the crucifixion extend to the past as well as to the future.

4. Calming the Storm (Matthew 8:23-27)

After a day of exhausting ministry, Jesus and the disciples get into a boat to cross the Sea of Galilee. Jesus relaxes and soon falls asleep as they begin to make the eight-mile crossing to the eastern shore. As they sail, "suddenly a great tempest arose on the sea." As the surging waves rise, the boat takes on water, and the disciples fear for their lives. The term "tempest," translated from the Greek word *seismos*, speaks of a violent shaking. We recognize the word in relationship to seismology, the science of measuring earthquakes. Matthew is describing a storm that has Peter, James, and John—all experienced fishermen—shaking in their boots!

The Sea of Galilee is 680 feet below sea level and is bordered on the east by high hills, so the geographic and atmospheric conditions can suddenly turn the sea into a raging wind tunnel, producing violent storms. This is the setting and the situation.

During the whole episode, Jesus sleeps like a baby. When the disciples finally jar him out of his deep sleep, they cry out for him to help. But what do they expect him to do? The most common answer is to stop the storm. However, I believe this is reading too much into the text. The disciples do not yet realize that Jesus is divine. Do they want him to help bail out the water? Another hand will not solve their problem. Most likely they want him to pray to God on their behalf. They know he has a direct line to God.

Look how Jesus responds. "Why are you fearful, O you of little faith?" He chides these tough sailors for being cowardly, and then he labels their faith as miniscule. Earlier in the day, he called attention to the Gentile centurion's "great faith" (Matthew 8:10).

They freak out when they should trust God to see them through the storm. After all, isn't this what Jesus does? He is so trusting of his Father that he sleeps and doesn't bother to get up as the storm rages. In fact, when Jesus first gets into the boat, he commands, "Depart to the other side" (verse 18). He actually expects to make it across the lake from the start.

We are no different from the disciples on this stormy night. We lose our focus and become frantic, forgetting that Jesus is with us in every crisis.

Finally, Jesus stands in the boat and rebukes the winds and the sea, "and there was great calm." Jesus deals with storms the same way he deals with demons. This may be Matthew's way of letting us know that this is no ordinary storm, but is demonically controlled.

If you think the disciples are terrified during the storm, they must be scared stiff after it is over! In their astonishment they ask each other, "Who can this be, that even the winds and the sea obey him?" This question proves the disciples were still confused about Jesus's identity. It may be easier for us, living on this side of the resurrection, to answer their question. One thing is for sure—the disciples were not expecting Jesus to calm the sea.

Here is an interesting side note that should help us understand the significance of this miracle. The Sea of Galilee was also called Lake Tiberius, named in honor of Emperor Tiberius Caesar, who reigns over the Roman Empire at the time of Jesus's ministry. Tiberius holds the title Master of the Sea, indicating that even the sea is under his control. Everything that comes out of the sea rightfully belongs to him. Therefore, every haul a fisherman drags to shore is viewed as benevolence from the hand of Caesar. All blessings flow down from his throne to the masses. But Satan is the real power behind the throne. He controls the kingdoms of the world. The usurper claims the land and sea for himself, which may help to explain why Jesus rebukes the storm, showing his power to be greater than that of Caesar or Satan.

5. Healing a Paralytic (Matthew 9:1-8)

Our next kingdom miracle opens with the words, "So He got into a boat, crossed over, and came to His own city," a reference to Capernaum. Matthew then tells of a paralytic man whose friends carry him to Jesus. Luke's Gospel recounts their heroic effort to lower him down through a hole in the roof because they can't get through the front door for the press of the crowds desiring to see Jesus (Luke 5:17-19). Both texts comment that after Jesus notices their faith, he turns to the crippled man and says, "Your sins are forgiven you" (Matthew 9:2; Luke 5:20).

Wait a minute! What a strange thing to say! These men have faith for their friend's healing, not for his forgiveness. So why does Jesus make such a statement? Can he forgive sin based on someone else's faith? Of course not!

What seems strange to us made perfect sense in Jesus's day. Many Jews believed sickness was the result of sin and that healing could not take place until a person was first forgiven. So possibly Jesus decides to deal with the root problem that, according to tradition, opens the way for healing. But when he declares the man forgiven, the scribes murmur, "This Man blasphemes" (Matthew 9:3) and declare that only God can forgive sins (Luke 5:21).

Their assertion, however, is inaccurate. The high priest, himself only a man, had authority to forgive sins because he represented God. Jesus claims the same right. He is God's authorized spokesperson, God's high priest. Caiaphas, the usurper, is appointed by Rome, not God.

After accusing the religious leaders of being evil, Jesus asks, "For which is easier, to say, 'Your sins are forgiven you,' or to say, 'Arise and walk'?"

No one can see a forgiven sin, so the first statement is easier to make than the second. But walking is another story. Either the person walks or he doesn't. It is obvious to all.

To the scribes and Pharisees, Jesus says, "But that you may know that the Son of Man has power on earth to forgive sins..." And then, turning to the paralytic, he commands, "Arise, take up your bed, and go to your house." The man walks home of his own accord.

The miracle proves Jesus has the authority, or "power on earth," to forgive sin and heal disease. After his resurrection, Jesus avows that his authority has been expanded to include heaven and earth (Matthew 28:18). As you read this book, Jesus Christ sits at God's right hand as the exalted ruler of the universe. He reigns as King over all creation and calls on all people everywhere to pledge their allegiance to him.

Matthew concludes, "Now when the multitudes saw it, they marveled and glorified God, who had given such power *to men*." How excited do you think these people became? How about the man's four friends or his wife and family? They must have been beside themselves. I doubt that anyone who was present ever forgot that day. In fact, we're still talking about it!

How excited are you over this miracle? Do you want to become even more excited? Then read verse 8 again. Notice the word "men" is plural, not singular. Jesus is not the only one who has been given power, or authority. It is available to us as well.

In the Great Commission, Jesus commands *the apostles* to preach "forgiveness of sins" (Luke 24:47 NRSV), and he instructs them, "If *you forgive the sins* of any, they are forgiven them; if you retain the sins of any, they are retained" (John 20:23). On another occasion, Jesus predicts his imminent death and resurrection and tells of his plans to build his church. He then gives authority to the apostles to bind and loose on earth what God binds and loosens (Matthew 16:13-19), a reference to forgiving sins. He again speaks to the issue when teaching on relationships in the church.

> If your brother sins against you, go and tell him his fault between you and him alone. If he hears you, you have gained your brother. But if he will not hear, take with you one or two more, that "by the mouth of two or three witnesses every word may be established." And if he refuses to hear them, tell it to the church. But if he refuses even to hear the church, let him be to you like a heathen and a tax collector.
>
> Assuredly, I say to you, whatever you bind on earth will be bound in heaven, and whatever you loose on earth will be loosed in heaven (Matthew 18:15-18).

If the Great Commission applies to us, as most interpreters believe, then all believers (not just apostles) are authorized to forgive sins. The Roman Catholic Church uses these verses to support its rite of Confession, but it claims the priesthood alone possesses the authority to forgive sins. Protestants, however, have shied away from confessing sins to each other because it smacks of Roman Catholicism. Both groups miss the bull's-eye.

In God's view, all believers are priests in his kingdom, serving and representing him on earth. We have the high privilege of proclaiming the gospel of the kingdom and calling on the lost to repent of their sins. We can promise and pronounce forgiveness when they respond in obedience. On the Day of Pentecost, the apostle Peter is the first to do so. He announces, "Repent, and let every one of you be baptized in the name of Jesus Christ for the remission of sins; and you shall receive the gift of the Holy Spirit. For the promise is to you and to your children, and to all who are afar off, as many as the Lord our God will call" (Acts 2:38-39).

6–7. Healing Jairus's Daughter and the Bleeding Woman (Matthew 9:18-26)

We will consider these two miracles together, as the Scriptures do.

As Jesus eats a meal at Levi's house, a well-known but uninvited guest, a ruler of the synagogue named Jairus (Mark 5:22), interrupts the lively after-dinner discussion. Jairus announces his emergency situation: "My daughter has just died, but come and lay Your hand on her and she will live."

Why does he come to Jesus? Possibly he witnessed Jesus heal someone in his synagogue. Or maybe he heard stories of Jesus's miraculous powers. In any case, his urgent plea moves Jesus to respond. "Jesus arose and followed him, and so did His disciples." But then comes an unexpected interruption—suddenly, a woman with a 12-year-old blood condition comes from behind and touches the hem of Jesus's robe and says to herself, "If only I may touch His garment, I shall be made well." In Mark's fuller account of the incident, we learn that the press of the crowd is so great that the procession moves only at a snail's pace toward Jairus's house. And now this woman with a chronic illness brings the advancement to a complete halt.

I don't know about you, but if I were Jairus, I would be frustrated and angry. After all, I have an emergency on my hands, and this lady with a noncritical and prolonged illness literally grabs Jesus's attention. To make matters worse, he turns and responds, "Be of good cheer, daughter; your faith has made you well." Matthew adds, "And the woman was made well from that hour." With the daughter's life hanging in the balance, every second counts. This unnecessary delay seems unconscionable.

But Matthew is sure to let us know that the bleeding woman has faith that Jesus will heal her. Thus, she and Jairus have something in common. They both exhibit an unqualified faith.

With the woman's problem resolved, Jesus heads toward Jairus's house. Upon arrival, he confronts a wake in progress, replete with flute players and professional mourners. Everyone is wailing as their emotions run deep over the death of the ruler's daughter. When Jesus, disturbed by the sight, commands the crowd to "make room, for the girl is not dead, but sleeping," the mourners ridicule him.

In ancient times, prior to scientific tools, it was difficult to tell if a person had actually died. Some Bible commentators believe Jesus uses the word "sleep" euphemistically as a substitute for death. This is unlikely because he states categorically, "The girl is not dead." He discerns she is alive indeed "but sleeping." Today, we would say she is in a coma.

Matthew continues the account: "But when the crowd was put outside, He went in and took her by the hand, and the girl arose." The phrase "put outside" means the mourners are removed or expelled by force. This is the same word used to describe how Jesus casts out demons. With the doubters no longer an obstacle, Jesus raises the girl from a fate worse than death. He keeps her from being buried alive!

Matthew concludes, "And the report of this went out into all that land."

Interestingly, Jairus's daughter is 12 years old, or on the verge of womanhood, and the bleeding woman has been ill for 12 years. She has been sick as long as the girl has been alive. Both are beyond help. They are physically bound with no way out.

In Jewish thought, numbers have symbolic significance. So it is no surprise to find the case of two persons linked in one passage by the number 12. To the Jewish mind, 12 represents the nation of Israel. There are 12 tribes, 12 stones on the high priest's breastplate, and 12 loaves of showbread. The Gospel writers likely view these two women as emblematic of Israel.

Jesus's healings, exorcisms, and other miracles point graphically to the defeat of evil that keeps God's people down. Kingdom miracles also serve as enacted parables, showing that Rome and Satan are losing their physical, economic, and political hold on Israel. So Jesus's demonstrations of kingdom power serve as hidden messages that proclaim deliverance.

God's kingdom is invading enemy territory and gaining one victory at a time. As God's kingdom increases, Satan's kingdom suffers loss.

8. Healing Two Blind Men (Matthew 9:27-31)

"When Jesus departed from there, two blind men followed Him, crying out and saying, 'Son of David, have mercy on us!'" Two things jump off the page. First, the title Son of David is a designation for the

Messiah and has similar meaning to Son of God, or King. The blind men perceive Jesus to be Israel's messianic King who will usher in the kingdom. The title is given a prominent place in the first verse of Matthew's Gospel: "The book of the genealogy of Jesus Christ [or Messiah], the Son of David, the Son of Abraham." As Son of David, Jesus fulfills the Davidic covenant and is heir to David's throne (2 Samuel 7:12-16). Just as David was the king of the Jews, so Jesus now takes the moniker. He, not Herod, is God's authorized ruler over Israel. All promises and hopes for the nation rest with him. The blind men recognize Jesus as David's successor.

Second, their call, "Have mercy on us," contains covenant language. These men are pleading for God to keep his covenant promises by extending loving compassion or mercy to them through his newly revealed Son of David.

As they follow him into a house, he replies, "Do you believe that I am able to do this?" "Yes, Lord" is their simple reply. Their positive answer motivates Jesus to touch them and say, "According to your faith let it be to you." The miracle is instantaneous: "And their eyes were opened."

Again, notice the importance of faith. Few things thrill God more than people trusting him and taking him at his word. In fact, the writer of Hebrews says, "Without faith it is impossible to please Him" (Hebrews 11:6). Faith is an important kingdom principle. God's kingdom power is released on earth when we exhibit faith. There are no limits in the kingdom when we walk by faith and not by sight.

9. Healing a Mute Man (Matthew 9:32-34)

We now look at yet another healing that points to the kingdom of God. "As they [likely Jesus, the disciples, and the formerly blind men] went out, behold, they brought to Him a man, mute and demon-possessed." This shows Jesus's popularity. No sooner does he heal one person than others are waiting in the wings for their miracle. A non-stop flow of people come to him for healing. We too should be seeking his healing touch.

On this occasion the prevailing problem is satanic. In the West today, we give little credence to demon-related sickness. But it is real. Some diseases and illnesses that do not respond to medicine and therapy may have a demonic source. This is one such case. Jesus, recognizing the cause of the trouble, casts out the demon, and the mute speaks.

As I mentioned previously, there is more to these miracles than meets the eye. The Old Testament prophets told of a future day when miracles would accompany the arrival of God's kingdom.

> Then the eyes of the blind shall be opened,
> And the ears of the deaf shall be unstopped.
> Then the lame shall leap like a deer,
> And the tongue of the dumb sing (Isaiah 35:5-6).

These things are happening in Jesus's ministry. As God's appointed and anointed King, Jesus brings the kingdom to the people in word and deed. He is the messenger and mediator of the kingdom.

Those who witness the healing of the mute man marvel and exclaim they have never seen anything like this before in all of Israel. Yet the Pharisees decry, "He casts out demons by the ruler of the demons."

The masses of common people recognize Jesus's healing as unique in the history of Israel, but the religious leaders oppose Jesus's ministry. Instead of recognizing that Jesus possesses the power of God, the Pharisees accuse him of being in league with the prince of demons, or Beelzebub. A line is drawn in the sand with supporters on one side and the opposition on the other.

On another occasion, when Jesus heals a demon-possessed man who is both blind and mute, the Pharisees again accuse him of casting out demons by the power Satan (Matthew 12:22-24). After exposing their claims as nonsensical, Jesus counters with, "But if I cast out demons by the Spirit of God, *surely the kingdom of God has come upon you.*" Exorcisms demonstrate the present reign of God.

Like Matthew's original audience, we must choose sides. Are we on the side of the kingdom of God or on the side of tradition? Do we view healings and miracles with suspicion and contempt by labeling them as demonic, or do we embrace the validity of God's healing power as evidence that the kingdom has arrived on earth and that we are the beneficiaries? Are we persons of faith or doubt?

Miracles will move you toward the kingdom or away from it. The Gospel writers include accounts of miracles so their readers will embrace the kingdom not only as a future hope but also as a present reality that can be experienced here and now on earth.

This section of Matthew's Gospel concludes with this summary: "Then Jesus went about all the cities and villages, teaching in their synagogues, preaching the gospel of the kingdom, and healing every sickness and every disease among the people" (Matthew 9:35). This descriptive statement is a repeat of Matthew 4:23. I guess Matthew doesn't want us to miss the point. Jesus had a unique Spirit-empowered ministry.

10. Feeding the 5000 (John 6:1-15)

I have chosen one account from the Gospel of John because of its clear connection to the kingdom of God. The feeding of the 5000 takes place on a hillside near the Sea of Galilee in the final year of Jesus's ministry. When Jesus asks his disciples where they might buy food to feed the hungering crowd, Philip replies that they can't afford such a large purchase. Jesus asks the question to test their creative resolve and to see if they can come up with a solution, but he already has a plan in mind.

When Andrew mentions in passing that a boy in the crowd has five barley loaves and two tiny fish, he never anticipates what is about to happen. After instructing the disciples to arrange the people in rows, Jesus takes the child's lunch and tells the disciples to distribute it to the 5000. The food begins to multiply in their hands and never runs out!

> So when they were filled, He said to His disciples, "Gather up the fragments that remain, so that nothing is lost." Therefore they gathered them up, and filled twelve baskets with the fragments of the five barley loaves which were left over by those who had eaten. Then those men, when they had seen the sign that Jesus did, said, "This is truly the Prophet who is to come into the world" (John 6:12-14).

When I was a seminary student a number of years ago, Professor Lowell Hazard told our class a story from his life in London during WWII. As a newly ordained minister, he was leading an afternoon Bible study for college students when the Germans began bombing London. The students enjoyed gathering each week to open God's Word and then break for afternoon tea. When bombing raids increased, the group discussed whether they should suspend their weekly study. One student suggested they keep meeting until the sugar bowl was empty. That would be the sign to stop. The sugar never ran out! Each teaspoon of sugar used for tea mysteriously reappeared. Professor Hazard says it was a genuine miracle, reminding us that sugar was rationed during the war and in very short supply.

The bread and fish are never exhausted. The people proclaim Jesus to be the Prophet—a reference to the long-expected prophet as foretold in Deuteronomy 18:15-16, who will lead God's people in a new Exodus. In this case, they are expecting deliverance from Roman tyranny. The prophet will be Israel's new king, the head of God's government on earth. Earlier in the Gospel of John, the priests and Levites ask John the Baptist if he is the Prophet. He answers no (John 1:21).

The crowd interprets the feeding of the 5000 to be a sign that Jesus is the Messiah-King. On the Day of Pentecost, the apostle Peter likewise describes Jesus as "a Man attested by God to you by miracles, wonders, and signs which God did through Him in your midst" (Acts 2:22).

Jesus orders the disciples to gather the leftovers and place them into 12 baskets so "*nothing is lost.*" This is another clue that the miracle points to the kingdom. As we have noted previously, the number 12 is often a symbol for Israel. If such is the case here, the collecting of the fragments might represent the ingathering of the broken and scattered tribes, which will occur when God restores the kingdom to Israel. If so, this miracle serves as yet another enacted prophecy that speaks of God saving his people. This makes sense in light of Jesus's discourse on the bread of heaven later in the same chapter:

> I am the bread of life. He who comes to Me shall never hunger, and he who believes in Me shall never thirst...This

is the will of the Father who sent Me, that of all He has given Me I should *lose nothing*, but should raise it up at the last day (John 6:35,39).

John ends his account of the feeding miracle this way: "Therefore when Jesus perceived that they were about to come and take Him by force *to make Him king*, He departed again to the mountain by Himself alone."

Again we see the kingdom focus. The crowd decides unanimously to draft Jesus as their King. Their intentions are honorable but misguided and ill-conceived. Jesus knows God's kingdom will be established on earth not by a violent revolution, but by the ultimate act of faith, laying down his life for the sheep and trusting God to raise it up again (see Matthew 11:12).

Jesus Empowers His Followers to Perform Miracles

As we have seen, with much to do and so little time to accomplish it, Jesus deputizes a group of followers to help him reach the masses. "Then He called His twelve disciples together and gave them power and authority over all demons, and to cure diseases. He sent them to *preach the kingdom of God and to heal the sick*" (Luke 9:1-2). Prior to their calling, the disciples have no ability to perform miraculous feats. This capacity comes only after Jesus empowers them.

As representatives of Jesus, the apostles are mostly successful in their endeavors, although as we have seen, at least on one occasion they fail in their attempt to cure a demon-related illness (Mark 9:17-18).

Then a day arrives when Jesus discloses his plan to transfer his kingdom powers to his disciples in a more permanent way. They will carry on a kingdom-focused ministry after his departure. Reclining at the Last Supper, Jesus prepares them for their assignment in his absence (John 14:1-6). When they inquire about his destination, Jesus says he is going to the Father, the one who has worked through him to perform all the miracles. Knowing they do not grasp his unique relationship with the Father, he asks, "Do you not believe that I am in the Father, and the Father in Me?" He then offers an explanation.

> The words that I speak to you I do not speak on My own authority; but the Father who dwells in Me does the works. Believe Me that I am in the Father and the Father in Me, or else believe Me for the sake of the works themselves (verses 10-11).

In this conversation Jesus emphasizes the words "believe" and "works." First, the disciples must believe that Jesus is in the Father and the Father is in him. In fact he commands them to believe it! This concept must be as confusing to them as it is for us. Second, if they have trouble accepting or understanding Jesus's claim of having a special relationship with the Father, they need to believe "for the sake of *the works* themselves." His miracles are proof of his claim. This leads to one of Jesus's most controversial sayings in the New Testament.

> Most assuredly, I say to you, he who believes in Me, the works that I do he will do also; and greater works than these he will do, because I go to My Father. And whatever you ask in My name, that will I do, that the Father may be glorified in the Son (verses 12-13).

This is a remarkable promise. Jesus offers the apostles carte blanche, giving them unlimited power and authority to perform kingdom deeds in his absence.

When we look carefully at the promise, we notice it contains two actions. The first action relates to the disciples. They shall perform the same works—and even greater works than Jesus. The promise is made to the apostles, but it is not limited to them alone. It has a broader application, for Jesus says, "*He who believes* in Me, the works that I do *he will do* also; and greater works than these he will do." That includes us. Notice it does not say that we *might* do greater works, but that we *will* do them.

The second action relates to Jesus. "Whatever you ask...*that will I do*." This means we work together: "He will do" and "I will do." They go together. The believer has a part, and Jesus has a part.

The basis for the promise involves him going to the Father. But what is it about Jesus traveling to heaven that guarantees his promise will be kept? We know that his departure is followed by the end-time pouring out of the Spirit (John 14:26). The Spirit is the power behind the works and greater works.

Although the promise is unlimited, it contains a conditional clause. Certain requirements must be met before the promise is fulfilled. "Most assuredly, I say to you, he who *believes* in Me, the works that I do he will do also." We must believe. If we lack confidence that he will keep his word, we will see no results.

Additionally, Jesus says all our requests must be in his name. But what does this entail? To make a request in the name of someone else means to do it with his full support. If I give you my credit card to buy yourself a pair of shoes, you buy them in my name, but you receive the benefit. When the bill comes due, I will pay it. Here is a question for you to ponder: Who bought the shoes—you, me, or both of us?

We can make our request without presumption because Jesus authorizes it. We have his word, and we have the power of the end-time Spirit. In a sense, the Spirit is like a credit card, or better yet, a debit card accessing cash on hand to cover all charges.

Jesus answers our requests "that the Father may be glorified in the Son." When Jesus fulfills his promise, he extols God and reveals his goodness for all to see. That's the goal. Miracles are not ends in themselves, but means to a greater end—the glorification of God, which is what the kingdom is all about.

Now we come to the $64,000 question: What are the "greater works"? They are acts of God, which include answers to prayer as well as his ministry through us, which produces exorcisms, healings, and other miracles. Jesus had already authorized first the Twelve and then 70 others to heal the sick and cast out demons (Luke 9:1-6; 10:1,9,17), so we shouldn't be surprised that he empowers other believers to do miraculous works after his ascension. In the book of Acts we read of ordinary Christians accomplishing mighty works. People are healed of a whole range of diseases. The blind see, the lame walk, the deaf hear, and the dead are brought back to life (Acts 3:1-10; 14:3,8-10; 16:16-18; 19:11-17; 20:7-12; 28:1-6). These are signs that the kingdom has arrived.

Just as in Jesus's ministry, we see in the book of Acts that preaching the gospel of the kingdom and miracles are interconnected. For example, Luke specifically writes that Philip, a layman, goes to Samaria and preaches "the things concerning the kingdom of God." Many people believe and are baptized, including Simon the sorcerer, who is amazed by the miracles and signs done by the hands of Philip (Acts 8:12-13).

Philip, Timothy, and Barnabas are not apostles in the traditional sense of the word, yet God uses them to perform great feats. After Jesus ascends and takes his seat at God's right hand, he sends the Spirit and gives spiritual gifts to ordinary believers. Both the end-time Spirit and the gifts come from the exalted Jesus, as Paul makes clear.

> To each one of us grace was given according to the measure
> of Christ's gift. Therefore He says:
>
> "When He ascended on high,
> He led captivity captive,
> And gave gifts to men" (Ephesians 4:7-8).

These are gifts from the reigning King to his people on earth. They contribute to the fulfilling of Jesus's prayer, "Your kingdom come, your will be done on earth as it is in heaven."

Although our works cannot be greater in *quality* than those of Jesus (what can be greater than raising a person from the dead!), they are greater in *quantity*. When Jesus was on earth, his ministry was limited geographically to the land of Israel, and it lasted for three years only. But for the past 2000 years, Christ has ministered through the church, his corporate body, which consists of millions of Spirit-empowered believers. Jesus commissions us to continue demonstrating the power of the kingdom to the end of the age.

Greater Works in the Twenty-First Century

Healings and miracles may fill the pages of the Bible, but where are they today? Although Jesus promises greater works, we rarely see *any* of them! Why not? This is a difficult question to answer. Here are three considerations.

First, as I mentioned in chapter 6, religion has taken a backseat to science in the Western world since the Enlightenment. Naturalism has supplanted supernaturalism. This shift affects the way people think. Simply put, most people no longer believe in a Jesus who performs miracles through them or for them. The minority who still hold to such a belief are often labeled fanatics, superstitious, mentally imbalanced, or worse.[1]

Second, healings and other miracles are signs that point to the arrival of the kingdom, and they validate the claims of the true gospel. If we fail to see miracles in our churches, possibly we are not preaching the authentic gospel—the gospel of the kingdom. We place too much emphasis on individual salvation of the soul or going to heaven and not enough on experiencing the kingdom of heaven here and now on earth.

Third, our theology often gets in the way. At an impressionable age, many of us (including me) were introduced to and embraced theological systems that explained away modern-day miracles, arguing that miracles ended when the last apostle died or the canon of Scripture was completed. When coupled with the paucity of miracles in the Western world, the case seems ironclad.

Our opinion of miracles might be different, however, if we didn't approach the text from a preconceived theological perspective or a set of Enlightenment presuppositions. I often encourage my students to apply the Mars principle when reading a text. It goes something like this: If visitors from Mars (who had no understanding of theology and had not been influenced by the Enlightenment) came to earth and read the Bible for the first time, what would they think about the relevancy of healing or miracles for today?

Or consider the many remote villages of the world that have been reached for Christ over the centuries but that remain unaffected by the Enlightenment. Persons living in these regions have little difficulty believing in and receiving miracles. These simple folk have mustard-seed faith. They experience the blessings of the kingdom on their part of the earth.

Putting On Our Thinking Caps

Do you realize that God provided Old Testament believers with divine health and healed them when necessary? For example, "Moses was one hundred and twenty years old when he died. His eyes were not dim nor his natural vigor diminished" (Deuteronomy 34:7). This means he didn't need eyeglasses or Viagra. He had the strength of a young man!

To ancient Israel, God promises, "You shall serve the Lord your God, and He will bless your bread and your water. And *I will take sickness away* from the midst of you. No one shall suffer miscarriage or be barren in your land; I will fulfill the number of your days" (Exodus 23:25-26). Does he keep his promise?

Ask Miriam how her leprosy was healed (Numbers 12:1-15), or Hannah how her barrenness was reversed (1 Samuel 1:9-20), or the two widows how their sons were raised from the dead (1 Kings 17:17-24; 2 Kings 4:18-37), or Naaman how the miracle waters cured his leprosy (2 Kings 5:1-14), or the dead man how his limp body came back to life when it touched Elisha's bones (2 Kings 13:21), or King Hezekiah how he was given 15 more years of life after being at death's door (Isaiah 38:1-8), or the multitudes how they were cured of venomous snake bites when they glanced up at a pole (Numbers 21:4-9).

Don't you wish you lived in Old Testament times? The psalmist praised God for spiritual and physical blessings.

> Bless the Lord, O my soul;
> And all that is within me, bless His holy name!
> Bless the Lord, O my soul,
> And forget not all His benefits:
> Who forgives all your iniquities,
> Who heals all your diseases (Psalm 103:1-3).

The psalmist says that *both* forgiveness and healing are part of the benefit package for Old Testament saints. If God healed his people under the old covenant, will he do any less under the new covenant? After all, isn't the new covenant supposed to be better than the old? How can promises connected with the dawning of God's kingdom be less efficacious than those made to Old Testament saints?

Conclusion

Healings and miracles are evidence that the eschatological reign of God is breaking into time and space. Wherever the gospel of the kingdom is preached, the powers of darkness lose their grip on the affairs of humankind. Salvation is holistic and includes deliverance of both soul *and* body. On the cross Christ reversed the curse, and healing is one of the firstfruits of the kingdom that is available to us.

The kingdom began with Jesus and his ministry. He was God's appointed and anointed King. At first, the kingdom was geographically limited to one man and one location, but it grew like a tiny mustard seed, expanding to include apostles and 70 lay ministers. When Jesus ascended and gave the eschatological Spirit to the first-century church, the kingdom expanded throughout the Roman Empire. Over the centuries, its impact moved across land and sea. The kingdom can now be found wherever believers preach the gospel of the kingdom and allow God to manifest kingdom power through them. At Christ's return the fullness of the kingdom will come on the earth. Therefore the kingdom is both a present reality and a future hope. Or, as we said in a previous chapter, it is "already but not yet." It is here now but always coming.

8

Kingdom Responsibilities

Blessed are the poor in spirit, for theirs is the kingdom of heaven.

MATTHEW 5:3

Citizens everywhere are expected to obey their nation's established laws. Those of us who belong to the kingdom of God are no different. We get to enjoy the benefits of the kingdom, but we also are expected to abide by its moral code. Soon after Jesus launches into his public ministry, he delivers a lengthy treatise on responsibilities of kingdom citizenship.

Kingdom Ethics: Living as Kingdom Citizens

We will limit our study to the Sermon on the Mount (Matthew 5–7), referring to other Gospel accounts only as they shed additional light. Jesus begins his discourse with the Beatitudes.

> Blessed *are* the poor in spirit,
>   For theirs is the kingdom of heaven.
> Blessed *are* those who mourn,
>   For they shall be comforted.
> Blessed *are* the meek,
>   For they shall inherit the earth.
> Blessed *are* those who hunger and thirst for righteousness,

> For they shall be filled.
> Blessed *are* the merciful,
>   For they shall obtain mercy.
> Blessed *are* the pure in heart,
>   For they shall see God.
> Blessed *are* the peacemakers,
>   For they shall be called sons of God.
> Blessed *are* those who are persecuted for righteousness' sake,
>   For theirs is the kingdom of heaven (Matthew 5:3-10).

As we read these well-known and beloved words, our attention is drawn to two things. First, we notice that some people are blessed. We have seen that under the old covenant, those who were faithful to the covenant were blessed, but those breaking the covenant were cursed. Here, the blessed people include the faithful remnant, or those who reorient their lives toward the kingdom. The popular British New Testament commentator William Barclay believes the Beatitudes should not be viewed as statements of facts but as exclamations or exultations: "Oh, the blessedness of…" or "Oh, the sheer happiness of…" This is because the verb "are" is not part of the original Greek text (as indicated by the italics in the NKJV and some other translations), lending to an exclamation more than to a statement of fact. Either way, the bottom line is the same—God's blessing rests on those whose lives exhibit certain characteristics.

Second, we notice that each beatitude is followed by the word "for," which means "because" and gives the reason or basis for the blessedness. Let's look briefly at the eight Beatitudes to determine how each relates to our living as kingdom citizens.

The Poor in Spirit

What does it mean to be poor in spirit? The term "poor" refers to people living in extreme poverty, people who are powerless and disenfranchised and brought to their knees. In the Roman Empire, these people survived by finding a patron, begging, stealing, or turning to prostitution or crime. Others survived by their wits.

Jesus is referring not to all poor people but only to God's poor people. He is addressing his disciples (verse 1) who live on the margins as peasants. To be poor in spirit has to do with one's attitude. Unlike the masses, who take pride in their survival skills, Christ's disciples show themselves humble and trust God to meet their needs.

For Matthew's original audience, including many who lived on the economic edge of society and had never heard Jesus speak in person, this message is an important one. How should they respond to their poverty? They may be tempted to follow the route of Roman society by entering into a patron-client relationship or something more extreme. Jesus's words provide encouragement and hope: "Oh, the blessedness of the poor in spirit!"

Next Jesus explains why they are blessed, even in the throes of financial scarcity: "For theirs is the kingdom of heaven." Notice that he didn't say, "Theirs *will be* the kingdom of heaven." The kingdom is theirs already. It is a present possession, here and now, on earth. The blessings are presently theirs in accord with Jesus's prayer, "Your will be done on earth as it is in heaven." In a later chapter we see what these kingdom blessings entail, but I'll give you a hint. In a kingdom-driven church, all members, despite the lack of resources, have their needs met.

Action Points

- Be humble in spirit.
- Join a kingdom-driven church.
- Trust God to meet your needs.
- Recognize and rejoice that you are blessed.

Those Who Mourn

Many Christians mistakenly think these words refer to those who mourn over their sins. Sin should sadden us, but this is not the intent of Jesus's statement. Notice that he makes no reference whatsoever to sin. I believe the Phillips translation catches the gist of the meaning:

"How happy are those who know what sorrow means." Blessing in sorrow seems like an oxymoron. The two don't go together. But in Jesus's kingdom they are compatible.

You may have experienced such sorrow. Perhaps you've cried your eyes out over the loss of a child or a spouse. You may have been spurned by a friend. You might feel as if your world is falling apart. Perhaps this lyric expresses your feelings: "Nobody knows the trouble I've seen, nobody knows my sorrows…Tell all my friends I'm coming to heaven." I have good news for you. Heaven is indeed a place of comfort, but you don't have to wait to go to heaven before finding relief.

Jesus continues, "For they shall be comforted." Who will comfort them? When will they be comforted? Where does the comfort take place? From other words of Jesus, we learn that the Holy Spirit, God's gift to the church, is the divine Comforter (or Paraclete). God's Spirit, also called the Spirit of Christ, ministers whenever the kingdom-driven church comes together.

Action Points

- Count your blessings when feeling sad.

- Remember that God has not forsaken you.

- Don't allow your sorrows to sidetrack you from living in the present.

- Find a kingdom-focused church whose members minister to each other.

The Meek

Blessing resides with disciples who have servant hearts, who are self-effacing and gentle. Rather than grasping for recognition or attempting to get their own way at the expense of others, they calmly trust God for the desired outcome. Meekness is the opposite of being self-willed, overzealous, and aggressive. Many people in Jesus's day were calling for the forceful and violent overthrow of the Roman government. The meek do not follow this path.

Jesus serves as the perfect example of a humble servant. Even with the armies of heaven and his disciples at his beck and call, he chooses nonviolent means to achieve his kingdom goals. In the garden of Gethsemane, when Peter draws a sword to stave off the arresting posse, Jesus orders him, "Put your sword in its place, for all who take the sword will perish by the sword. Or do you think that I cannot now pray to My Father, and He will provide Me with more than twelve legions of angels?" (Matthew 26:52-53). And when facing Pilate, his executioner, Jesus refuses violence as a means of overthrowing Rome and ushering in his kingdom (John 18:36). Rather, he humbly submits to his Father's will and trusts him to bring about the kingdom as he sees fit. Jesus faces death like a lamb facing the slaughter. Ironically, God inaugurates the worldwide spread of his kingdom by means of Christ's death and resurrection, as foretold in the Old Testament Scriptures (Matthew 26:54).

The meek live a blessed existence, knowing "they shall inherit the earth." Notice that the goal is not going to heaven, but receiving the title deed to the earth. An inheritance is not a reward for good performance, but a birthright given to an heir.

Just as God had deeded the promised land to Israel, so now he bequests the earth to us. Even before taking actual possession of it, we can enjoy and care for the earth as a gift from the hand of God.

Action Points

- Identify three areas in your life where you demonstrate self-will rather than humility and take steps to change.

- If you viewed the land around you as a future inheritance, how would you treat it differently? Make a game plan to become more environmentally conscious and responsible. Think in terms of recycling and beautification.

Those Who Hunger and Thirst for Righteousness

"Hunger" and "thirst" are highly significant words for our study. In the first century, people often went to bed hungry. The average peasant labored in the fields and earned a denarius a day—just enough money to cover the cost of food. Agricultural workers depended on good weather for their livelihood, so when it rained, they were not paid. Unless they had saved money for a rainy day, they might go hungry.

Likewise, fresh water was not in plentiful supply in Israel, so thirst was a reality. And because water quality was poor, it had to be mixed with wine to be drinkable.

Jesus says the person who craves goodness and justice above all is blessed right now. Our desire for the Lord's will to be done on earth must be greater than our desire for food or water. Like David, each of us is to be a person after God's own heart. Our testimony should be, "As the deer pants for the water brooks, so pants my soul for You, O God" (Psalm 42:1).

These people are blessed because "they shall be filled," or satisfied. What does this mean? How shall we be filled? It likely means that if we place righteousness above all else, our daily needs will be met. If correct, this beatitude is similar to Jesus's later statement, "Seek first the kingdom of God and His righteousness, and all these things [daily provisions] shall be added to you" (Matthew 6:33).

When John R. Mott, the great missionary statesman and recipient of the Nobel Prize for Peace, was a student at Cornell University and a nominal Christian, he happened to walk in on a lecture by C.T. Studd, the famous English cricketer and guest lecturer. Studd had just reached the crescendo of his speech and proclaimed, "Seek ye great things for yourself? Seek them not! Seek ye first the kingdom of God, and these things will be added unto you." The words struck Mott right between the eyes, and in a sobering moment of self-reflection, he realized he had been trifling with the Christian life. God was now calling him to be a kingdom citizen!

One day justice will fill the earth as water fills the seas, but until then, it can fill your part of the world.

Action Points

- Make a list of the things you desire most.

- Consider where righteousness and justice fit on the list.

- Determine steps you can take to develop a heart for God's kingdom.

The Merciful

"Mercy" is an important word for Jews. It speaks of compassion and loving-kindness toward God's people. When God forms Israel into a nation, he desires for them to live by a set of ethical standards that are different from those of their surrounding neighbors. These standards include making loans without interest, not defrauding one's neighbor, and caring for the poor, widows, orphans, and disenfranchised. The list goes on. The Jews agree to God's terms and enter into a covenant with God. In turn, God promises to protect them and meet all their needs. All they have to do is abide by the covenant and trust God.

In return for obedience, God promises to bless the people. If they break the covenant, they can expect curses. Unfortunately, they fail miserably. But through the prophet Micah, God continues to make his appeal.

> He has shown you, O man, what is good;
> And what does the LORD require of you
> But to do justly,
> To love mercy,
> And to walk humbly with your God? (Micah 6:8).

Do these words sound familiar? Can you see the striking resemblance to the Beatitudes? When Jesus says God blesses the merciful, he is not teaching anything new. He is calling them to renew their covenant with God.

Jesus explains why the merciful are presently blessed: "For they shall obtain mercy." Instead of being judged on the last day for our numerous acts of disobedience, we will be recipients of God's compassion. This assurance provides us with great joy, even now.

Action Points

- Think of individuals or families in your church who may be hurting because of abandonment by spouses or by adult children. Become God's compassionate hand of mercy toward them.

- Bob Pierce, the founder of World Vision, cried, "Lord, break my heart with the things that break your heart." When God answered, Bob's life was changed forever. Dare to make this prayer your own.

The Pure in Heart

Jesus is speaking here about issues of the heart. Pure-heartedness speaks of motives and intent. What do people with pure hearts look like? First, their inward desires are chaste and unsullied. The opposite of a pure heart is a tainted heart. Jesus describes an adulterer as one who "looks at a woman to lust for her" (Matthew 5:28). His objectives are impure.

Second, pure-hearted people have pure motives, or reasons for doing things. By definition, mixed motives are impure motives. Many people say and do things for the wrong reasons. The New Testament portrays Pharisees in this manner, and Jesus calls them hypocrites. The apostle Peter reminds and exhorts, "Since you have purified your souls in obeying the truth through the Spirit in sincere love of the brethren, love one another fervently with a *pure heart*, having been born again" (1 Peter 1:22-23).

Third, people with a pure heart are single-minded—that is, they trust God unequivocally. The epistle of James exhorts, when a believer makes a request of God, "let him ask in faith, with no doubting, for he who doubts is like a wave of the sea driven and tossed by the wind. For let not that man suppose that he will receive anything from the Lord; he is a double-minded man, unstable in all his ways" (James 1:6-8).

Why are the pure of heart blessed? "They shall see God." What a remarkable statement, especially in light of other verses that say no one can see God (Exodus 33:20; John 1:18; 1 Timothy 6:15-16; 1 John 4:12). But one day it will become a reality. In our glorified bodies created for kingdom existence, we shall see the glory of God in its fullness.

Action Points

- Conduct a reality check of your heart. What do your motives and intents reveal? Do you say and act certain ways for self-aggrandizement and self-promotion?

- Consider this question: Why do we profess faith in Christ for ultimate salvation but sometimes doubt he will care for us day by day?

The Peacemakers

Don't confuse peacemakers with peacekeepers. The United Nations sends troops into hot spots around the world as peacekeepers to keep people from killing each other. They serve as a buffer between two opposing factions. To accomplish the goal, they carry weapons and use them as needed.

Peacemakers are different. We are mediators who attempt to reconcile enemies. Our goal is to bring them together, not keep them apart. In the world we are committed to a ministry of reconciliation. Like the apostle Paul, we cry out to the lost, "We are ambassadors for Christ, as though God were pleading through us: we implore you on Christ's behalf, be reconciled to God" (2 Corinthians 5:20). In our families and churches we show people how to forgive and receive forgiveness.

The Roman Empire claimed that its greatest contribution to humankind was *Pax Romana*, or Roman peace. Rome guaranteed peace and security to all nations who came under its rule. It maintained peace through law and order. Nations that refused the offer became subject to military attack and were forced into submission. Rome's peace through strength was successful only at a high cost to human life. For Rome, collateral damage was the price of peace.

Jesus's peace is the opposite. It is accomplished through mediation and humility. Peacemakers are blessed, "for they shall be called sons of God." This is the same royal title given to Jesus at his baptism. Could you receive any higher accolade than to be called a child of God? As God's royal priesthood, we stretch out our arms. With one hand we grasp the hand of God, and with the other we grasp the hand of man to bring them together.

Action Points

- Consider whether you are known in your church as a person who stirs up controversy and causes division or as a reconciler.

- Encourage your church to develop a policy of reconciliation that spells out steps to be taken when two believers are at odds with each other.

Those Who Are Persecuted for Righteousness' Sake

This speaks of intimidation, mistreatment, discrimination, torture, and even death for doing right. The early Christians suffered unjustly at the hands of the state, the synagogue, and at times, even their own relatives (Mark 13:9,12). For instance, believers paid dearly when they refused to pour out libations in honor of Caesar because of their exclusive loyalty to Christ as Lord. Others were put out of synagogues when they acknowledged Jesus as the Jewish Messiah (John 9:22,34).

Years later the apostle Peter reiterates Jesus's words when he says, "Even if you should suffer for righteousness' sake, you are blessed" (1 Peter 3:14). Under these circumstances, he says, we can have a clear conscience and need not be ashamed of jail time or torture (verse 16).

Christians living in the Western world know little or nothing about persecution. At times we may be overlooked for a raise or promotion, or be shunned by the popular crowd. For instance, evangelicals are not usually hired for positions in the science departments of secular universities. These minor irritants pale in comparison to the persecution our brothers and sisters experience in some Muslim and Communist countries.

Peter also writes that believers should avoid suffering for doing evil (verse 17). Unfortunately, some kingdom citizens erroneously believe the end justifies the means, and they resort to unscrupulous methods and even violence in the name of a good cause.

Jesus explains why victims of injustices are blessed: "For theirs is the kingdom of heaven." Notice three things. First, the reason for blessing in this last beatitude is exactly the same as the reason given in the first beatitude. Together they form bookends around the beatitudes. Second, they both relate to the kingdom. Third, the verb is in the present tense. The kingdom *is* ours here and now on earth.

Action Points

- Determine beforehand how you will respond if faced with persecution. If you have a plan, you will not be caught off guard.

- Discover the areas of the world where believers are presently being persecuted for their faith and begin to pray for them. You might want to involve Christian friends or start a prayer ministry team in your church. A good resource for statistics and materials is Voice of the Martyrs (www.persecution.com).

Salt and Light

After expounding on the blessings that covenant keepers receive, Jesus tells his followers how to live in the world as kingdom citizens.

> You are the salt of the earth; but if the salt loses its flavor, how shall it be seasoned? It is then good for nothing but to be thrown out and trampled underfoot by men.
>
> You are the light of the world. A city that is set on a hill cannot be hidden. Nor do they light a lamp and put it under a basket, but on a lampstand, and it gives light to all who are in the house. Let your light so shine before men, that they may see your good works and glorify your Father in heaven (Matthew 5:13-16).

Contemporary readers may be familiar with these words, but they usually don't understand them correctly.

We notice immediately that Jesus uses two metaphors. Salt and light have a few things in common. Both penetrate things—salt penetrates meat, and light penetrates darkness. With each, a small amount can have a significant result. Jesus uses these metaphors to drive home a single point: We can have an effect on a corrupt and dark society. Let's take a closer look at each metaphor.

Salt

Jesus says, "You are the salt of the earth." To whom does he refer? The pronoun "you" in the Greek text stands apart from the verb, which means it is to be emphasized. Jesus is speaking to specific people, not to people in general. Only his followers are salt. If you are a believer, you are like salt. But what are you to preserve? The earth. Obviously, Jesus is not speaking about dirt, but about society or humankind.

When we analyze these words, we see that Jesus makes an explicit assertion (we are salt) and gives an implicit admonition (we must preserve society from moral decay). The first tells us who we are, and the second, what we must do.

These words have implications for us as kingdom citizens. We must not become isolationists. When Christians withdraw from the world, they have no effect on their society. On the other hand, we must not be conformists. We are called to be in the world but not of it (John 17:16; Romans 12:1-2). Many Christians in democratic societies believe they can make an impact on society by becoming part of the system. Their attempts rarely produce the desired results. What about Christians living in countries where oppression and tyranny are the rule? They are forbidden to take an active role in politics or governmental affairs. This was mainly the case for Jesus and his disciples under the domination of the Roman Empire. Peasants had no rights. When Jesus describes his followers as salt, he is not making a universal call for all to become cultural warriors. The majority of believers throughout history simply have not been afforded such a luxury. Therefore, Jesus must mean something different.

Additionally, Jesus is not calling for us to stand against culture, especially in an aggressive and violent manner. There is a time and place for followers to exercise a prophetic role in society, as we shall see in another chapter, but we must not view ourselves as crusaders.

Jesus's main point follows his assertion that believers are salt. He asks, "But if the salt loses its flavor, how shall it be seasoned?" One translation puts the question like this: "If the salt loses its saltiness, how shall it become salty again?" The answer is, it can't!

How does salt lose its strength? Having lived the first half of my life in a region that gets a couple feet of snow each winter, I can answer the question with certainty. Salt can lose its potency in two ways. The first is by getting wet. As snow begins to fall, many cities send their road crews into action putting salt on the streets. At first, the salt works well, but as the snow continues to fall and melt, the salt becomes diluted, losing its strength. Before long, the salt loses the battle, and the snow piles up high.

The second way salt loses its strength is by becoming defiled or corrupted. Some cities in the southern United States add foreign substances (like sand) to salt to increase their supply. In doing so, they inadvertently make the salt less effective. When a large snowstorm hits unexpectedly, the impure salt does little good.

Jesus then answers his own question. "It is then good for nothing but to be thrown out and trampled underfoot by men." Unable to stem decay, it is worthless.

Jesus is not speaking about salt, but about Christians. We are like salt. When we become watered down or diluted by compromise or conformity, we cannot impact our world. When sin, pride, the quest for power, or ambition infiltrates the church, God's people lose their ability to effect change in the world around them. The church becomes weakened.

You might think that if you compromise just a little, you can gain the respect of the lost, the power brokers, or the movers and shakers. But in the end, they lose respect for you and reject you.

A kingdom citizen does not compromise. "In the world but not of it" is a difficult principle to maintain.

Light

"You are the light of the world." Jesus again uses an emphatic pronoun, which means he is speaking of his followers. When light dispels darkness, people can see things as they really are. Light reveals, attracts, and guides.

Jesus's disciples are like a light to the world—that is, to humankind or the nations. Isaiah (representing the nation of Israel) was the first to be called by this title (Isaiah 49:6), and Matthew applies it to Jesus (Matthew 4:15-16). Jesus applies it to himself (John 8:12; 9:5) and to us. Notice that Jesus does not say *a* light or one among many lights, but *the* light—the one and only light. We are a revelation of God to others.

Jesus continues, "A city that is set on a hill cannot be hidden." Likewise, there is no mistaking a follower of Jesus.

To make his point, Jesus gives another truism: "Nor do they light a lamp and put it under a basket, but on a lampstand, and it gives light to all who are in the house." You don't light a lamp in order to hide it, but so it can shine and provide light. Isolationists and separatists fail to comprehend this principle.

Did you notice the digression from a city to a house, or from a large group of people to a family? We have a responsibility to reveal God to both.

Now Jesus makes the application by giving a command: "Let your light so shine before men." This is *what* we are to do and *where* we are to do it. This verse supplies the application for Matthew 5:3-15. The "what" involves shining our light. The "where" is "before men," which is the equivalent of the terms Jesus used previously—"earth" and "world."

Next, Jesus gives two reasons for shining our light. The first is "that they may see your good works." This revealing phrase defines what it means to shine our light. It involves doing good works. What kind of deeds? Those listed in the Beatitudes (verses 3-11) and others, such as almsgiving, washing feet, caring for widows and orphans, all of which reflect the light of the kingdom of God. Good deeds draw attention.

The second reason for shining our light is "that they may...glorify your Father in heaven." The ultimate purpose is for God to receive praise. Unfortunately, some people are like the Pharisees, who did good deeds occasionally to be seen and to receive praise for themselves (Matthew 6:1-2)! We must always check our motives.

According to Jesus, when we perform good works, our light shines in the world, and God receives praise. If you want to see people giving God praise, then start doing good in real-life situations today! Peter tells Cornelius, the Roman centurion, "Jesus of Nazareth...went about doing good" (Acts 10:38). Shouldn't we follow our Master's example?

Good Works in the New Testament

(The verses in this sidebar are taken from the New International Version.)

"*Let us not become weary in doing good*, for at the proper time we will reap a harvest if we do not give up. Therefore, as we have opportunity, *let us do good to all people*, especially to those who belong to the family of believers" (Galatians 6:9-10).

"We are God's handiwork, *created in Christ Jesus to do good works,* which God prepared in advance for us to do" (Ephesians 2:10).

"[We pray] that you may live a life worthy of the Lord and please him in every way: *bearing fruit in every good work*, growing in the knowledge of God" (Colossians 1:10).

"I also want the women to dress modestly, with decency and propriety, adorning themselves, not with elaborate hairstyles or gold or pearls or expensive clothes, *but with good deeds*, appropriate for women who profess to worship God" (1 Timothy 2:9-10).

"No widow may be put on the list of widows unless she is over sixty, has been faithful to her husband, and is *well known for her good deeds*, such as bringing up children, showing hospitality, washing the feet of the Lord's people, helping those in trouble and *devoting herself to all kinds of good deeds*" (1 Timothy 5:9-10).

"The sins of some are obvious, reaching the place of judgment ahead of them; the sins of others trail behind them. In the same way, *good deeds are obvious*, and even those that are not obvious cannot remain hidden forever" (1 Timothy 5:24-25).

"Command those who are rich in this present world not to be arrogant nor to put their hope in wealth, which is so uncertain, but to put their hope in God, who richly provides us with everything for our enjoyment. *Command them to do good, to be rich in good deeds*, and to be generous and willing to share" (1 Timothy 6:17-18).

"Those who cleanse themselves from the latter will be instruments for special purposes, made holy, useful to the Master and *prepared to do any good work*" (2 Timothy 2:21).

"All Scripture is God-breathed and is useful for teaching, rebuking, correcting and training in righteousness, so that the servant of God may be thoroughly equipped *for every good work*" (2 Timothy 3:16-17).

"Let us consider how we may *spur one another on toward love and good deeds*" (Hebrews 10:24).

"Do not forget to *do good and to share with others*, for with such sacrifices God is pleased" (Hebrews 13:16).

"*What good is it, my brothers and sisters, if someone claims to have faith but has no deeds? Can such faith save them?* Suppose a brother or sister is without clothes and daily food. If one of you says to them, 'Go in peace; keep warm and well fed,' but does nothing about their physical needs, what good is it? In the same way, faith by itself, if it is not accompanied by action, is dead.

"But someone will say, 'You have faith; I have deeds.'

"Show me your faith without deeds, and I will show you my faith by my deeds. You believe that there is one God. Good! Even the demons believe that—and shudder.

"You foolish person, do you want evidence that *faith without deeds is useless?*" (James 2:14-20).

"Who is wise and understanding among you? *Let them show it by their good life, by deeds done in the humility* that comes from wisdom" (James 3:13).

"I want you to stress these things, so that those who have trusted in God may be careful to *devote themselves to doing what is good.* These things are excellent and profitable for everyone" (Titus 3:8).

When we perform good deeds, our light shines in the world, and God recieves praise.

The Law and the Kingdom

Jesus affirms strongly that the law is still in effect and binding on God's people. He says, "Do not think that I came to destroy the Law or the Prophets. I did not come to destroy but to fulfill" (Matthew 5:17). With these words Jesus dispels any misconceptions some people have about his opinion of the law. Evidently, a rumor is circulating that Jesus has come to destroy or set aside the law. Most likely these reports can be traced back to Pharisees and scribes, who accuse him of abolishing

Israel's moral code. Jesus denies these erroneous claims and says his goal is to fulfill the law.

Instead, Jesus desires to destroy their false ideas about the law. He will do this by explaining the meaning of the law and keeping the law to its fullest measure as God intended from the start. The religious leaders are the ones responsible for distorting and destroying the law. As God's spokesperson, Jesus will elucidate the fullness of the law so people will see its potential to impact their lives and community.

The Duration of the Law

After stating his intention of fulfilling the law, Jesus explains, "For assuredly, I say to you, till heaven and earth pass away, one jot or one tittle will by no means pass from the law till all is fulfilled" (Matthew 5:18). Here Jesus gives assurance that the law will remain intact and in effect until God's plan for the ages is complete. The law has a purpose in God's end-time plan. This means the law is still in full force today. The problem is not with the law—it is good. But people do not interpret and practice it correctly. They change its sense and cheapen it. Jesus gives the correct and fuller meaning of the law and shows how to observe it.

Then Jesus gives the results of cheapening the law: "Whoever therefore breaks one of the least of these commandments, and teaches men so, shall be called least in the kingdom of heaven; but whoever does and teaches them, he shall be called great in the kingdom of heaven" (verse 19). The "whoever" in this verse are the people of God, which he divides into two categories. The first group consists of those guilty of committing two errors. First, they break minor laws. The word "break" in this verse has the same root word as "destroy" (verse 17). Lawbreakers destroy the law because they treat it as if it doesn't exist. Second, they instruct others to do likewise. Jesus is speaking specifically of teachers or religious leaders who are responsible for those under their charge.

We know Jesus's words are meant to be a warning because he gives the result of such practices. The offenders will one day be recognized as least in God's kingdom. How unfortunate for professors, pastors, and Sunday school workers who lead others astray. Rather than accepting Jesus's fuller meaning of the law, they either interpret it according to tradition or teach that it is not relevant under the new covenant.

The second group keeps and teaches the law the way Jesus intended. They will be recognized as great in God's kingdom.

Up to this point Jesus has been speaking about his followers and their place in the future kingdom. Next he issues a far more serious warning: "For I say to you, that unless your righteousness exceeds the righteousness of the scribes and Pharisees, you will by no means enter the kingdom of heaven" (verse 20). It is one thing to be the least in the kingdom, but it is another thing entirely to be excluded from the kingdom altogether. The scribes and Pharisees observe the law but not as God intended. Through their traditions, they creatively twist the law to suit their fancy, and in doing so, they transform the Word of God into the word of man, which carries no divine authority. Those calling themselves disciples of Christ who do the same will find themselves outside the kingdom.

Two things should be gleaned from this passage. First, Jesus is God's authoritative interpreter of the law. Second, law and kingdom go hand in hand. A correct perspective of the law affects one's position in the kingdom.

But what does Jesus mean when he says our righteousness must exceed that of the religious traditionalists? A few moments of reflection provides the answer. The scribes and Pharisees emphasized carrying out the letter of the law—don't work on the Sabbath, wash your hands, don't touch unclean things, and so on. Jesus is less interested in formalities and rituals and more concerned about one's inner motives and the hidden intent of the law.

Jesus and the Law (Matthew 5:21-48)

By use of a literary device known as thesis and antithesis ("You've heard it was said to those of old...but I say to you"), Jesus gives us six ways his understanding of the law exceeds that of the scribes and Pharisees. He provides us with the true meaning and intent of the law. The theses deal with the outward form of the law as his contemporaries understood and practiced it, but the antitheses go deeper, dealing with the inner life and hearkening back to the Beatitudes, which focus on issues of the heart.

Jesus sets the bar higher. His ethical standards are more demanding. By discovering how Jesus handles the law, we learn how we should observe it.

Verses 21-26	**Thesis 1**	Do not commit murder (the sixth commandment), or you will be judged.
	Antithesis	If you are angry (Greek, *orgé*, inner rage) with your brother, you have already committed murder. You are in danger of a far worse judgment.
Verses 27-30	**Thesis 2**	Do not commit adultery (the seventh commandment).
	Antithesis	If you desire to use a woman for your own sexual gratification, you have already committed adultery in your heart. You are in danger of hell.
Verses 31-32	**Thesis 3**	Divorce is permissible with a certificate of divorcement.
	Antithesis	Divorce is permissible only on the grounds of marital infidelity. Those who divorce for any other reason may have a hard heart, and if they remarry, they are guilty of adultery.
Verses 33-37	**Thesis 4**	Do not break promises when you have invoked God's name (the third commandment). Stay faithful to your oaths. Otherwise you perjure yourself and face a legal penalty. (Jews would get around this by swearing on something other than God's name, such as the city of Jerusalem.)
	Antithesis	Never invoke God's name in order to give weight to your promises. The issue is not oaths, but keeping your word. Your word should be your bond. A simple yes or no is sufficient. Saying more implies your word is not reliable and raises doubt as to your veracity. If you take oaths, you may have a heart problem.
Verses 38-42	**Thesis 5**	Make sure the punishment fits the crime—an eye for an eye. Do not go beyond the limits of justice.
	Antithesis	Do not retaliate in kind when treated unfairly or physically harassed. (Unlike Shakespeare's Shylock, we need not seek a pound of flesh.) The proper response is to turn the other cheek and go the extra mile. Taking a hit is better than responding in like manner. Grace trumps justice.

Thesis 6	Love your neighbor and hate your enemy. (Jews attempted to get around this law by asking, "Who is my neighbor?")
Antithesis	"Love your enemies, bless those who curse you, do good to those who hate you, and pray for those who spitefully use you and persecute you" (Matthew 5:44). Any question about the neighbor's identity is moot. We are to love everyone. This is how God treats all people. His sun shines and his rain falls on his enemies as well as his friends. God's law can be summed up by the word "love." "Therefore you shall be perfect, just as your Father in heaven is perfect" (verse 48). To be perfect does not mean to be sinless, but to follow God's example of love—to be charitable to others whether they deserve it or not.

Verses 43-48

The law served as Israel's legal code and marked the identity of a child of God. A good Jew was a person who kept the law. Israel based its civil code of conduct on God's commandments. Lawbreakers were brought to court and their cases adjudicated. The elders and judges and eventually the rabbis provided clarification when a particular application of the law was needed. Punishments included reparations, fines, sacrifices, beatings, and on occasion, death, depending on the severity of the crime. On the whole, the interpretation of the law was stilted and legalistic.

The surrounding pagan nations did not observe the law God had handed down to Moses.

Jesus infuses the Old Testament law with a fuller meaning. He demonstrates the new norm for living under the present reign of God. Jesus speaks to matters of the heart that lie behind the letter of the law. Under the old system, one could keep the law outwardly and yet sin in the heart without being detected. Jesus sets a higher standard and takes the law to the next level. Jesus's requirements for keeping the law are more severe. The kingdom of God demands total commitment and not lip service. Those confronted by the gospel of the kingdom are called to make an about-face (repentance) and pledge their loyalty (faith) to Christ their King.

9

AM and FM Christians

Behold, I stand at the door and knock. If anyone
hears My voice and opens the door, I will come in
to him and dine with him, and he with Me.

Revelation 3:20

The kingdom of God is located wherever God's end-time Spirit is present and welcomed. When first-century believers gathered, they knew God was there with them. They expected him to speak and minister to them and through them. In this sense, they carried on the kingdom ministry that Jesus started.

From the Scriptures we can recreate what a church gathering might look like. Believers in attendance reclined on couches and ate a leisurely meal in typical Roman banquet fashion, but they did so in the name of Jesus. In the book of Acts, Luke describes this Lord's Supper as the "breaking of bread" (Acts 2:42,46; 20:7,11), a phrase still used in modern times to denote eating with friends. The practice of eating a wafer and sipping a little wine or grape juice was unknown in the early church.

After the meal and a toast offered to the Lord Jesus (1 Corinthians 11:24-25), the believers transitioned into an hour or two of Spirit-led and empowered activities that included prayer, teaching, prophecy, the laying on of hands for healing, ministering of spiritual gifts, the reading of letters, and much more. On special occasions, the gathering lasted well past midnight (Acts 20:7).

We would be hard pressed today to find similar church meetings. Why is this? Can you imagine a situation in which the presence and power of God's Spirit is so real that you didn't want to go home? It seems that early church members, despite their many problems, failures, and excesses, knew God was in their midst when they came together. Why don't we?

The answer probably has something to do with our tendency to leave little room for God to move among us. If we allot only one hour a week to corporate worship and have every moment of that hour planned ahead of time, what are the chances we will even recognize God in our midst? Quite frankly, we don't expect him to show up. In many ways, we are like the church at Laodicea (Revelation 3:20). Jesus knocks on the door trying to get our attention, but we don't hear him. Why not?

A Personal Word

When I started my decade-long journey on the road to discovering the kingdom of God, I was forced to grapple with a God who speaks. As Francis Schaeffer wrote, "He is there and he is not silent." The record is clear. God speaks to Adam and Eve when he gives them dominion over the earth. He speaks to his kingdom saints under the old covenant. He speaks at Jesus's birth when he appoints him King. He speaks at his baptism when he anoints him King. He speaks at Pentecost when his end-time Spirit manifests the kingdom through the church. He speaks to his angels and those around his heavenly throne. He speaks when his ultimate kingdom comes to earth at Christ's return. Shouldn't he be speaking today?

Why don't many twenty-first-century kingdom citizens hear God's voice? We surely need his guidance as much as believers in the past and his assurance of "Well done, good and faithful servant" as much as those at the end of the age. Hearing God's voice is a privilege of being a member of God's kingdom.

In this chapter I will explore the ways God's people hear his voice individually and corporately.

Lamps and Radios

I have a favorite leather chair in my living room that sits by the fireplace. That's where you can find me early each morning sipping a freshly brewed cup of coffee and working on the *New York Times* crossword puzzle. A tall floor lamp is situated by my chair. What if I turn on the switch but the light doesn't shine? I know immediately something is wrong. Usually I find an unconnected plug lying on the floor or a burned-out lightbulb. In either case, I can remedy the matter. No one in his right mind would ignore the problem indefinitely and remain in the darkness for the next 30 years!

Let's move across the room and listen to the radio. What if I turn it on but get no sound? As with the lamp, I check the cord to see if it's plugged into the outlet. With the problem fixed, the radio powers up, but all I hear is static. Now I have a different problem. I adjust the tuner and find the right signal. Voilà! My favorite news channel, KRLD-AM, comes across crisp and clear.

But suppose I want to listen to NPR-FM. I make an additional adjustment. I switch from AM to FM frequency. If my radio doesn't receive FM signals, I'm out of luck.

AM and FM Christians

Most Christians function like an AM receiver. Their capacity for hearing God is limited to one signal—the written Word of God. These believers operate mainly at a cognitive level. They enjoy sermons and read their Bibles daily. God speaks to them through his written Word. They may take notes and jot comments in the margins of their Bibles. AM Christians receive and perceive information mainly through their five senses. They hear the voice of God with their conscious minds, analyze it, and seek to live by it.

FM Christians, on the other hand, operate on an additional frequency. God speaks not only to their conscious mind but also at a subconscious level. FM Christians are tuned in to the still, small voice of God. They listen with their inner ears and see God's future plans for them with their spiritual eyes. As a result, they live in the moment and believe God guides them intuitively. They often take giant steps of faith, which others might deem unreasonable, because they have an internal sense that God has revealed his will. They are aware of God's presence as he motivates them to act or speak on his behalf.

Which category best describes your experience? Are you more like an AM or FM Christian? I do not use these categories to infer one kind of Christian is morally deficient or superior to the other. They are simply ways of explaining how believers hear God's voice. All genuine believers are equipped to receive spiritual AM *and* FM signals, but many don't realize it. As a result, they miss out on what God wants to say to them.

God Wants to Speak to You

To hear God's voice like an FM Christian, two things are imperative. First, we need to be plugged in to the divine power source. If you are a follower of Jesus Christ, you are already connected. God's Spirit surges through you. Second, we must be tuned in to the right frequency.

If you are a born-again follower of Jesus, you have the spiritual resources and power you need to hear the voice of God and minister with power. But you may be operating on the AM dial only.

Hearing God's inner voice requires fine tuning. You have to switch to your spiritual FM dial and then make adjustments until the static is gone and God's voice comes across loud and clear.

How to Become an FM Christian

Get Plugged In

The vast majority of people in the world have no relationship with God. They are like an unplugged lamp or radio. As a result, they have no power surging through them. They are like the walking dead. They have physical life but no spiritual life. Until God breathed into Adam, the first man was nothing more than a lump of clay. The Spirit is the power source. In his meeting with Nicodemus, a very religious man, Jesus warns, "Unless one is born again, he *cannot see the kingdom of God*" (John 3:3). Notice that Jesus uses the word "cannot," which speaks of inability. Apart from a new birth, a person lacks the equipment to hear God's voice. This means that natural birth alone is insufficient to discern, see, or understand things relating to God's kingdom. It takes a second birth, a supernatural birth of the Spirit. That's why Jesus adds, "That which is born of the flesh is flesh, and that which is born of the Spirit is spirit. Do not marvel that I said to you, 'You *must* be born again'" (verses 6-7). It is not optional. It is mandatory.

The apostle Paul makes a related statement when he says, "The natural man does not receive the things of the Spirit of God, for they are foolishness to him; nor can he know them, because they are spiritually discerned" (1 Corinthians 2:14). If we desire to hear God speak to us, we must be connected to the divine power source. This is a necessary first step.

If you are already plugged in, you are ready to take the next step.

Get Tuned In

After you turn on your spiritual radio, you need to tune in to the right spiritual frequency. For many of us this means switching from an "analysis mode" (AM) to a "faith mode" (FM). We hear God speak to us through the ears of faith (Galatians 3:2; James 1:5-6). Proverbs admonishes children of God, "Trust in the LORD with all your heart, and lean not on your own understanding" (Proverbs 3:5).

Hearing God on Your FM Dial

Here is a six-part process I follow to hear God's voice. Try it to see if it works for you.

First, decide on a time in your schedule when you will not be distracted by phone calls, children, or normal daily household or work-related tasks. Morning is best for many people. But if you are a night owl, later may be better, after everyone else is asleep and you have time to yourself. Some busy people take 15 or 20 minutes of their lunch for this purpose. Experiment with different times to see which works best for you.

Second, choose a quiet place where you can relax in solitude. It is important that you are away from other people, including family, friends, neighbors, coworkers, and strangers. In other words, a bench in the mall is not appropriate.

Third, settle into a comfortable chair. You should sit up straight but be relaxed. Don't slouch or cross your legs, which actually contorts your body or ties it in knots. Rest your arms comfortably in your lap or on the arms of the chair. Over the next few minutes you want to reach a state of complete relaxation.

Fourth, close your eyes. This will help you to tune out the world and tune in to God.

Fifth, begin taking slow breaths. You might start by closing your mouth and exhaling the air from your lungs through your nose. When all the air is expelled, your body will automatically inhale air. On this first in-breath, notice how your abdomen expands. This is called diaphragmatic breathing. Have you ever watched a baby breathing as it lies on its back? Its abdomen rises and falls. This kind of breathing exercise relaxes the body within a few minutes.

Sixth, relax your mind. It is imperative that you do not allow your conscious mind to run wild or remain active. It is not enough for your body to be relaxed. Your brain needs a rest too. As long as you are thinking your own thoughts, you cannot hear God's thoughts. God commands the psalmist, "Be still, and know that I am God" (Psalm 46:10).

But how do you get your mind as relaxed as your body? It's very simple. Allow your mind to become synchronized with your breathing. With each in-breath, mentally pray the words, "Lord Jesus." With each out-breath, pray, "Speak to me." Make sure each phrase is prayed the full length of each breath. Focus completely and totally on the prayer. Do not allow any other thoughts to interrupt the prayer. If your mind starts to wander, recognize what happened and return to your relaxing breathing and praying. An old Gospel song speaks of what happens:

> Turn your eyes upon Jesus,
> Look full in His wonderful face,
> And the things of earth will grow strangely dim,
> In the light of His glory and grace.[2]

As you practice this discipline of silence, you will discover your mind and body are relaxed and in sync. The psalmist advises his readers, "Rest in the LORD, and wait patiently for Him" (Psalm 37:7).

When you open your eyes at the end of the 15– to 20–minute exercise, you will have a sense of calm and peace. You will notice this feeling abides with you for some time. As you continue in this daily spiritual discipline, the state will remain with you progressively longer. You will be more relaxed throughout the day and have a sense of God's presence. You will discover that you think more clearly, respond differently to crises, and detect God's guiding hand. You will become more intuitive, knowing when to speak or act in a given situation. This is the voice of God speaking to the inner you. You are now an FM Christian!

Occasionally in your daily spiritual exercise of breathing and prayer, God might bring an unexpected thought or idea to your mind. It might come in the form of words or pictures. This may shock you at first because you know it is not of your own making. Do not fear. This is exactly what you have been praying: "Lord Jesus, speak to me." Accept it but don't dwell on it. Return to your normal routine. You can later ponder the words or vision to determine what God is saying to you or may want you to do.

Jesus Is Our Model

The Gospels give many examples of Jesus getting off by himself to commune with his heavenly Father. "Now in the morning, having risen a long while before daylight, He went out and departed to a solitary place; and there He prayed" (Mark 1:35). Luke calls it "a deserted place" (Luke 4:42). When the crowds start to arrive, seeking a healing touch, no one can find him. Finally the disciples search him out and complain, "Everyone is looking for you." But instead of returning to the needy crowd, he moves on to the next town. Time alone with the Father is paramount for him to discern God's will.

This is not an isolated experience. "When He had sent the multitudes away, He went up on the mountain by Himself to pray. Now when evening came, He was alone there" (Matthew 14:23).

From this passage we learn that Jesus takes time to pray not only in the morning but also at night. And he secludes himself from the crowds despite their apparent needs.

The insensitive disciples sometimes interrupted his private time with the Father. "And it happened, as He was alone praying, that His disciples joined Him, and He asked them, saying, 'Who do the crowds say that I am?'" (Luke 9:18). This leads to a prolonged discussion.

On the night of Jesus's betrayal, we find him and three apostles heading to the garden of Gethsemane, where he says to them, "Sit here while I go and pray over there" (Matthew 26:36). If Jesus, the appointed and anointed King, must get away to receive instructions from his Father, I certainly think we ought to do likewise. In fact, he instructs all his disciples to do so: "When you pray, go into your room, and when you have shut your door, pray to your Father who is in the secret place; and your Father who sees in secret will reward you openly" (Matthew 6:6).

Jesus Hears God Speak

As Jesus spends time alone in communion with his heavenly Father, he hears God's voice. With his FM receiver turned on and tuned in, Jesus gets his marching orders. The fourth Gospel focuses on this important aspect of Jesus's devotional life. On one occasion, Jesus reminds his disciples, "'I speak to the world those things which *I heard from Him.*' They did not understand that He spoke to them of the Father" (John 8:26-27). He goes on to explain, "When you lift up the Son of Man, then you will know that I am He, and that I do nothing of Myself; but *as My Father taught Me*, I speak these things. And He who sent Me is with Me. The Father has not left Me alone, for I always do those things that please Him."

Turning then to the Pharisees, he excoriates them for obeying the voice of Satan instead of God's voice and adds, "*I speak what I have seen with My Father*, and you do what you have seen with your father" (John 8:38).

This reveals that two voices constantly seek our attention—God's and the devil's. Jesus is unique because he never gives in to the voice of the enemy, but always follows the other Voice. What a far cry from Adam's and Eve's experience!

Still again Jesus asserts, "I have not spoken on My own authority; but *the Father who sent Me gave Me a command*, what I should say and what I should speak. And I know that His command is everlasting life.

Therefore, whatever I speak, just *as the Father has told Me*, so I speak" (John 12:49-50).

Remember Jesus discussing his upcoming departure back to heaven and to God? This leads Philip to ask, "Lord, show us the Father, and it is sufficient for us." Notice how Jesus responds.

> Have I been with you so long, and yet you have not known Me, Philip? He who has seen Me has seen the Father; so how can you say, "Show us the Father"? Do you not believe that I am in the Father, and the Father in Me? *The words that I speak to you I do not speak on My own authority; but the Father who dwells in Me does the works.* Believe Me that I am in the Father and the Father in Me, or else believe Me for the sake of the works themselves (John 14:8-11).

Jesus hears God's voice and obeys. This Voice shows him what to do and to say, and when. Jesus can discern these words of instruction because of his reciprocal relationship with the Father. He refers to a mutual indwelling of Father and Son.

In some situations, as we have already seen, Jesus leaves people in a state of sickness, and at other times he heals everyone. What explains such seemingly erratic behavior? The only satisfactory answer is that Jesus does not speak or act unless God directs him. The healing at the pool of Bethsaida is a case in point. The pool was an ancient Fountain of Lourdes, where people flocked to be healed, believing that an angel periodically stirred the waters. When this happened, whoever touched the water first was healed. The pool had five porches. "In these lay a great multitude of sick people, blind, lame, paralyzed, waiting for the moving of the water" (John 5:3). Yet Jesus picks one man out of the crowd and asks, "Do you want to be made well?" This is the person the Father directs Jesus to heal. He obeys.

What would have happened had Jesus told others around the pool, "Rise, take up your bed and walk"?

The Gospel of Luke gives us a clue about how Jesus knew when to attempt healing. "Now it happened on a certain day, as He was teaching, that there were Pharisees and teachers of the law sitting by, who had come out of every town of Galilee, Judea, and Jerusalem. And the power of the Lord was present to heal them" (Luke 5:17). This suggests that the power of God is sometimes not available to heal. Therefore Jesus speaks and acts only when he is aware of God directing him (also see John 5:17; 11:38-44; 17:8).

We find a similar circumstance when Peter and John heal the lame man at the gate of the temple. Every day the man is brought there to beg, and every day they pass him on their way to pray (Acts 3:1-5). But on this particular day they stop and command, "In the name of Jesus Christ of Nazareth, rise up and walk." What is it about this day? Why not another day? What causes them to stop and speak with such assurance? Do they hear the Voice? Do they sense that God is guiding them to do it? As a result of the miracle, Peter has an opportunity to preach the gospel to those watching in amazement.

God Speaks to New Testament Believers

All followers of King Jesus are equipped to hear the Savior's voice. Jesus says, "My sheep *hear My voice*, and I know them, and they follow Me. And I give them eternal life, and they shall never perish; neither shall anyone snatch them out of My hand" (John 10:27-28). To hear Christ's voice is as much a reality as receiving eternal life and having assurance of one's salvation.

Jesus speaks only what he hears from his Father, so to hear Christ's voice is to hear the Father's voice. This was as true for the early church as it was for the original apostles.

During the symposium portion of his Last Supper, Jesus talks about his upcoming departure.

> I still have many things to say to you, but you cannot bear them now. However, when He, the Spirit of truth, has come, He will guide you into all truth; for He will not speak on His own authority, but whatever He hears *He will speak*; and He will tell you things to come. He will glorify Me, for He will take of what is Mine and declare it to you. All things that the Father has are Mine. Therefore I said that He will take of Mine and declare it to you (John 16:12-15).

This means further revelation, guidance, and understanding are to follow after Jesus's return to heaven. The communication will come through the Holy Spirit. Just as Jesus heard his Father's voice through the Spirit, so the disciples will hear Jesus's voice after he returns to heaven.

The ability to hear the Voice is not limited to the apostles. In his first epistle, John writes to the members of a church, "You have an anointing from the Holy One, and you know all things" (1 John 2:20). The Spirit speaks to them as well.

Likewise, Paul confirms, "Now we have received, not the spirit of the world, but the Spirit who is from God, that we might know the things that have been freely given to us by God. These things we also speak, not in words which man's wisdom teaches but *which the Holy Spirit teaches*" (1 Corinthians 2:12-13).

The book of Acts is replete with God speaking in many ways, including tongues, visions, prophecies, and other forms of inspired utterance.

On the Day of Pentecost, 120 believers "were all filled with the Holy Spirit and began to speak with other tongues, *as the Spirit gave them utterance*" (Acts 2:4).

At one church meeting in Jerusalem, "the place where they were assembled together was shaken; and they were all *filled with the Holy Spirit, and they spoke the word of God* with boldness" (Acts 4:31).

Luke gives this account of Stephen ministering in a synagogue: "Stephen, full of faith and power, did great wonders and signs among the people. Then there arose some from what is called the Synagogue of the Freedmen (Cyrenians, Alexandrians, and those from Cilicia and Asia), disputing with Stephen. And they were not able to resist the wisdom and *the Spirit by which he spoke*" (Acts 6:8-10).

We also read in the book of Acts that Philip, in obedience to the Voice, shares the gospel with the Ethiopian eunuch. "Then *the Spirit said* to Philip, 'Go near and overtake this chariot'" (Acts 8:29-30). When Philip caught the eunuch's chariot, he preached Jesus to him and baptized him. Apart from the Spirit speaking and Philip heeding the Voice, a gospel opportunity would be missed.

We find Peter at Joppa on a housetop, where he goes to pray without being disturbed (Acts 10:9). As he communes with God, he falls into a trance and sees a vision of a sheet filled with "all kinds of four-footed animals of the earth, wild beasts, creeping things, and birds of the air.

And *a voice came to him*, 'Rise, Peter; kill and eat.'" Peter recoils at the command to eat unclean creatures and even argues with God by saying, "Not so, Lord." So the Voice speaks a second and third time, reiterating the command.

Peter sees a vision and hears a Voice. Does he perceive with his physical eyes and hear with his corporeal ears? Not likely because he is entranced. Nonetheless, the communication from above is real. As Peter ponders the event, three men arrive from the home of Cornelius, a Roman soldier, and inquire of Peter's whereabouts. They are to bring him back with them so he can preach the gospel to this unclean Gentile and his family.

Luke tells us that Peter was still on the roof thinking about the vision when "*the Spirit said* to him, 'Behold, three men are seeking you. Arise therefore, go down and go with them, doubting nothing; for I have sent them.'"

Peter reports back to the church at Jerusalem sometime later. "At that very moment, three men stood before the house where I was, having been sent to me from Caesarea. Then *the Spirit told me* to go with them, doubting nothing" (11:11-12).

Consider also how the exalted Jesus speaks to Paul on the road to Damascus and then to Ananias (Acts 9:3,10,17; 22:6-10; 26:12-18).

Additionally, notice that the very first missionary journey begins with a word from God.

> As they ministered to the Lord and fasted, *the Holy Spirit said*, "Now separate to Me Barnabas and Saul for the work to which I have called them." Then, having fasted and prayed, and laid hands on them, they sent them away.

> So, being *sent out by the Holy Spirit*, they went down to Seleucia, and from there they sailed to Cyprus (Acts 13:2-4).

Paul's second missionary journey was also directed by the Spirit.

> Now when they had gone through Phrygia and the region of Galatia, they were *forbidden by the Holy Spirit* to preach the word in Asia. After they had come to Mysia, they tried

to go into Bithynia, but *the Spirit did not permit them*. So passing by Mysia, they came down to Troas. And *a vision appeared* to Paul in the night. A man of Macedonia stood and pleaded with him, saying, "Come over to Macedonia and help us." Now after he had seen the vision, immediately we sought to go to Macedonia, *concluding that the Lord had called us* to preach the gospel to them (Acts 16:6-10).

Through God's direct intervention and guidance, the gospel is carried westward into Europe. Had the missionaries not heeded the Voice and vision, the gospel would have moved eastward into Asia. This shows the importance of being able to hear God speak. He is the one who sets the kingdom agenda.

When Timothy and Silas meet up with Paul in Corinth, Luke records that "Paul was *compelled by the Spirit*, and testified to the Jews that Jesus is the Christ" (Acts 18:5). And notice what happens when Paul is threatened with persecution.

The Lord spoke to Paul in the night *by a vision*, "Do not be afraid, but speak, and do not keep silent; for I am with you, and no one will attack you to hurt you; for I have many people in this city." And he continued there a year and six months, teaching the word of God among them (verses 9-11).

Agabus the prophet is mentioned twice in the book of Acts. The first time we meet him, he predicts a food crisis throughout the Empire. "In these days prophets came from Jerusalem to Antioch. Then one of them, named Agabus, stood up and *showed by the Spirit* that there was going to be a great famine throughout all the world, which also happened in the days of Claudius Caesar" (Acts 11:27-28). The disciples take seriously this warning of the Spirit and "send relief to the brethren dwelling in Judea...by the hands of Barnabas and Saul."

We meet Agabus again in the home of Philip at Caesarea, where he warns Paul of the dangers of going to Jerusalem. He binds his own hands and feet with Paul's belt and declares, "*Thus says the Holy Spirit,*

'So shall the Jews at Jerusalem bind the man who owns this belt, and deliver him into the hands of the Gentiles'" (Acts 21:11).

On several occasions Paul receives similar God-inspired warnings from other prophets. In his farewell to the Ephesian elders, Paul mentions the difficulty he will face in Jerusalem: "The *Holy Spirit testifies* in every city, saying that chains and tribulations await me" (Acts 20:23). And when Paul stayed with disciples at Tyre, "they told Paul *through the Spirit* not to go up to Jerusalem" (Acts 21:4).

Sailing to Rome as a prisoner, Paul is warned supernaturally of an impending shipwreck. He informs the sailors and assures them that no life will be lost.

> For there stood by me this night an angel of the God to whom I belong and whom I serve, saying, "Do not be afraid, Paul; you must be brought before Caesar; and indeed God has granted you all those who sail with you." Therefore take heart, men, for I believe God that it will be just *as it was told me* (Acts 27:23-25).

The Holy Spirit presently resides within individual believers and the corporate church. We have already established that wherever the Spirit is, there the kingdom of God is also. It is only logical to expect him to be active in our lives and the life of the church. What else could Paul mean when he declares, "For as many as are *led by the Spirit of God*, these are sons of God" (Romans 8:14)? God's end-time Spirit guides his people as we head toward the ultimate kingdom.

Paul reminds the believers at Corinth of his first visit to their city: "My speech and my preaching were not with persuasive words of human wisdom, but *in demonstration of the Spirit* and of power, that your faith should not be in the wisdom of men but in the power of God (1 Corinthians 2:4-5).

Later in the letter he explains how members should minister to one another following the Lord's Supper. He mentions prophecy and words of knowledge and wisdom, among other gifts (1 Corinthians 12–14). He especially wishes them to prophesy (1 Corinthians 14:1). He also instructs them to test all utterances to make sure they are words from God (14:29). He reminds them, "No one *speaking by the Spirit of*

God calls Jesus accursed, and no one can say that Jesus is Lord except by the Holy Spirit" (12:3).

Paul exhorts the church at Colossae, "Let the word of Christ dwell in you richly in all wisdom, teaching and admonishing one another in psalms and hymns and spiritual songs, singing with grace in your hearts to the Lord" (Colossians 3:16).

Paul writes to young Timothy, who is discouraged because church members at Ephesus are dropping by the wayside, and reminds him that this is to be expected. "*The Spirit expressly says* that in latter times some will depart from the faith, giving heed to deceiving spirits and doctrines of demons" (1 Timothy 4:1).

John receives the Apocalypse in its entirety through a series of Spirit-induced revelations, voices, and visions.

> I was in the Spirit on the Lord's Day, and I *heard behind me a loud voice*, as of a trumpet, saying, "I am the Alpha and the Omega, the First and the Last," and, "What you see, write in a book and send it to the seven churches which are in Asia: to Ephesus, to Smyrna, to Pergamos, to Thyatira, to Sardis, to Philadelphia, and to Laodicea" (Revelation 1:10-11).

Then to the seven churches, the exalted Jesus says, "He who has an ear, let him hear what *the Spirit says to the churches*" (Revelation 2:7,11,17,29; 3:6,13,22).

Do you have ears to hear what the Spirit is speaking to you? Are you an AM Christian or an FM Christian?

The book of Revelation concludes with this exhortation: "*The Spirit and the bride say, 'Come!' And let him who hears say, 'Come!' And let him who thirsts come. Whoever desires, let him take the water of life freely*" (Revelation 22:17).

The evidence is overwhelming. God desires to speak to his people. Therefore the real question becomes, are you willing to tune in to the Voice? Will you allow the Spirit of Christ to speak through you to your church?

To the church at Laodicea, Jesus pleads, "Behold, I stand at the door and knock. *If anyone hears My voice* and opens the door, I will come in to him and dine with him, and he with Me" (Revelation 3:20). Will you be that person?

The Voice as Evidence of the Kingdom

After the writing of Malachi, salvation history enters 400 silent years, when God's voice is no longer heard in the land. With the opening of the Gospels, however, we are introduced to John the Baptist, "a man sent from God" (John 1:6), a prophet through whom God begins to speak. His message is clear: "The kingdom of God is at hand. Repent, and believe in the gospel" (Mark 1:15). Then at the baptism of Jesus, God speaks again and declares Jesus to be his anointed King. The return of God's voice in the land is a sign of the kingdom's imminent arrival and presence.

From the sending of the Holy Spirit on the Day of Pentecost up until the present, many people have heard God speak (Acts 2:17-18). This signifies that the end of the age is upon us. By the Spirit, both Jesus and his Father speak to and through us to guide and empower us as we live as kingdom citizens. Since the beginning of the Christian era, God has continued to speak in visions, dreams, and prophecies. He speaks through angels, by impressions, and in a still, small voice. These communications are evidence that God is with us.

Some Christians believe God speaks through the Scriptures alone, but they are hard pressed to explain how he guided his people during the era when Christian Bibles were not available. The New Testament as we know it was virtually inaccessible to God's people for centuries. Even after it was compiled and canonized, handwritten copies of the Bible were rare. Only the rich could afford them. It was only after Gutenberg invented the printing press in the 1440s that hard copies of the Bible could be obtained. And nearly a century passed before Tyndale translated the Bible into English (approximately 1526). Did God leave those living prior to the printing press without a word? This sounds more like 1400 silent years than the arrival of the kingdom of God!

Jesus's reception of the Spirit at his baptism and the believers' reception of the Spirit at Pentecost change everything. God's voice is heard once again, as the apostle Peter explains.

This is what was spoken by the prophet Joel:

> "And it shall come to pass *in the last days*, says God,
> That I will pour out of My Spirit on all flesh;
> Your sons and your daughters *shall prophesy*,
> Your young men shall *see visions*,
> Your old men shall *dream dreams*.
> And on My menservants and on My maidservants
> I will pour out My Spirit in those days;
> And they *shall prophesy*" (Acts 2:16-18).

Are You Hearing the Voice of God?

In Paul's two earliest epistles, 1 Thessalonians and 1 Corinthians, the apostle explains how to judge, test, or evaluate an inspired utterance given in a congregational setting. We might liken the church at Thessalonica to a modern-day fundamentalist church and the church at Corinth to a charismatic church. When each assembled, God spoke prophetically. Each church reacted in its own inappropriate way. Both needed correction.

1 Thessalonians 5	1 Corinthians 14
Do not quench the Spirit (verse 19).	Desire...that you may prophesy (verse 1).
Do not despise prophecies (verse 20).	Let two or three prophets speak (verse 29).
Test all things (verse 21).	Let the others judge (verse 29).
Hold fast what is good (verse 21).	Desire earnestly to prophesy (verse 39).
Abstain from every form of evil (verse 22).	Let all things be done decently and in order (verse 40).

Paul encourages the Corinthians to desire to prophesy and to embrace prophecy in their assembly. To the Thessalonians he gives a negative command: "Do not quench the Spirit." By using a present-tense verb, Paul likely means, "Stop quenching the Spirit," which indicates they are currently doing so. This implies that the Spirit's ministry can be hampered by the community. A move of the Spirit is not an irresistible force, but is susceptible to human opposition. As Paul writes, "The spirits of the prophets are subject to the prophets" (1 Corinthians 14:32).

Paul's second exhortation to the Thessalonians provides a clue as to how they are quenching the Spirit: "Do not despise prophecies" (1 Thessalonians 5:20). This suggests that certain church members are treating the Spirit's utterances as valueless or as aggravations. By treating as despicable the inspired instructions, they quench the Spirit and thus miss out on the exalted Christ's will for the church. This command, like the first (verse 19), is in the negative present tense, so it might be translated, "Stop your continuous disregard for prophetic utterances."

Although the identity of those opposing the Voice is not mentioned in verses 19-23, they are possibly congregational leaders who view the prophetic utterances as a hindrance to church order.

Paul offers the Thessalonians a corrective in verse 21 by issuing a third command: "Test all things." Paul's readers must not quench the Spirit or show contempt for prophetic utterances, but neither must they simply accept every word as coming from the Spirit. Each prophecy ("all things") must be put to the test. This is the same advice Paul gives to the Corinthians: "Let the others judge" (1 Corinthians 14:29). This implies that words can be spoken from a source other than God.

The responsibility of testing prophecies rests with the members of the church and not with the prophets only. This tradition of testing prophecy is carried over from the Old Testament (Deuteronomy 18:21-22).

The Thessalonians, despite their apprehensions, are told to receive the spoken prophecies and then scrutinize them. The Corinthians, who enthusiastically embrace prophecy but have allowed it to run amok, are given the same instructions. So we have two different churches and two different circumstances but the same solution.

How does a congregation go about evaluating or examining the validity of a prophecy? If Paul's instructions to the Corinthians and Thessalonians are any indication, those with the gift of discernment are to weigh the prophecy to determine if it proclaims Jesus as Lord (1 Corinthians 12:3), comforts and edifies the saints (1 Corinthians 14:3), and conforms to the traditions that have been passed down by word or epistle (2 Thessalonians 2:15). Those that do not pass muster are to be rejected as originating from a source other than the Spirit, either human or demonic. The New Testament is filled with warnings about false prophets and teachers who bring messages contrary to Christ. Such counterfeiters are to be identified and exposed (2 Peter 2:1; 1 John 4:1; Jude 4; Revelation 2:2,20).

Rather than searching for the actual genesis of the prophecy, Paul recommends they examine the content of the prophecy. Once the prophetic content is judged, Paul gives two further instructions in 1 Thessalonians 5:21-22, one a positive and the other a negative: "Hold fast what is good," and "Abstain from every form of evil." These commands tell them what to do with the test results. After all, the goal is to discern God's will for the community. The church should embrace the prophecies that may prove beneficial and avoid those that are detrimental.

So charismatic as well as fundamentalist extremes are to be avoided. The churches must neither restrict the voice of God nor allow matters to get out of hand. As Paul says, "Let all things be done decently and in order."

Summary

God wishes to speak to the hearts of individual believers and to his people when they gather. I am not advocating in any way New Age mysticism, but New Testament Christianity. I am repulsed by church services where believers work themselves into a wild-eyed frenzy or throw back their heads and begin spouting off ridiculous nonsense, which they claim comes from the Lord. This form of Corinthian chaos is more akin to spirit possession found in voodoo than to being filled by the *Holy* Spirit.

God can speak quietly to the heart, or he can speak aloud through human lips. He is God. People who hear God's voice are those who exhibit the fruit of the Spirit, which includes not only love, joy, and peace, but also patience, kindness, goodness, faithfulness, gentleness, and self-control (Galatians 5:22-23). They are not mystics or maniacs. They are men and women of God—FM Christians—who have learned to hear the Voice, which is a sign of the kingdom in their midst.

10

The Church and Its Worldwide Mission

You are Peter, and on this rock I will build My church...
And I will give you the keys of the kingdom of heaven.

Matthew 16:18-19

Part 1: The Church Jesus Built

While passing through Caesarea Philippi, Jesus asks his disciples how others view him (Matthew 16:13). He refers to himself as "the Son of Man," the title Daniel used.

> Behold, One like the Son of Man, coming with the clouds of heaven! He came to the Ancient of Days, and they brought Him near before Him. Then to Him was given dominion and glory and a kingdom, that all peoples, nations, and languages should serve Him. His dominion is an everlasting dominion, which shall not pass away, and His kingdom the one which shall not be destroyed (Daniel 7:13-14).

Because Jesus identified himself as the Son of Man, there is little doubt that "Jesus believed Himself to be the Messiah, the instrument and embodiment of the Reign of God."[1] His question to the disciples is designed to discover if anyone else has a correct understanding of his role in establishing the kingdom of God.

Peter responds that the consensus opinion among them is that Jesus is an end-time prophet. Based on apocalyptic literature at the time, Jews believed that a God-sent prophet would appear prior to the advent of the Messiah (see 2 Esdras 2:16-18; 2 Maccabees 15:14). Malachi names Elijah as the forerunner (4:5).

This leads Jesus to ask, "But who do you say that I am?" Simon Peter replies, "You are the Christ, the Son of the living God."

"Christ" is the Greek equivalent of the Hebrew word "Messiah." It is a title, not a name, and refers to the God-sent representative who restores the kingdom to Israel. In similar fashion, "Son of God" refers to God's chosen king who reigns on earth from the throne of David (Psalm 2:7). Peter's reply, therefore, is all about the kingdom of God. We must not assume that Peter understands Jesus to be a Savior in the sense of taking people to heaven after they die. This concept is foreign to the Jewish mind in the first century.

Jewish hopes were earthly hopes. They looked forward to the day when God would set up his kingdom once again in Jerusalem, fulfilling his covenant with King David.

Jesus commends Peter. "Blessed are you, Simon Bar-Jonah, for flesh and blood has not revealed this to you, but My Father who is in heaven" (Matthew 16:17). In other words, Peter hits the nail on the head and correctly identifies Jesus as the Messiah. He does not follow public opinion. Peter's response leads Jesus to make two declarations. He begins each with "I will."

"And I also say to you that you are Peter, and on this rock *I will build* My church...And *I will give* you the keys of the kingdom of heaven."

I Will Build My Church

This declaration must be a shock to the disciples. If Jesus is the Messiah, he should defeat Rome and establish the kingdom of God. What is this talk about building a church? The Messiah is a kingdom builder, not a church builder! It seems as if Jesus's agenda is different from the expected one.

When we twenty-first-century believers look at Jesus's pronounce-ment, it does not seem shocking at all. The church has been around for 2000 years. We've gotten used to it. But for the disciples, it was another matter.

But even we might be shocked if we understood more clearly the nature of the church Jesus planned to build. It doesn't look like many churches today.

The Church as a Voluntary Association

Until recently, most biblical scholars have viewed the church in New Testament times as something akin to a Christian version of the Jewish synagogue. This understanding, while partially correct, causes more confusion than clarity. The Greek word *ekklesia*, trans-lated "church" in most Bibles, was commonly used in the first century to describe a voluntary association or meal club. Churches and syna-gogues fell into this category.

Within the Roman Empire, voluntary associations (*collegia* in Latin) were social organizations, or more specifically, supper clubs. Each association had its own goals and purposes for existence. Some were professional or occupational guilds. Others were religious or cul-tic groups whose members honored a particular deity. A number were funeral societies that provided financial assistance for burials. Still oth-ers were household or ethnic associations that kept alive one's family or native heritage. These groups placed much emphasis on fellowship and benevolence. Regardless of their stated purpose, all associations had one thing in common—their meetings revolved around meals.

Many people, especially peasants and artisans, belonged to associa-tions. Meetings were held monthly and always included a meal. Some people belonged to more than one association, such as an occupational one and an ethnic one. The poorer and smaller associations usually held their meetings in homes or common areas.

New Testament scholar Kathleen Corley argues that the voluntary association serves as "the primary analogue" for understanding the for-mation of the church. She shows that the same Greek terms used to describe voluntary associations and their members in the first century were used also to describe Christian churches and their members.[2] For instance, churches and voluntary associations were both called *ekklesiai*. Three words used to describe church members—*adelphoi* (brethren), *episkopos* (overseer, bishop), and *diakonos* (servant, deacon)—were common terms first used to designate association members.[3] Synagogues, also considered to be voluntary associations, called some of their leading male members by the title *presbuteroi* (elders). The churches adopted this term as well.

Jesus's first Jewish followers attended synagogue association meetings, where they were viewed as a messianic movement within Judaism and not as a stand-alone religion. We might liken the early Jesus movement to Methodism at the time of John Wesley, which was a movement within the Church of England.

Regardless of the precise nature of each association, they all had one thing in common—they were supper clubs. They held regular reclining banquets, usually at monthly intervals.

A typical Roman banquet usually lasted three or four hours. It was divided into two sections—the full-course meal, called a *deipnon*, followed by a prolonged period of leisurely drinking called a *symposion* (Greek) or *convivium* (Latin), which included entertainment or discussion.

These two segments were joined together by a ceremonial act known as a libation, or drink offering of mixed wine, followed by a hymn honoring the deities or, on special occasions, a patriotic song in remembrance of a great battle.

As we discussed in chapter 4, Rome imposed two obligations upon all associations. Their libations had to be offered in the name of the emperor, and during the *symposion*, they could not engage in any discussion or actions against the state. These regulations enabled Rome to keep its subjects in line with the Empire's political agenda.

If the *ekklesia* Jesus built was structured after a Roman *ekklesia*, or voluntary association, a picture of the New Testament church emerges that makes more sense. When Acts and the epistles are read in this context, we understand why the church meets weekly for a community meal. This is what similar voluntary associations did.

Although the Christian communal meal looked much like a typical Roman banquet, it had a different purpose. The three- to four-hour *deipnon* and *symposion* constituted the entirety of Christian worship. In the first hour or so believers reclined on couches and ate a leisurely meal, followed by a toast to Jesus—not to Caesar—as Lord. They spent another hour or so singing anti-imperial hymns about Jesus (who overcame death at the hands of the Roman authorities), teaching about God's kingdom plans to bring all empires under his reign, praying for daily sustenance, reading aloud apostolic letters that instructed them how to live according to the ethics of the kingdom of God, and ministering to each other through supercharged spiritual gifts.

This mealtime gathering in Jesus's name was a politically subversive act, challenging Rome's ideological claims and right to rule the world and upholding Christ's right to rule the world as God's authorized King. In essence, the Christian banquet was a behind-the-scenes act of nonviolent resistance.

So when Jesus says he will build his *ekklesia* (church), his disciples likely understand him to be speaking of a new voluntary association.

Five Characteristics of the Ekklesia Jesus Built

First, Jesus is the architect. He says, "*I* will build my church" (Matthew 16:18). He chooses the people who make up the composite materials of his *ekklesia*, or voluntary association. These building materials are people, not wood and bricks. Peter, writing years later, speaks of believers as "living stones...being *built up a spiritual house*, a holy priesthood, to offer up spiritual sacrifices acceptable to God through Jesus Christ" (1 Peter 2:5).

Second, the church is a future entity. Jesus says, "I *will build* my church." At the time of his pronouncement, the church has not yet been built. Jesus reveals later in the discussion with the disciples that he must first die and be raised from the dead (Matthew 16:21). This must confuse the disciples. They are not expecting him to die, but to overthrow Rome.

Third, the church belongs to Jesus. He calls it "*my* church." This distinguishes it from other voluntary associations whose members make sacrifices to pagan deities or meet for other purposes. Members of Jesus's church pledge their loyalty to worship and serve him alone. Based on Peter's identification of Jesus as Christ and Son of God, we can say it is a messianic association.

Fourth, the church has a rock-solid foundation. After Simon correctly identifies Jesus as the Christ, Jesus calls him *petros* (Rock) and then declares, "And on this rock (*petra*) I will build my church." This pronouncement requires some examination because of a major controversy about the identity of the rock. There are three main theories.

Theory 1. Peter's confession ("You are the Christ, the Son of the living God") is the foundation of the church. John Chrysostom (AD 347–407), one of the early church fathers and the greatest preacher of his era, was a proponent of this theory. Many evangelical Christians today also embrace this position.

Theory 2. Jesus is the foundation of the church. Earlier in Matthew's Gospel, we find Jesus telling a story of a wise man whose house withstands the onslaught of the raging elements because "it was founded on the rock" (Matthew 7:21-25). In his epistle, Peter calls Jesus a "rock of offense" (1 Peter 2:8, quoting Isaiah 8:14). The apostle Paul identifies Jesus as the one and only foundation of God's building (1 Corinthians 3:11). Saint Augustine (AD 354–430), bishop of Hippo, held to this position (*Retractationes* I, 21). Likewise, an equal amount of modern-day believers hold to this position.

Theory 3. Peter (Greek, *petros*) is the foundation. This is the official position of the Roman Catholic Church. Many evangelicals reject this theory, noting that Matthew uses two different Greek words for "rock" in the verse—*petros* and *petra*. Peter (*petros*) cannot be the rock (*petra*).

But a renowned New Testament scholar, Oscar Cullmann, exposed such logic as an exegetical fallacy when he observed that Jesus spoke in Aramaic, not in Greek. Aramaic has only one word for rock: *Kepha*. Therefore, Jesus actually said, "You are *Kepha*, and on this *Kepha* I will build My church." The person and the foundation are identical. According to Cullmann, Peter is the rock upon which the church will be built.[4] Then how did we end up with two Greek words? The translator rendered *Kepha* in two different ways—*petra* and *petros*. He likely did this for the sake of variety and not to make a distinction between the two.

This explanation seems more contextually supportable, especially since Jesus identifies himself in this passage as the builder and not the foundation of the *ekklesia*.

Many Protestants reject this interpretation because the Roman Catholic Church has used it to build its doctrine of apostolic succession to designate Peter as the first pope. However, the passage makes no mention of Peter's successors. We can accept Peter as the rock without having to accept the Catholic belief in papal authority. If we accept that the first *ekklesia* in Jerusalem is a messianic voluntary association, then Peter as its foundation makes good sense. After all, Peter is the leading apostle in Acts 1–12, and he opens the door of salvation to Jews (Acts 2:14-41), Samaritans (Acts 8:14-17), and Gentiles (Acts 10:1–11:18). Through his preaching and/or laying on of hands, these three different ethnic groups receive the Holy Spirit.

Fifth, the *ekklesia* will endure. Jesus says, "The gates of Hades [death] *shall not prevail* against it." What does Jesus mean by the phrase "gates of Hades"? Similar imagery is found in the Old Testament as a metaphor for death. Jonah describes death as an inescapable prison with bars or gates that have been slammed shut (Jonah 2:6). Likewise, Job equates "the gates of Sheol" with death (Job 17:16; 38:17). King David celebrates when God rescues him from the "gates of death" (Psalm 9:13). And when facing a terminal illness, King Hezekiah laments, "In the prime of my life I shall go to the gates of Sheol; I am deprived of the remainder of my life" (Isaiah 38:10).

Since the Hebrew Bible uses gates to refer to death, Jesus likely does the same thing. If so, this implies that the *ekklesia* exists at a time when death is present and continues to claim victims. Death, our last enemy, will not be destroyed until the kingdom arrives in its fullness, so the church lives in the interim period. Its mission takes place between the inauguration and consummation of the kingdom. Therefore, the disciples should not expect the kingdom to be restored to Israel in their immediate future.

Now let's look at the phrase "shall not prevail against it." What does

Jesus mean? Here are three options: (1) The church can expect persecution and even martyrdom, yet it will survive. (2) The church will preach the gospel of the kingdom and snatch souls out of death's grip. (3) The church will heal the sick and raise the dead.

Whatever the exact meaning, the intention is clear. Death will not defeat the church or halt its mission. Death will not be victorious over the church because Jesus conquered death and the church shares in Christ's resurrection power.

I Will Give You the Keys of the Kingdom of Heaven

After Jesus declares, "I will build my church" and elaborates on it, he makes a second declaration: "And I will give you the keys of the kingdom of heaven, and whatever you bind on earth will be bound in heaven, and whatever you loose on earth will be loosed in heaven" (Matthew 16:19).

From this pronouncement we learn two things. First, the *ekklesia* (church) and the kingdom are not the same.[5] The church serves the kingdom. As a messianic voluntary association, it carries out the Messiah's agenda, just as other voluntary associations carried out Caesar's agenda.

Second, if Jesus gives the keys of the kingdom, then they are his to give. He holds the keys and has authority to pass them on to the disciples. Of course, Jesus is speaking metaphorically. People use keys to open and close doors. The apostles will be given the privilege of opening and closing the doors of the kingdom. The Jewish leaders, who should be leading people into the kingdom, have chosen instead to serve the Roman Empire, and Jesus scolds them: "Woe to you, scribes and Pharisees, hypocrites! For *you shut up the kingdom of heaven* against men; for you neither go in yourselves, nor do you allow those who are entering to go in" (Matthew 23:13). Jesus is replacing Israel's leaders with those of his own who will do the right thing. They will possess the keys of the kingdom.

What do these keys represent? Although Jesus does not get specific, they likely represent the good news of the kingdom, which calls on people to repent and believe. Jesus preached the kingdom and summoned his hearers to change and pledge their allegiance to God, so he would logically expect his church to do likewise after his departure. The church is at the center of Christ's kingdom plans from the time of his ascension to his return at the end of the age. He uses people to carry out his mission.

This leads him to say, "Whatever you bind on earth will be bound in heaven, and whatever you loose on earth will be loosed in heaven" (Matthew 16:19). Those responding positively to the gospel are loosed from their sins and eligible to enter the kingdom. Those who do not respond are bound by their sins and cannot gain entrance.

Binding and loosing were common legal terms in Jesus's day. To bind people was to hold them responsible for their actions and incarcerate them. To loose someone was to acquit them. This action is theologically equivalent to the Christian concept of justification, or the forgiveness of sins. In Matthew's Gospel, binding and loosing relates to being bound to sin or forgiven of sin. The authority to bind and loose is not given to Peter alone, but to the entire church as well (see Matthew 18:15-18).

Jesus says whenever something is bound or loosed on earth, the same is being done in heaven. This means that after Jesus's death and departure, the apostles will represent God on earth. Just as Jesus pronounces forgiveness and judgment when he ministers, so can the church in his absence (as Peter does in Acts 2:38-41).

PART 2: THE WORLDWIDE MISSION OF THE CHURCH

After Jesus's death and glorification, the church becomes God's agent on earth, pointing people toward the kingdom. This eschatological mission involves, among other things, preaching the true gospel. For instance, during a discussion about the last days, the disciples ask, "What will be the sign of Your coming, and of the end of the age?" (Matthew 24:3). After speaking about a variety of events that will precede his coming, Jesus gives the ultimate sign. "This gospel of the kingdom will be preached in all the world as a witness to all the nations, and then the end will come" (Matthew 24:14). To the same question, Mark records Jesus's answer this way, "The gospel must first be preached to all the nations" (Mark 13:10). In this case the emphasis is on the *necessity* of the gospel reaching the world before the end comes.

The Great Commission reiterates these themes. Jesus says, "Go therefore and make disciples of *all the nations*…and lo, I am with you always, even to the end of the age" (Matthew 28:18-20).

In Luke's version, Jesus says the gospel "should be preached in His name to all nations, beginning at Jerusalem" (Luke 24:47). The task starts in Jerusalem but continues to the ends of the earth.

Before Jesus's ascension, the apostles ask him, "Lord, will You at this time restore the kingdom to Israel?" (Acts 1:6). This is his response:

> It is not for you to know times or seasons which the Father has put in His own authority. But you shall receive power when the Holy Spirit has come upon you; and you shall be witnesses to Me in Jerusalem, and in all Judea and Samaria, and to *the end of the earth* (Acts 1:7-8).

Jesus explains that the timing of the kingdom is God's responsibility. But we too have a responsibility. Between now and the time when the kingdom is restored, we must take the gospel to the far reaches of the world.

Who Are the Nations?

"The nations" likely refers to the Gentile nations, in fulfillment of God's promise to Abraham that through him all the families of the earth will be blessed (Genesis 12:3). In that context, the nations are the ones listed in the table of nations (Genesis 10–11). These same nations are mentioned in Isaiah 66 as having a part in God's end-time plans:

> For I know their works and their thoughts. It shall be that I will gather *all nations* and tongues, and they shall come and see My glory. I will set a sign among them; and those among them who escape I will send to the nations: to Tarshish and Pul and Lud, who draw the bow, and Tubal

and Javan, to the coastlands afar off who have not heard
My fame nor seen My glory. And they shall declare My
glory among the *Gentiles*. Then they shall bring all your
brethren for an offering to the LORD out of *all nations* (Isaiah 66:18-20).

When preaching to the philosophers on Mars Hill, Paul says God
determines the borders of *every nation* and that he "now commands all
men everywhere to repent" (Acts 17:26,30). God wants Gentiles to be
included among his people.

One of Israel's main tasks was to be a light to the Gentiles. Even a
portion of the temple was available to Gentiles who would come and
worship. But Israel lost sight of its divine mission. By the first century,
the court of the Gentiles was used as a market for vendors and money-
changers. Israel's disobedience eventually leads to Christ commission-
ing his disciples (Matthew 24:14; Mark 13:10). The mission to the
nations must be completed before the end arrives. God's purpose for
the present stage of redemptive history, and the church's mission, is to
announce the good news of his kingdom to the Gentiles.

The selected history of the church in the book of Acts is an account
of the church reaching the ends of the known world (the Roman
Empire of their day) with the gospel of the kingdom. Along the way
as people responded, new *ekklesiai* were established in various locales.
Each served as a messianic association where fellow believers and curiosity seekers gathered for an evening meal and ministry.

World evangelization of the Gentiles is a sign of the last days, so
each succeeding generation during this final stage of redemptive history must proclaim the gospel of the kingdom anew to the nations,
regardless of whether the previous generation fulfilled its evangelistic
obligation.

God has appointed the church—with the keys of the kingdom in
hand—to be his means of getting his gospel to the nations. The church
must ever be kingdom focused and kingdom driven.

From the book of Revelation, we know that in the end the mission
will be accomplished.

After these things I looked, and behold, a great multitude
which no one could number, of all nations, tribes, peoples,
and tongues, standing before the throne and before the
Lamb...crying out with a loud voice, saying, "Salvation
belongs to God who sits on the throne, and to the Lamb!"
(Revelation 7:9-10).

11

The Final Week

You say rightly that I am a king. For this cause I was
born, and for this cause I have come into the world.

JOHN 18:37

After ministering in Galilee, Jesus works his way toward Jerusalem,
where he will celebrate the Passover and prepare for his reign as
Israel's King. As he approaches, he decides to ride into the city as a symbolic gesture of his kingly status.

The Triumphal Entry

Many key events in Jesus's life portray some facet of the kingdom of
God, and the triumphal entry into Jerusalem is no exception (Matthew
21:1-11; Mark 11:1-11; Luke 19:28-44; John 12:12-19). As Jesus rides into
the Jewish capital, a crowd of enthusiasts give him the red-carpet treatment as they line the highway, wave palm branches, and spread their
clothes in front of him. The event is reminiscent of Jehu's enthronement as king of Israel (2 Kings 9:13).

It also reminds us of Solomon's grand entry before his installation
as Israel's new monarch. With the aging of King David, the question of
his successor is on everyone's mind (1 Kings 1:1-4). Adonijah, David's
son by Haggith, declares presumptuously, "I will be king" and arranges

a parade of chariots, horsemen, and foot soldiers to go ahead of him. When word reaches Nathan the prophet that Adonijah has named himself king, he gets word to David, who takes decisive action. He begins by reiterating his promise to Bathsheba.

> As the Lord lives, who has redeemed my life from every distress, just as I swore to you by the Lord God of Israel, saying, "Assuredly Solomon your son shall be king after me, and he shall sit on my throne in my place," so I certainly will do this day (verses 29-30).

He then gives orders to Zadok the priest, Nathan the prophet, and Benaiah the son of Jehoida.

> Take with you the servants of your lord, and have Solomon my son ride on my own mule, and bring him down to Gihon. There let Zadok the priest and Nathan the prophet anoint him king over Israel; and blow the horn, and say, "Long live King Solomon!" Then you shall come up after him, and he shall come and sit on my throne, and he shall be king in my place. For I have appointed him to be ruler over Israel and Judah (verses 33-35).

With orders in hand, David's loyal servants place Solomon on the king's mule and lead him to the Gihon River, where Zadok anoints Solomon as king. With the blowing of the trumpet, the people shout, "Long live King Solomon!" (verses 38-39).

What makes this story of particular interest is that Gihon is the spring alongside the temple mount. Here Solomon is anointed before he makes his grand entry and is installed as king. So we note a parallel between Jesus's triumphal entry and Solomon's. Just as Solomon is anointed with oil at the site of water (Gihon), so Jesus was anointed with the Holy Spirit at the site of water (Jordan), and both acts prepared the anointed ones for kingship. Likewise, both ride on a lowly animal, signifying that they are to rule as servant-kings. Unfortunately, Solomon fails in this respect and becomes an imperial king. Jesus, however, succeeds and replaces David as God's eschatological Servant-King, whose kingdom will be unending.

Those watching the events unfold along the dusty road this first Palm Sunday morning do not miss the symbolism. Jesus is Israel's new King David, long foretold by the prophets (Ezekiel 37:24).

Matthew and the other Gospel writers associate Jesus's entry into Jerusalem with Zechariah's prophecy: "Rejoice greatly, O daughter Zion! Shout aloud, O daughter Jerusalem! Lo, your king comes to you; triumphant and victorious is he, humble and riding on a donkey, on a colt, the foal of a donkey" (Zechariah 9:9 NRSV). Describing the event in self-effacing terms, Zechariah suggests that Yahweh's new king will be "triumphant and victorious" and yet "humble and riding on a donkey." The babe in a manger, the baptismal dove, and the lowly donkey all point to an anti-imperial monarchy that will serve the people in humility rather than ruling by force.

Zechariah's prophecy concludes with Yahweh announcing that his newly installed King will bring an end to war and reunite his people through a new covenant.

> He will cut off the chariot from Ephraim
>   and the war-horse from Jerusalem;
> and the battle bow shall be cut off,
>   and he shall command peace to the nations;
> his dominion shall be from sea to sea,
>   and from the River to the ends of the earth.
> As for you also, because of the blood of my covenant with you,
>   I will set your prisoners free from the waterless pit.
> Return to your stronghold, O prisoners of hope
> (Zechariah 9:10-12 NRSV).

In Jesus's partial fulfillment of Zechariah's prophecy, the throng of onlookers cries out, "Blessed is the King who comes in the name of the LORD! Peace in heaven and glory in the highest!" The reaction from the Pharisees, however, is condescending: "Teacher, rebuke Your disciples" (Luke 19:38-39).

Notice that the crowd calls Jesus the King, but the Pharisees address him as simply a teacher.

Instead of kowtowing to their demands, Jesus answers, "I tell you

that if these should keep silent, the stones would immediately cry out."
With this response Jesus is affirming the crowd's evaluation of him.
Even the rocks have better sense than the Pharisees. (This is the last ref-
erence to the Pharisees in Luke's Gospel.)

Matthew tells of the crowds shouting, "Hosanna to the Son of
David! 'Blessed is He who comes in the name of the LORD!' Hosanna
in the highest!" (Matthew 21:9).

The people rightly interpret the messianic and kingly symbolism of
Jesus's triumphal entry, but they fail to grasp the means by which he
will secure their peace. They expect him to establish God's universal
peace by overthrowing Rome's government. Realizing their hopes are
misguided, Jesus weeps over the city.

> If you had known, even you, especially in this your day, the
> things that make for your peace! But now they are hidden
> from your eyes. For days will come upon you when your
> enemies will build an embankment around you, surround
> you and close you in on every side, and level you, and your
> children within you, to the ground; and they will not leave
> in you one stone upon another, because you did not know
> the time of your visitation (Luke 19:42-44).

Jerusalem will be razed, and multitudes, including children, will be
slaughtered because of their failure to recognize the time of their visitation. Zacharias had spoken of this visitation: "Blessed is the Lord God
of Israel, for He has visited and redeemed His people, and has raised
up a horn of salvation for us in the house of His servant David" (Luke
1:68-69). In Jesus, God visits his people, but their failure to recognize
this leads to Israel's destruction as a nation.

Their unwillingness to accept the nature of Jesus's kingdom mission
leads the people to turn against him and in a few days cry, "Crucify!"

Borg and Crossan trigger our historical imaginations when they
compare and contrast Jesus and Pilate, who entered Jerusalem from
opposite directions on the Sunday before Easter. One, a Roman-
appointed governor atop a charger, commands a procession of
6000 foot soldiers. The other, a Jewish prophet on a donkey, leads a

procession of peasant pilgrims. Pilate's grand entrance is designed to drive the fear of Caesar into all who might be contemplating a violent demonstration during the Passover season. The display of sheer physical force can deter even the bravest insurgent from shattering the *Pax Romana*. By contrast, Jesus prearranges his humble entrance to coincide with the governor's arrival, which is intended to mock and mimic him. When understood in this way, the triumphal entry might be viewed as a subversive anti-imperial act, possibly even as a performance of guerrilla theater.

The two processions represent two opposing kingdoms. The one is personified by Pilate and is built on brute strength and maintained at all cost. The other is typified by Jesus riding on a beast of burden and offers an alternative vision for humankind—the kingdom of God built on humility, sacrifice, and servitude. By the end of the week the kingdoms will clash, and men and women will align with one or the other. Nearly all will follow Rome.

Jesus's parabolic ride into the city ends at the temple mount, where he challenges the Jewish elites.

The Temple and the Kingdom

The next defining kingdom-oriented event in Jesus's ministry is the cleansing of the temple, which graphically serves as another call for Israel to repent and return to God.

The temple was originally built as a house of prayer for Jew and Gentile alike (Isaiah 56:7) and as a holy space where priests serve as intermediaries between God and his people, but it had lost its focus. As far back as the days of Jeremiah, God conditionally promises his people access to the temple and Jerusalem as a permanent dwelling place.

> If you thoroughly amend your ways and your doings, if you thoroughly execute judgment between a man and his neighbor, if you do not oppress the stranger, the fatherless, and the widow, and do not shed innocent blood in this place, or walk after other gods to your hurt, then I will cause you to dwell in this place, in the land that I gave to your fathers forever and ever (Jeremiah 7:5-7).

But Israel chooses to ignore this period of grace and continues in its abominations, turning God's house into "a den of thieves" (verse 11). So the city is destroyed, and the people are scattered and taken into captivity. A partial return occurs under Medo-Persian rule, but except for a brief period just before the time of Christ, Israel remains under foreign oppressive rule during the Greek and Roman Empires.

Under Roman leadership, the temple in Jerusalem devolves into a center of political domination and economic oppression. The priests, who are members of Jewish aristocratic families, are appointed by the Roman prefect and are responsible for collecting tribute and taxes from Jews on behalf of Caesar. The priests derive their wealth and status by doing Rome's bidding, so ordinary Jews may fear them, but few respect them.

Jesus confronts the situation head-on. "He went into the temple and began to drive out those who bought and sold in it, saying to them, 'It is written, "My house is a house of prayer," but you have made it a "den of thieves"'" (Luke 19:45-46; see also Matthew 21:12-13). The phrase "drive out" is the same used elsewhere to describe Jesus exorcizing or casting out demons, which might be intended to show us that the real power behind temple affairs is demonic.

Merchandise tables and money-changing booths fill the court of the Gentiles, leaving no space for God-fearing Gentiles to worship. The priests, like their counterparts in Jeremiah's day, oppress rather than serve God's people.

The cleansing of the temple should be viewed as much more than a literal overturning of the tables of commerce. It also has symbolic and prophetic significance, pointing to the ultimate removal of Israel's corrupt priesthood and the destruction of the temple. The purification of the temple is necessary preparation for the kingdom of God as the usurpers are replaced by God's anointed kingly priest, the Messiah.

Jeremiah is not the only Old Testament prophet to pronounce judgment on the people and predict the destruction of the temple. "Because of the evil of their deeds I will drive them from My house; I will love them no more. All their princes are rebellious" (Hosea 9:15). "Behold, I send My messenger, and he will prepare the way before Me.

And the Lord, whom you seek, will suddenly come to His temple, Even the Messenger of the covenant" (Malachi 3:1).

So Jesus seems to fulfill the role of God's messenger who prepares the way for the kingdom by first coming to the temple. Seen in this light, the cleansing of the temple serves as another enacted prophecy, warning of the judgment to come. But the symbolism doesn't stop here.

> Then the blind and the lame came to Him in the temple, and He healed them. But when the chief priests and scribes saw the wonderful things that He did, and the children crying out in the temple and saying, "Hosanna to the Son of David!" they were indignant and said to Him, "Do You hear what these are saying?"
>
> And Jesus said to them, "Yes. Have you never read,
>
> 'Out of the mouth of babes and nursing infants,
> You have perfected praise'?" (Matthew 21:14-16).

Three things speak of the dawning of the new age. First, the blind and the lame come into the temple. According to 2 Samuel 5:8, the blind and lame are forbidden to enter God's house. Something has now changed. Second, Jesus heals these two conditions, a sign of the kingdom's arrival (Isaiah 35:5-6). Third, the children cry out, "Hosanna to the Son of David," or "Deliver us now, Messiah." The chief interpreters of the law and priests try to stop them, but Jesus calls this "perfected praise."

With the cleansing of the temple, a new messianic community is being formed, comprised of the blind, the lame, children, and others on the margins.

The Last Supper

Jesus's Last Supper with his disciples, which is actually a Passover meal, has a clear connection to the kingdom of God. We might say it is a Passover with a difference. According to the Exodus account, the Hebrew slaves hastily ate the original Passover meal as they prepared for their escape from Pharaoh's totalitarian regime. Each family participated in this subversive supper in anticipation of their divine emancipation from Egyptian oppression. The meal, however, was much more than a pre-celebration event. It actually effectuated their release. They smeared the blood of the lamb (the meat portion of the supper) on their doorposts as a signal for the angel of death to pass over their homes and destroy only the firstborn of Egypt, thus leading to the Exodus. Later, the Passover meal became a symbol of Israel's liberation.

Except for short periods of self-rule, Israel falls victim to one tyrannical empire after another (722 BC to AD 70). Captivity is God's judgment on the nation for its disobedience. Even during independence (167–63 BC), its corrupt priestly rulers choose to fill their own stomachs and coffers while the masses are deprived of food and justice.

By the time of Christ, the Jews find themselves living again under foreign rule. Like Egypt, Rome uses military might and other oppressive means to control the masses. Each spring when Jews from far and wide congregate in Jerusalem to celebrate the Passover, they not only remember the original Exodus but also yearn for God to rescue them from the present authoritarian regime and their own traitorous priests. They look in anticipation for a deliverer to lead a new exodus, culminating in a new age and a new Passover celebration under the reign of God (Ezekiel 45:21-22).

Jesus's Final Passover

> When the hour came, he took his place at the table, and the apostles with him. He said to them, "I have eagerly desired to eat this Passover with you before I suffer; for I tell you, I will not eat it [again] until it is fulfilled in the kingdom of God" (Luke 22:14-16 NRSV).

Jesus has a deep desire to eat this final Passover with his disciples. When he says, "I will not eat it [again] until it is fulfilled in the kingdom of God," he implies that in its present form the Passover is a type that prefigures or foreshadows something greater—the messianic banquet in the future kingdom. The next time he eats the meal with them, it will be no ordinary Passover, but a kingdom Passover feast that celebrates ultimate deliverance from the powers of darkness and oppression!

Jesus's statement about the coming kingdom and a messianic banquet must thrill his table companions, but it implies that he will die sometime between the Last Supper and the messianic banquet. He will not be around. This must confuse the disciples. What does he mean? Will the kingdom be delayed?

The phrase "until it is fulfilled in the kingdom of God," leads to the question, when will this fulfillment take place? Will the Passover find its fulfillment in the Lord's Supper eaten by the early church or not until the messianic banquet at the second coming? Additionally, does a relationship exist between the original Passover, Jesus's Last Supper, the Lord's Supper, and the messianic banquet at the end of the age? If so, what is the connection? Let's keep reading.

> Then he took a cup, and after giving thanks he said, "Take this and divide it among yourselves; for I tell you that from now on I will not drink of the fruit of the vine until the kingdom of God comes" (Luke 22:17-18 NRSV).

With his lifting of the cup, Jesus refers a second time to the kingdom. His next meal with them will take place in the kingdom. He expects to die, but he will eat and drink again with them in the future. He expects to be resurrected. To the Jewish mind this implies a resurrection at the end of the age, immediately before the arrival of the kingdom.

> Then he took a loaf of bread, and when he had given thanks, he broke it and gave it to them, saying, "This is my body, which is given for you. Do this in remembrance of me." And he did the same with the cup after supper, saying, "This cup that is poured out for you is the new covenant in my blood" (verses 19-20 NRSV).

Jesus follows standard Passover procedure by blessing, breaking, and distributing the unleavened bread, which is called the "bread of affliction" in Deuteronomy 16:3. Jesus next departs from tradition by reinterpreting the Passover, connecting the bread with his person: "This is my body." That he speaks metaphorically is evident because his actual body is reclining on the couch beside them. Therefore "is my body" means "represents my body" or "represents me." Jesus sees himself as taking the affliction of the people. This is not the ordinary meaning assigned to unleavened bread at a typical Passover feast, so Jesus is reinterpreting the Passover.

Then he says, "Do this in remembrance of me." Normally Jews remembered the Exodus from Egypt. His disciples are to remember him instead. This implies that when they eat subsequent annual Passover meals, he will not be there to eat with them.

He then picks up the cup, but not until after supper. He says two things about the cup. First, he calls it "the cup that is poured out for you," which brings to mind Old Testament animal sacrifice. In his letter to Timothy, Paul uses the phrase metaphorically to describe his own impending death (2 Timothy 4:6). When Jesus mentions being poured out, therefore, he is speaking of his vicarious death. These words may be an allusion to Isaiah 53:12 (NRSV):

> Therefore I will allot him a portion with the great,
>   and he shall divide the spoil with the strong;
> because he *poured out himself to death,*
>   and was numbered with the transgressors;
> yet he bore the sin of many,
>   and made intercession for the transgressors.

Second, Jesus says the cup represents a new covenant—another Old Testament allusion.

> The days are surely coming, says the Lord, when I will make a new covenant with the house of Israel and the house of Judah. It will not be like the covenant that I made with their ancestors when I took them by the hand to bring them out of the land of Egypt—a covenant that they broke, though I was their husband, says the Lord (Jeremiah 31:31-32 NRSV).

The new covenant is actually a covenant of renewal God makes with the house of Israel and the house of Judah, and it implies a return to the Lord in repentance and a reuniting of the tribes.

> But this is the covenant that I will make with the house
> of Israel after those days, says the LORD: I will put my law
> within them, and I will write it on their hearts; and I will
> be their God, and they shall be my people. No longer shall
> they teach one another, or say to each other, "Know the
> LORD," for they shall all know me, from the least of them to
> the greatest, says the LORD; for I will forgive their iniquity,
> and remember their sin no more (Jeremiah 31:33-34 NRSV).

The phrase "after those days" is the prophet's way of speaking of the kingdom of God that follows Israel's exile and its return to the land.

Jesus says the new covenant is in his blood, so he likely views his impending death as the means by which God fulfills his eschatological promise to Israel. Jesus's second use of the prepositional phrase "for you," read in light of Jeremiah 31:31, where the covenant is to be made with the united nation, infers that the 12 apostles represent the nation as a whole and are the firstfruits of God's newly restored Israel. The apostle Paul will later say that God purchased the church with his own blood (Acts 20:28).

In Matthew's parallel of Luke 22:20, Jesus adds the words, "for the remission of sins" (Matthew 26:28). New Testament scholar Warren Carter notes this reference should not be limited to forgiving personal or individual sins. The term translated "remission" (or "forgiveness" or "release") is the same word used in the Greek Septuagint translation of Leviticus 25, where it is translated 14 times as "a Jubilee" and "year of Jubilee," referring to a social and economic restructuring of Israel.[1] So Matthew interprets Jesus's teaching about the new covenant in his blood to mean that his death will bring about an end-time Jubilee, when those under sin (that is, living in a world ruled by evil oppressors) will be released from bondage to live in a renewed world where God reigns.

What runs through the apostles' minds as Jesus speaks of these things? They must have mixed emotions. On one hand, he speaks of his death. On the other, he offers hope for the future. It must be confusing. Most likely, they are thinking in traditional terms: "God will overthrow Rome and restore the kingdom to Israel in the immediate future."

After speaking of his demise and the new covenant through his blood, Jesus announces he will be betrayed by one sitting at the table. This causes each to wonder if he is the one (Luke 22:21-23). Ironically, the apostles immediately switch their focus from who is the worst among them to who is the best, or greatest. Their humility turns to pride. Their competition for superior ranking leads Jesus to exhort them.

> The kings of the Gentiles lord it over them; and those in authority over them are called benefactors. But not so with you; rather the greatest among you must become like the youngest, and the leader like one who serves. For who is greater, the one who is at the table or the one who serves? Is it not the one at the table? But I am among you as one who serves (Luke 22:25-27 NRSV).

Jesus corrects their faulty concept, which is based on the Roman model of greatness expressed in the patron-client relationship. Jesus points specifically to kings and benefactors who operate on the principle of wielding power over others. A king uses might to "lord it over" his clients, and the lesser benefactors, or patrons, gain status by sponsoring banquets for their clients. In exchange for this benefaction, clients heap praise on the patrons and pledge their loyalty to them. The patron-client relationship was part of the Roman domination system, which assured that power always resided with a select few and that the king was the ultimate benefactor. The kingdoms of this world operate on such principles.

Jesus declares, "But not so with you." Jesus reverses the principle by saying the greatest person at a table is not the host, but "the one who serves"—slaves rather than kings or benefactors. He redefines greatness. His followers are not to mimic followers of the Empire.

He calls on those who are part of God's new society to practice a different ethic. When they embrace and implement this alternative behavior, the watching world will perceive the vast contrast between the social and economic foundations of the Empire and the kingdom of God.

Jesus then offers himself as the prime example: "I am among you as one who serves." As the one who provides the Passover meal, Jesus is a benefactor, but not the kind found in the Roman world. According to John's Gospel, Jesus stops in the middle of the meal and shows what greatness looks like by performing the task of a slave. He washes the disciples' feet (probably including the feet of Judas Iscariot). Jesus insinuates that greatness is not defined by status but by actions. He teaches that in God's kingdom, those with the greatest authority are not those who lord it over others but those who serve others.

Jesus then concludes his Passover meal teaching with these words about the kingdom of God:

> You are those who have stood by me in my trials; and I confer on you, just as my Father has conferred on me, a kingdom, so that you may eat and drink at my table in my kingdom, and you will sit on thrones judging the twelve tribes of Israel (Luke 22:28-30 NRSV).

In essence, this is Jesus's last will and testament. He makes a bequest, which he identifies as "my kingdom."

What does he mean by this? He is not speaking of them merely entering the kingdom, but rather ruling over the kingdom, which likely refers to the ultimate kingdom at the end of the age. This is the same kingdom he receives from his heavenly Father. His use of "so that" provides a purpose statement or result of receiving the kingdom. He says, "I confer on you…a kingdom, so that you may eat and drink at my table in my kingdom, and you will sit on thrones judging the twelve tribes of Israel."

This purpose statement contains two points. First, the apostles will partake of this eschatological meal ("my table") in the future kingdom ("my kingdom"). Jesus sees himself as a central figure in the kingdom, where the Passover meal reaches its highest objective.

Second, the apostles "will sit on thrones judging the twelve tribes of Israel." For their loyalty to Christ in this age ("you are those who have stood by me in my trials"), these faithful ones will receive positions of leadership in the reconstituted kingdom of Israel in the age to come. This promise does not mean things will be easy between now and then. The apostles must guide the affairs of the "already" kingdom, which

Christ implements through his death on the cross. Their faithful work during the interim stage of the kingdom will be rewarded in the "not yet" kingdom to come.

It is interesting that Jesus chooses to explain the significance of his death at his last meal with his disciples. He possibly selects this time and venue so the ideas will be fresh in their minds following his death and resurrection.

Gethsemane: The Last Temptation

After dinner, Jesus and his disciples make a short trek to the garden of Gethsemane, where Jesus faces his last temptation. En route, Jesus must be thinking of his impending death because upon arrival he says privately to Peter, James, and John, "My soul is exceedingly sorrowful, even to death. Stay here and watch with Me" (Matthew 26:38). As he heads farther into the garden, he prays, and suddenly falling facedown to the ground he cries, "O My Father, if it is possible, let this cup pass from Me." Jesus realizes his death is necessary to establish God's kingdom, but he dreads having to face it. Despite the temptation to walk away unscathed, he resolves to fulfill his Spirit-anointed mission and adds, "Nevertheless, not as I will, but as You will."

Within minutes a posse led by Judas Iscariot arrives to arrest him. Addressing the chief priests and other arresting officers, Jesus reminds them that they were unable to take him into custody during the past week, and then he adds, "But this is your hour, and the power of darkness" (Luke 22:53). With this statement Jesus reveals two important truths. First, God is in control of everything. He permits this arrest. Second, the Jewish officials are under the sway of evil. Jesus's murder is orchestrated by Satan.

Jesus Before the Sanhedrin

According to Luke's version of the events, Jesus is brought before the Sanhedrin at morning light. The question before the court is whether Jesus claims to be the Messiah, so they ask, "If You are the Christ, tell us." Jesus responds, "If I tell you, you will by no means believe. And if I also ask you, you will by no means answer Me or let Me go. Hereafter the Son of Man will sit on the right hand of the power of God" (Luke 22:66-69).

In the garden, Jesus had spoken of the power of evil. Standing before the council, he mentions the power of God and claims he will be exalted to God's right hand.

The Sanhedrin shoots back, "Are You then the Son of God [the Messiah]?" Jesus answers, "You rightly say that I am." Matthew and Mark each add that the high priest tears his clothes and charges Jesus with blasphemy (Matthew 26:65; Mark 14:63-64).

Jesus seals his fate. The court concludes, "What further testimony do we need? For we have heard it ourselves from His own mouth" (Luke 22:71). Jesus is condemned to die (Matthew 26:66; Mark 14:64).

Jesus Before Pilate

The Jewish authorities deliver Jesus to Roman governor Pontius Pilate, charging, "We found this fellow perverting the nation...saying that He Himself is Christ, a King" (Luke 23:2). In John's Gospel the accusation against Jesus reads, "He made Himself the Son of God" (John 19:7). The allegation has profound political ramifications for both Jews and Romans. For the Jews, "Son of God" is a messianic designation. The fact that they charge Jesus with claiming the title for himself shows they personally do not believe him to be the Messiah. For the Romans, to take for oneself the designation "Son of God" is a challenge to Caesar's exclusive claim to that title. Therefore, from both a Jewish and a Roman standpoint, Jesus is deemed worthy of death.

To make sure the charges are true, Pilate directly questions Jesus and asks, "Are You a king then?" Jesus replies, "You say rightly that I am a king. For this cause I was born, and for this cause I have come into the world, that I should bear witness to the truth. Everyone who is of the truth hears My voice" (John 18:37).

From this exchange, Jesus affirms he is God's chosen King and was born to this end. We also learn that truth seekers will accept his claim, which implies others will not.

Following the preliminary hearing, Jesus is scourged and handed over to the soldiers, who "twisted a crown of thorns and put it on His head" and place a purple robe over his shoulders as they mockingly declare, "Hail, King of the Jews!" (John 19:1-3; also see Matthew 27:27-31).

At the urging of his wife, and believing this messianic pretender has suffered enough, Pilate seeks to release Jesus, but the Jewish leaders play their trump card. "If you let this Man go, you are not Caesar's friend. Whoever makes himself a king speaks against Caesar" (John 19:12). Pilate finds himself between a rock and a hard place. If they can make the charge stick, according to Roman law, Pilate has no choice but to execute Jesus as a political enemy of the state. Rather than call their bluff, Pilate brings Jesus before the judgment seat in full public view and announces to the Jews, "Behold your King!" He then asks, "Shall I crucify your King?" Speaking for the mob, the chief priests answer, "We have no king but Caesar!" So Jesus is led away to execution hill.

By applying Rome's ultimate weapon of domination—crucifixion—Pilate likely hopes to drive the fear of Rome into any person or group that might be plotting an armed uprising during Passover week. At the same time, he can satisfy the demands of the Jewish religious establishment.

The Crucifixion

The Gospel writers say very little about the horrors of crucifixion, possibly because their first-century readers need no explanation. Crucifixion is one of the most agonizing forms of capital punishment ever devised by humankind.

The King on the Cross

I believe the Gospel writers want us to comprehend three things from their accounts of Jesus's death. First, the Empire and its Jewish retainers are putting to death God's chosen King. The Gospel of John, more than the others, makes sure we can't miss this point.

> Now Pilate wrote a title and put it on the cross. And the writing was:
>
> JESUS OF NAZARETH, THE KING OF THE JEWS.
>
> Then many of the Jews read this title, for the place where Jesus was crucified was near the city; and it was written in Hebrew, Greek, and Latin.

Therefore the chief priests of the Jews said to Pilate, "Do not write, 'The King of the Jews,' but, 'He said, "I am the King of the Jews.""'"

Pilate answered, "What I have written, I have written" (John 19:19-22).

According to Luke, Jewish rulers, Roman soldiers, and a condemned criminal each goad Jesus:

- "He saved others; let Him save Himself if He is the Christ, the chosen of God" (Luke 23:35).

- "If You are the King of the Jews, save Yourself" (verse 37).

- "If You are the Christ, save Yourself and us" (verse 39).

In Mark's version, the Jewish rulers taunt, "Let the Christ, the King of Israel, descend now from the cross, that we may see and believe" (Mark 15:32). But Mark also tells of a Roman centurion who witnesses Jesus's death and then proclaims, "Truly this Man was the Son of God!" (verse 39). This public avowal might be viewed as treasonous, considering the centurion's allegiance to Caesar as the only son of god—the divinely appointed leader of the world.

All four Gospel writers agree that the Empire and its collaborators are executing the rightful King of Israel.

The Necessity of the Crucifixion

The second thing the Gospel writers want us to understand from their accounts of the Messiah's death is that God's kingdom plan depends on it. Each Gospel says in effect that Jesus's death is a fulfillment of Old Testament prophecy.

- "They crucified Him, and divided His garments" (Matthew 27:35; see Psalm 22:18).

- "My God, My God, why have You forsaken Me?" (Matthew 27:46; see Psalm 22:1).

- "He was numbered with the transgressors" (Mark 15:28; see Isaiah 53:12).

- "Father, 'into Your hands I commit My spirit'" (Luke 23:46; see Psalm 31:5).

- "Not one of His bones shall be broken" (John 19:36; see Psalm 34:20).

- "They shall look on Him whom they pierced" (John 19:37; see Zechariah 12:10).

Apart from the cross, the kingdom is not possible. This has been God's plan all along, as he revealed to the Old Testament prophets. For example, when interpreted in light of Christ and the end times, Psalm 22 lays out God's kingdom plans. It opens with the Messiah's cry of being forsaken (verse 1), moves to his suffering (verses 6-21), and reaches an apex with this doxology:

> All the ends of the world
> Shall remember and turn to the LORD,
> And all the families of the nations
> Shall worship before You.
> For the kingdom is the LORD's,
> And He rules over the nations (verses 27-28).

The vast majority of first-century Jews miss one of the important aspects of the Messiah's mission—that he must suffer before bringing in the kingdom. The Messiah is not a triumphal warrior who destroys his enemies with a sword. Quite the opposite. He is a suffering servant who defeats the enemy by succumbing to death.

New Testament scholar N.T. Wright shows convincingly that Isaiah 52–55 lays out the sequence of events necessary to usher in God's kingdom.[2] Here are the five steps in the progression and a sampling of verses.

1. God announces that the kingdom is at hand (Isaiah 52:1-12).

> How beautiful upon the mountains
> Are the feet of him who brings good news,
> Who proclaims peace,
> Who brings glad tidings of good things,
> Who proclaims salvation,
> Who says to Zion,
> "Your God reigns!" (Isaiah 52:7).

2. The Messiah suffers and establishes God's covenant of peace (Isaiah 52:13–53:12).

> He was wounded for our transgressions,
> He was bruised for our iniquities;
> The chastisement for our peace was upon Him,
> And by His stripes we are healed.
> All we like sheep have gone astray;
> We have turned, every one, to his own way;
> And the LORD has laid on Him the iniquity of us all (Isaiah 53:5-6).

Likely the early church believes this prophecy to Israel is fulfilled in Jesus, its representative. He is the one who suffers and whom God glorifies. In fact, Jesus speaks about this to the doubting disciples on the road to Emmaus: "O foolish ones, and slow of heart to believe in all that the prophets have spoken! Ought not the Christ to have suffered these things and to enter into His glory?" (Luke 24:25-26).

3. God declares his love and invites the thirsty to drink of the Spirit (Isaiah 54:1–55:4).

> Your Maker is your husband,
> The LORD of hosts is His name;
> And your Redeemer is the Holy One of Israel;
> He is called the God of the whole earth (54:5).
>
> My kindness shall not depart from you,
> Nor shall My covenant of peace be removed (54:10).
>
> Ho! Everyone who thirsts,
> Come to the waters;
> And you who have no money,
> Come, buy and eat.
> Yes, come, buy wine and milk
> Without money and without price (55:1).

4. Gentiles rush into the kingdom (Isaiah 55:5-11).

> Surely you shall call a nation you do not know,
> And nations who do not know you shall run to you,

> Because of the LORD your God,
> And the Holy One of Israel;
> For He has glorified you (verse 5).

5. Creation is transformed (Isaiah 55:12-13).

> For you shall go out with joy,
> And be led out with peace;
> The mountains and the hills
> Shall break forth into singing before you,
> And all the trees of the field shall clap their hands.
> Instead of the thorn shall come up the cypress tree,
> And instead of the brier shall come up the myrtle tree;
> And it shall be to the LORD for a name,
> For an everlasting sign that shall not be cut off.

The sequence found in Isaiah 52–55 is the path Jesus must follow to bring in the kingdom of God. He announces that the kingdom is at hand, he suffers and establishes God's covenant of peace, he invites the thirsty to drink of the Spirit, Gentiles rush into the kingdom, and finally, creation will be transformed.

Most Christians think of the cross as a means of personal salvation, but the crucifixion has a bigger purpose. It is the means of initiating God's kingdom, and we are invited to become part of it.

Jesus Predicts His Death

Matthew 16:21-28	Luke 9:22-27
Matthew 20:17-19	Luke 18:31-34
Matthew 26:1-2	John 2:18-22
Mark 8:31-33	John 10:11
Mark 10:32-42	John 12:32-33

Jesus is a preacher of the kingdom. Yet on several occasions he speaks of his impending death as a necessity. In doing so he establishes a relationship between the two. Without his death there can be no kingdom.

Faith Trumps Force

The third thing the Gospel writers want us to comprehend from their accounts of the Messiah's death is that through faith, he conquers the powers of the world. As he faces the cross, rather than begging for his life or calling on his supporters to take up arms and fight for his release, Jesus places his faith in his heavenly Father alone. In doing so, he shows us the difference between Satan's kingdom and God's kingdom. One operates by force and the other by faith in God.

The cross exposes Rome as an evil bully who uses death as a weapon of fear and terror to dominate its subjects. The apostle Paul assures his readers, "Having disarmed principalities and powers, [Jesus] made a public spectacle of them, triumphing over them in [the cross]" (Colossians 2:15). In death, Jesus discloses Rome's moral bankruptcy and the eventual collapse of all governments and kingdoms that follow the demonic principles of domination and coercion.

On the cross Jesus secures a victory over the kingdoms of the world without lifting a finger, and he takes his rightful place as earth's King. Even before his resurrection, Christ wins his battle over the enemy, as foretold in Genesis 3:15.

From a literary perspective, we might view the crucifixion in terms of a Greek tragedy. The Roman and Jewish officials believe that by terminating Jesus, they can stop his influence and movement. However, their aggressive move becomes the very means to their own downfall.

But hindsight is 20–20. On the day of Jesus's death, the authorities believe *they* are the victors, and the disciples believe the messianic movement is over. As far as they are concerned, Jesus ends his life a dismal and disappointing failure and not as a superhero. What now?

12

The Present Reign of the Exalted Christ

For He [Christ] must reign till He [the Father]
has put all enemies under His feet.

1 CORINTHIANS 15:25

With their leader dead and their messianic hopes dashed, the apostles seek to avoid a similar fate by taking refuge in an upstairs room of a local friend. Other disciples head back to their hometowns after the Passover feast ends.

But on Sunday morning, things begin to change when reports trickle back that the tomb is empty and that God has brought Jesus back to life. When the rumors are confirmed as reality, the disciples are both elated and frightened. On several occasions Jesus suddenly appears to the disciples. They don't know if they are seeing a ghost or experiencing some form of mass hysteria.

Jesus looks different. His earthly body is transformed into a glorified body, not limited to time and space. He can walk through doors, travel distances in the blink of an eye, and appear and disappear in an instant. Yet he has the same body, complete with the marks of crucifixion. Jesus can speak, eat, drink, touch, and be touched. He is not a specter or figment of their imaginations. He stands before them as the once crucified but now living Lord, who is incapable of dying again.

I don't know about you, but to my way of thinking, nothing in human history compares to the resurrection of Jesus. A number of years ago I received a phone call that my father had died. I packed my bags and hopped the first plane going from Dallas to Baltimore. As I flew at 33,000 feet, memories of my dad flooded my mind. I thought of my father always working two jobs to meet our family's needs, of his faithfulness to my mother, and of the way he coached me and taught me to throw and hit a baseball. He was my hero. When I realized I would never again speak to my dad or give him another hug, a torrent of emotion rushed forth, and I cried like a baby. I was glad no one was sitting nearby.

After the funeral, I stayed at my mom's for a few days to help her get things in order. How do you suppose I would have reacted if one morning I walked nonchalantly out the door, looked up, and there before my eyes stood my dad?

"Hi, Al. Where ya going?"

Doing a double take, I reply, "Dad! Is that you?"

"Of course it's me. I haven't seen you for a while. When did you get into town?"

"Last week," I answer hesitantly.

"I brought along your baseball glove. I thought we might have a game of catch. What do ya say?"

For the next 20 minutes we play catch! Then he says, "Let's go get a bite to eat. I'm hungry."

How would my dad's coming back to life change things for my family? Would we still be grieving or keeping our appointment the next day to pick out a headstone? I don't think so. In fact we would advertise, "For sale: one slightly used cemetery plot. Make offer."

When Jesus appears to the disciples, everything changes. Rome and the Jewish leaders no longer have the final word. Jesus does. His resurrection is proof that faith in God is more powerful than the forces of evil. Despite their efforts to destroy him, Jesus emerges from the grave. In this battle of the ages, Christ, not Satan, is the winner. The early church declared emphatically, *Christus victor!*

> Low in the grave he lay, Jesus my Savior,
> Waiting the coming day, Jesus my Lord!

Up from the grave he arose,
With a mighty triumph o'er his foes;
He arose a victor from the dark domain,
And he lives forever, with his saints to reign.
He arose! He arose! Hallelujah! Christ arose!

The crucified Jesus is now the living Lord. After his resurrection, Jesus announces, "All authority has been given to Me in heaven and on earth" (Matthew 28:18). This declaration is pregnant with meaning. Notice several things. First, the authority Jesus receives is given, which means it is delegated. Second, his authority is total—*all* authority. He shares his authority with no other person. Third, his authority is not limited to heavenly or spiritual matters, but extends to earth, including political affairs and tangible matters. This means Christ has authority over all government and world leaders—good and bad—whether they realize it or not. Fourth, Christ has regained control of the territory that Satan, the usurper, seized from Adam and Eve. Fifth, Christ has begun to reign already over God's kingdom. This is the present dimension of the kingdom of God.

In the Gospel of Luke, the risen Jesus appears to the disciples on three occasions and explains that his death and resurrection as God's Messiah are necessary components of God's kingdom plan (Luke 24:13-46). On the road to Emmaus, his spiritually blinded and dejected disciples declare, "We were hoping that it was He who was going to redeem Israel" (Luke 24:21). This prompted a response from Jesus.

> "O foolish ones, and slow of heart to believe in all that the prophets have spoken! Ought not the Christ to have suffered these things and to enter into His glory?" And beginning at Moses and all the Prophets, He expounded to them in all the Scriptures the things concerning Himself (Luke 24:25-27).

When he later appears to the 11 remaining apostles, he teaches the same lesson.

> "These are the words which I spoke to you while I was still with you, that all things must be fulfilled which were written in the Law of Moses and the Prophets and the Psalms

concerning Me." And He opened their understanding, that
they might comprehend the Scriptures (Luke 24:44-45).

Without his death and resurrection there can be no redemption for
Israel. They are a part of the "all things" (including Psalms 16:10; 110:1-
2) that must be fulfilled.

Jesus Predicts His Resurrection

On several occasions during his earthly ministry, Jesus
predicts his resurrection.

Matthew 12:39	Matthew 27:63
Matthew 16:21	Mark 9:9
Matthew 17:9,23	Mark 9:31
Matthew 20:19	Mark 14:58
Matthew 26:32	Luke 9:22

Salvation is much bigger than any individual. It is about God
reclaiming his world and restoring his kingdom on earth. The good
news is, we can be part of it. Christians sometimes say, "If you were
the only person on earth, Christ would have died for you," and statements like this might solicit a round of amens. But it does an injustice
to God's larger and greater plan of redemption of the cosmos. "The
Son of Man has come to seek and to save that which was lost" (Luke
19:10)—that is, what was lost when Adam listened to the voice of Satan
rather than the voice of God. Through his cross and resurrection, Jesus
defeats the devil, liberates the earth, and begins to restore the kingdom.

In John's Gospel the resurrection and the kingdom of God are
linked when the glorified Jesus appears to his disciples, who are hud-
dled behind locked doors, fearing they too might be arrested and crucified (John 20:19). After calming them with words of peace and
showing them his wounds, Jesus charges, "As the Father has sent Me, I
also send you." This is John's version of the Great Commission.

Next John recounts, "He breathed on them, and said to them, 'Receive the Holy Spirit.'" The juxtaposition of breathing and the Spirit brings to mind Genesis 2:7 and Ezekiel 37:1-14. The former text deals with Adam, created from the dust of the earth, who remains inert until God breathes life into him. Once alive, he is empowered and given authority to carry out his God-given mission of ruling over God's earthly kingdom.

The latter text contains Ezekiel's famous vision of the valley of dry bones. The lifeless bones represent Israel, living in a state of exile under foreign domination. God instructs Ezekiel in his vision to breathe on the dead bones. Ezekiel complies, and the bones come to life and stand "upon their feet, an exceedingly great army" (Ezekiel 37:10).

Ezekiel 37:11-28 interprets the vision. This corporate resurrection encompasses "the whole house of Israel." God then speaks directly to his people: "I will put My Spirit in you, and you shall live, and I will place you in your own land. Then you shall know that I, the LORD, have spoken it and performed it." He adds that the nation will no longer be divided (north and south), but be reunited as a single kingdom. Yahweh promises them a new king and shepherd, whose rule will last forever. "Moreover," he adds, "I will make a covenant of peace with them," after which the nations will come to know the Lord.

When Jesus breathes on the apostles, he is acting out the prophecy of Ezekiel 37. As he breathes on them, the resurrection of Israel begins. The Old Testament Scriptures are being fulfilled in their sight. Alluding to Ezekiel 37:26, Jesus declares, "Peace to you!" He then commissions them, "As the Father has sent Me, I also send you" (John 20:21). The apostles and their Jewish converts will constitute the "great army" (Ezekiel 37:10) who represent the kingdom and make God known to the nations. After the commission he tells them, "If you forgive the sins of any, they are forgiven them; if you retain the sins of any, they are retained." The apostles now hold the keys of the kingdom.

The restoration of Israel has begun, but it is not yet completed. It starts with Jews and expands to include the Gentiles. In time, God will fulfill his covenants to Abraham and David.

The Nature of Christ's Present Reign

The nature of Christ's present reign is a far cry from what the first-century Jews expect. Instead of a Messiah riding into town on a charger, slaying his enemies and ushering in a golden age of prosperity for Israel, they get a suffering servant who dies a helpless victim. But those who have been given insight into the mysteries of the kingdom of heaven (Matthew 13:11) understand that his death and resurrection are precisely what qualify Jesus to be God's Messiah-King. In order to reign, Jesus must first be crucified and raised from the grave.

Peter's Sermon on the Day of Pentecost

Through the death and resurrection of his Son, God fulfills a pledge he made to King David. As the psalmist writes, "The LORD has sworn in truth to David; He will not turn from it: 'I will set upon your throne the fruit of your body'" (Psalm 132:11).

On the Day of Pentecost, the apostle Peter preaches that God's promise to David is the basis for Jesus's resurrection and his enthronement.

> Men and brethren, let me speak freely to you of the patriarch David, that he is both dead and buried, and his tomb is with us to this day. Therefore, being a prophet, and knowing that God had sworn with an oath to him that of the fruit of his body, according to the flesh, *He would raise up the Christ to sit on his throne* (Acts 2:29-30).

Notice the italicized phrase. God's oath to install a son of David on the throne finds its fulfillment in the resurrection of Christ. Peter goes on.

> He, foreseeing this, *spoke concerning the resurrection of the Christ*, that His soul was not left in Hades, nor did His flesh see corruption. *This Jesus God has raised up*, of which we are all witnesses. Therefore *being exalted to the right hand of God*, and having received from the Father the promise of the Holy Spirit, He poured out this which you now see and hear (verses 31-33).

Again, through the resurrection, the crucified Jesus takes his place of authority at God's right hand and reigns from this exalted position. All the extraordinary manifestations the people witness—the tongues of fire, the prophecies, abounding joy—come from the exalted Messiah. He is alive and in control of earthly affairs.

> For David did not ascend into the heavens, but he says himself:
>
> > "The LORD said to my Lord,
> > 'Sit at My right hand,
> > Till I make Your enemies Your footstool.'"
>
> Therefore let all the house of Israel know assuredly that God has made this Jesus, whom you crucified, both Lord and Christ (verses 34-36).

Peter here quotes from Psalm 110:1 and points out that King David is not referring to himself, but is prophesying of Jesus, whom Jewish authorities turned over to Pilate for execution. Despite charges to the contrary, God raises Jesus from the dead and thus vindicates him and declares him to be both Lord and Messiah-King. Taking his place at God's right hand, he is Israel's legitimate king and the world's rightful Lord. The church must get this message out, calling on all people to recognize this and submit to God's reign in Christ.

Psalm 110 in the New Testament

New Testament writers quote or allude to Psalm 110 more than any other psalm.

Matthew 22:44; 26:64	1 Corinthians 15:25
Mark 12:36; 14:62; 16:19	Ephesians 1:20,22
Luke 20:42-43; 22:69	Colossians 3:1
Acts 2:33-35; 5:31;	Hebrews 1:3,13; 8:1;
7:55-56	10:12-13; 12:2
Romans 8:34	1 Peter 3:22

> In each instance, the New Testament writer believes
> that this psalm supports the claim that Jesus, God's end-
> time Messiah, presently reigns over earth from his throne
> in heaven. This is the "already" dimension of the kingdom
> of God.

In Peter's quote, notice how long Jesus rules from his position at
God's right hand: "Till I [God] make Your enemies Your footstool."
His present reign continues until all earthly rebellion is put down. God
is the one who brings people to their knees, so he determines the dura-
tion of Christ's present rule from heaven. With his second coming,
Christ will descend to begin his rule *from earth*. The kingdom of God
will become a universal earthly reality.

Just prior to his ascension into heaven, the apostles ask when this
will occur, and Jesus responds, "It is not for you to know times or sea-
sons which the Father has put in His own authority" (Acts 1:7). The
timing is God's prerogative.

Paul's Teaching in Philippians

> He humbled Himself and became obedient to the point of
> death, even the death of the cross. *Therefore God also has
> highly exalted Him* and given Him the name which is above
> every name, that at the name of Jesus every knee should
> bow, of those in heaven, and of those on earth, and of those
> under the earth, and that every tongue should confess that
> Jesus Christ is Lord, to the glory of God the Father (Phi-
> lippians 2:8-11).

Does this sound familiar? The crucified Jesus is the exalted Lord. Do
you recognize the political nature of the message? First, he is crucified
on a Roman cross, which shows he is considered an enemy of the state.
Second, he dies willingly to fulfill God's kingdom plan. Third, God
exalts him to a place of prominence and gives him a name above all
others, which means he possesses ultimate authority. Fourth, the purpose of it all is that every knee will bend to Christ and that every tongue

will publicly declare that Jesus Christ (the Messiah) is Lord and that the Roman emperor is not! Fifth, all results in praise for God the Father.

The gospel of the kingdom that the early church preaches throughout the Jewish and Gentile sectors of the Roman Empire is that the person whom the Jews reject as a fake Messiah and the Roman officials dismiss as a troublemaking rabble-rouser is the one chosen by God to rule his universe. The apostles and evangelists travel at great risk to call on all, including elites and governmental leaders, to submit to King Jesus. They often quote from Psalm 2, which calls on the kings of the earth to "kiss the Son, lest He be angry" (Psalm 2:12).

Paul's Teaching in 1 Corinthians

The apostle Paul writes to the Corinthians in this same vein. After asserting the necessity for the Messiah's death and resurrection (1 Corinthians 15:1-8), Paul explains that Messiah is the first among many who will be brought back to life (verse 20). He then proceeds to give a chronology of end-time events as they will unfold, starting with Christ's resurrection.

> But each one in his own order: Christ the firstfruits, afterward those who are Christ's at His coming. Then comes the end, when He delivers the kingdom to God the Father, when He [the Father] puts an end to all rule and all authority and power. For He [Christ] must reign till He [the Father] has put all enemies under His feet. The last enemy that will be destroyed is death (verses 23-26).

From this passage we discover Paul's thinking about the sequential progression of future events.

1. Christ returns to earth and believers are raised from the dead.

2. The present evil age comes to an end.

3. Jesus turns the present ("already") kingdom over to the Father after God puts "an end to all rule and all authority and power"—that is, those who have opposed Christ.

4. The final enemy, death, is eradicated and thus loses its grip on us.

Here we have a description of how Christ's present heavenly rule over earth will come to an end. His descent from heaven begins his future earthly rule. Believers from all ages will join him in the ultimate kingdom.

Paul then offers a further clarification.

> For "He [the Father] has put all things under His [Christ's] feet." But when He says "all things are put under Him," it is evident that He [the Father] who put all things under Him is excepted. Now when all things are made subject to Him [the Father], then the Son Himself will also be subject to Him who put all things under Him, that God may be all in all (verses 27-28).

Jesus turns over the kingdom to his Father, and God is the supreme ruler. Jesus remains subservient to his Father. After all, he is the Son and not the Father.

Paul's Teaching in Ephesians

Paul begins his letter to the Ephesians speaking about God's eternal plan for the redemption of the world, which is accomplished in Christ, revealed by the gospel, and applied to the individual through faith by the Holy Spirit (Ephesians 1:1-14). Paul asks God to open their eyes of understanding and give them wisdom to know about the present blessings and future inheritance God has for them (verses 15-19).

> [His inheritance is] according to the working of His mighty power which He worked in Christ when He raised Him from the dead and *seated Him at His right hand in the heavenly places*, far above all principality and power and might and dominion, and every name that is named, not only in this age but also in that which is to come.

> And He put all things under His feet, and gave Him to be head over all things to the church, which is His body, the fullness of Him who fills all in all (verses 19-23).

That Paul calls on God to open the original readers' eyes shows that even in the early church many believers need encouragement and help to grasp the present aspect of the kingdom with all its blessings.

Peter Preaches After Healing the Lame Man

Peter's miraculous healing of the crippled beggar at the temple gate draws a crowd. After calling on the man to rise and walk in the name of Jesus, Peter preaches to the assembled throng.

> Men of Israel, why do you marvel at this? Or why look so intently at us, as though by our own power or godliness we had made this man walk? The God of Abraham, Isaac, and Jacob, the God of our fathers, glorified His Servant Jesus, whom you delivered up and denied in the presence of Pilate, when he was determined to let Him go. But you denied the Holy One and the Just, and asked for a murderer to be granted to you, and killed the *Prince of life, whom God raised from the dead*, of which we are witnesses. *And His name, through faith in His name, has made this man strong*, whom you see and know. Yes, the faith which comes through Him has given him this perfect soundness in the presence of you all (Acts 3:12-16).

What could be more shocking and controversial than Peter's claims? The man they nailed to a Roman stake is now alive and has healed this disabled man! What kind of authority must he possess—to overcome death and heal at long distance through his earthly followers?

> Yet now, brethren, I know that you did it in ignorance, as did also your rulers. But those things which God foretold by the mouth of all His prophets, that the Christ [Messiah] would suffer, *He has thus fulfilled*. Repent therefore and be converted, that your sins may be blotted out, so that times of refreshing may come from the presence of the Lord, and that He may send Jesus Christ, who was preached to you before, *whom heaven must receive until the times of restoration of all things*, which God has spoken by the mouth of all His holy prophets since the world began (verses 17-21).

In this second part of the sermon, Peter explains that the Messiah's death is a fulfillment of prophecy. For most Jews, this avowal is a stumbling block—a suffering Messiah doesn't fit into their preconceived picture of him. Peter also exhorts them to repent, to bring their lives in line with God's kingdom requirements for people of the new covenant. The purpose of this turnaround is threefold: that they might find forgiveness, that "times of refreshing may come from the presence of the Lord" (this refers to the present sending of the Spirit into their lives), and that God may send Jesus Christ, "whom heaven must receive until the times of restoration of all things." The latter phrase speaks of Christ's present reign in heaven, which lasts until he is sent from heaven to restore creation. Peter ends his sermon by saying this has been God's revealed plan since the world began. There was never a time when God did not intend to restore all things to their pristine beauty.

(Peter preaches this kingdom sermon without forethought or preparation. Does this sound like the typical gospel sermon being preached today? Something is dreadfully wrong.)

When the gospel of the kingdom is preached, people are either converted or outraged. There is rarely a middle ground. This occasion is no exception.

> Now as they spoke to the people, the priests, the captain of the temple, and the Sadducees came upon them, being greatly disturbed that they taught the people and preached in Jesus the resurrection from the dead. And they laid hands on them, and put them in custody until the next day, for it was already evening. However, many of those who heard the word believed; and the number of the men came to be about five thousand (Acts 4:1-4).

Would you be willing to preach the pure gospel and face jail time if you could see 2000 more people pledge their allegiance to King Jesus? (Peter's Pentecost sermon resulted in 3000 conversions, so the total has grown to 5000.) When brought before the court, Peter uses the opportunity to preach again.

> Then Peter, filled with the Holy Spirit, said to them, "Rulers of the people and elders of Israel: If we this day are judged for a good deed done to a helpless man, by what means he has been made well, let it be known to you all, and to all the people of Israel, that by the name of Jesus Christ of Nazareth, whom you crucified, whom God raised from the dead, by Him this man stands here before you whole" (Acts 4:8-10).

Peter contends that the crucified and resurrected Jesus is responsible for healing the lame man. Jesus, who sits at God's right hand, has all authority over earth—even over our bodies!

As believers we can come to King Jesus for our own healing and take Christ's healing touch to others. We each must ask, "Who possesses authority over my body?" The answer is determined by our actions. If we depend on the government to meet all our medical needs, then we believe the government controls our bodies. As members of God's kingdom, we should entrust all areas of our lives to King Jesus Christ.

I doubt any of the judges before whom Peter and John are standing ever receive a bodily healing from King Jesus. Why not? Most likely because they do not believe that he is alive or that he possesses authority over the earth in its entirety or over them individually.

After being released from jail, Peter and John report back to the church "all that the chief priests and elders had said to them." The congregation then breaks into praise and sings Psalm 2.

> Why do the nations rage,
> And the people plot a vain thing?
> The kings of the earth set themselves,
> And the rulers take counsel together,
> Against the LORD and against His Anointed (Acts 4:24-26).

Notice the kingdom content of this psalm and how the church interprets Peter's and John's jail time as a political act of persecution against King Jesus himself!

The Apostles Preach at the Temple

Using Solomon's Porch as their base for daily ministry, the apostles preach and heal the masses (Acts 5:12). As word spreads of the many being healed, who in turn pledge their loyalty to King Jesus, a surge of people from surrounding cities flock to the temple grounds to hear the gospel and experience the laying on of hands for themselves (verse 16). As usual, these activities draw the ire of the Jewish political leaders, and they arrest the apostles. After a miraculous release and subsequent confrontation with local authorities, who demand that they stop preaching in the name of Jesus, Peter proclaims, "We ought to obey God rather than men" (verse 29). Then he launches into a full-scale sermon about the kingdom and the present reign of Christ.

> The God of our fathers raised up Jesus whom you murdered by hanging on a tree. Him *God has exalted to His right hand* to be Prince [Greek *archēgon*, "chief ruler"] and Savior, to give repentance to Israel and forgiveness of sins. And we are His witnesses to these things, and so also is the Holy Spirit whom God has given to those who obey Him (verses 30-32).

Notice some salient kingdom features. First, Peter interprets Jesus's death to be a murder at the hands of Jewish leaders. It was like a lynching. Second, the God of the Jews brings Jesus back to life. This means God reverses the results of their heinous crime. Third, God exalts Jesus to the most privileged position and installs him as Israel's legitimate leader and deliverer in order to grant Israel repentance and forgiveness for its evil acts. Finally, Peter declares that these truths have both human and divine attestation.

The apostles are released and warned not to preach again. But do they obey? "Daily in the temple, and in every house, they did not cease teaching and preaching Jesus as the Christ" (verse 42).

Stephen Preaches to the Sanhedrin

The preaching of the kingdom in Jerusalem bears fruit: "The word of God spread, and the number of the disciples multiplied greatly in

Jerusalem, and a great many of the priests were obedient to the faith" (Acts 6:7). Stephen, a church deacon and "a man full of faith and the Holy Spirit" (verse 5) is one of those responsible for such results. He ministers regularly in the local synagogues, where he performs "great wonders and signs among the people" (verse 8). While he ministers at the Synagogue of the Freedmen, angry opponents "seized him, and brought him to the council," where false witnesses accuse him of blasphemy (verses 9-15). When Stephen is given the opportunity to answer the charges, he gives an overview of God's kingdom plan throughout history (Acts 7:1-53). As he works his way up to the first century, the hearers become hostile because they are "cut to the heart" by his word and they grind their teeth and growl at him.

> But he, being full of the Holy Spirit, gazed into heaven and saw the glory of God, and Jesus standing at the right hand of God, and said, "Look! I see the heavens opened and the Son of Man standing *at the right hand of God!*" (verses 55-56).

The history of God's kingdom strategy gradually crescendos, and then Stephen announces that Jesus is the man at God's right hand. Unwilling to submit to Jesus as their lawful King, those in the courtroom respond by crying out with a loud voice, and placing their hands over their ears, they rush toward Stephen like a vicious mob, driving him out of the city, where they stone him. Stephen prays, "Lord Jesus, receive my spirit." Next, he kneels down, and following the example of Jesus, he cries out, "Lord, do not charge them with this sin," and then dies.

Stephen's adherence and faithfulness to the kingdom and its King provides him with confidence as he stares death in the face. His master had placed his unreserved trust in God in similar circumstances, so Stephen follows suit. What a stark contrast between kingdom-focused Stephen and his opponents, the protectors of tradition. The one faces death calmly as the others seek to commit a murder.

In this passage we see two reactions when the pure gospel is preached. In the first instance, multitudes are saved and healed (Acts

6:7). But in the second, the crowd turns violent. This seems to be a pattern whenever people proclaim that the exalted Jesus is Lord over all. Little room is left for middle ground because the gospel of the kingdom calls for an all-or-nothing commitment. Those unwilling to surrender to the enthroned Christ become furious because they want to embrace the name Christian without relinquishing control of their lives to King Jesus.

Paul Preaches at Antioch of Pisidia

Early in their first missionary journey, Paul and Barnabas travel to Antioch of Pisidia, where they are invited to teach at the local synagogue. Paul takes the opportunity to preach the exalted Lord Jesus Christ. How Paul reaches this stage in his spiritual life is interesting.

As a rabbinical student of the famous Gamaliel, he is well trained in the Hebrew Scriptures and is a rising star among the Pharisees. He feels duty bound to protect Judaism from messianic Jews, whom he considers to be heretics. Paul is part of the original angry mob that stones Stephen and is likely the one to authorize the penalty (Acts 7:58–8:1). After Stephen's martyrdom, the church at Jerusalem faces great persecution. Many believers are hauled before the Jewish courts and imprisoned, and others seek refuge in other parts of Palestine (Acts 8:1). The church's main persecutor is none other than Paul, who in the Jewish community goes by his Hebrew name, Saul. "He made havoc of the church, entering every house, and dragging off men and women, committing them to prison" (verse 3).

On his way to Damascus to arrest Christians, the exalted Jesus appears in a bright light and speaks to Saul. When Saul realizes that Jesus, whom he assumed to be a dead false Messiah, is alive and that the heresy he has spent so much time and energy fighting against is actually true, he is radically converted! "Immediately he preached the Christ in the synagogues, that He is the Son of God" (Acts 9:20). The titles Christ and Son of God, as we have seen, refer to Jesus being God's authorized Messiah-King.

When Saul is converted to Jesus the Messiah, his former colleagues cast him as an enemy of the Pharisee branch of Judaism.

> Now after many days were past, the Jews plotted to kill him.
> But their plot became known to Saul. And they watched
> the gates day and night, to kill him. Then the disciples took
> him by night and let him down through the wall in a large
> basket (verses 23-25).

The former hunter becomes the hunted! Few conversion stories are more dramatic than this one, although the conversions of notable miscreants Saint Augustine, John Newton, and Chuck Colson give it a run for its money.

As we pick up with our story, Paul and Barnabas are on their first missionary journey, and they stop at Antioch of Pisidia, where they attend Sabbath services at a local synagogue. After the reading of the Scriptures, the elders ask if anyone has an exhortation for the people (Acts 13:14-15). Seeing an opening, Paul stands up and launches into one of the longest sermons in the book of Acts. Like Stephen before him, Paul presents a sweeping narrative of God's plan to raise "for Israel a Savior—Jesus" from the seed of David (Acts 13:22-23). He proceeds to explain that the Jewish rulers in Jerusalem turned Jesus over to Pilate "that He should be put to death" (verse 28). Paul explains this is all a fulfillment of the Old Testament Scriptures (verse 29).

> But God raised Him from the dead. He was seen for many
> days by those who came up with Him from Galilee to Jeru-
> salem, who are His witnesses to the people. And we declare
> to you glad tidings—that promise which was made to the
> fathers. God has fulfilled this for us their children, in that
> He has raised up Jesus. As it is also written in the second
> Psalm:
>
> "You are My Son,
> Today I have begotten You" (verses 30-33).

Like Peter and other gospel preachers before him, Paul quotes Psalm 2, a royal psalm, to tie Christ's resurrection to his status as exalted King. Let's not forget that at his resurrection, Jesus receives from the Father all authority in heaven and on earth. Thus, God's promise to send Israel a Messiah has been fulfilled. Israel, however, is caught off guard because

God's plans do not evolve as they anticipate. And rather than accept God's design for bringing in the kingdom, many tenaciously hold to their own preconceived views. For them, as for many today, tradition triumphs over the truth.

Following in Peter's sermonic footsteps, Paul quotes Psalm 16:10 to support his claim for the resurrection: "You will not allow Your Holy One to see corruption." He then explains that King David must be speaking of Christ because David himself is dead, and his lifeless body is decaying in a Jerusalem tomb.

> But He whom God raised up saw no corruption. Therefore let it be known to you, brethren, that through this Man is preached to you the forgiveness of sins; and by Him everyone who believes is justified from all things from which you could not be justified by the law of Moses (Acts 13:37-39).

The living King Jesus offers forgiveness under the new covenant, which sets the stage for the kingdom of God.

Paul concludes his sermon with a stern warning that is designed to sober those in the audience who might reject his message.

> Beware therefore, lest what has been spoken in the prophets come upon you:
>
> > "Behold, you despisers,
> > Marvel and perish!
> > For I work a work in your days,
> > A work which you will by no means believe,
> > Though one were to declare it to you" (verses 40-41).

This is the man who only a few years back would have marched into the same synagogue and arrested anyone who preached such "heresy." Now he is proclaiming Jesus as Lord.

What kind of response does his sermon elicit? The Gentile God-fearers want him to preach again the following Sabbath. Many Jews and Gentiles are converted and follow Paul and Barnabas out of the synagogue as he continues teaching and persuading them.

But that isn't the end of the story. Paul sticks around for another week as he waits for another opportunity to preach.

> On the next Sabbath almost the whole city came together to hear the word of God. But when the Jews saw the multitudes, they were filled with envy; and contradicting and blaspheming, they opposed the things spoken by Paul (Acts 13:44-45).

But Paul does not allow the synagogue shouters to have the last word. He and Barnabas boldly retort, "It was necessary that the word of God should be spoken to you first; but since you reject it, and judge yourselves unworthy of everlasting life, behold, we turn to the Gentiles" (verse 46). He tells them that this is his God-appointed mission. His announcement causes excitement among one group of people: "Now when the Gentiles heard this, they were glad and glorified the word of the Lord. And as many as had been appointed to eternal life believed" (verse 48).

Can you sense the struggle going on between the powers of good and evil over the souls of these people? This is more than a typical morning worship service and evangelistic message. Paul is seeking to plant a church in the heart of this city that will represent the kingdom of God to Jews and Gentiles long after he leaves. His plan causes a ruckus, but Luke adds this epilogue:

> And the word of the Lord was being spread throughout all the region. But the Jews stirred up the devout and prominent women and the chief men of the city, raised up persecution against Paul and Barnabas, and expelled them from their region. But they shook off the dust from their feet against them, and came to Iconium. And the disciples were filled with joy and with the Holy Spirit (verses 49-52).

The gospel of the kingdom stirs up a political hornets' nest and riles the religionists. The Jewish elders kick Paul and Barnabas out of the Jewish synagogue, and the Roman city officials run them out of town. If this were an isolated event, it would be bad enough. But it isn't.

Paul is beaten, jailed, or chased away in most cities he visits, including Iconium:

> The multitude of the city was divided: part sided with the Jews, and part with the apostles. And when a violent attempt was made by both the Gentiles and Jews, with their rulers, to abuse and stone them, they became aware of it and fled to Lystra and Derbe, cities of Lycaonia, and to the surrounding region. And they were preaching the gospel there (Acts 14:4-7).

At Lystra, Paul confronts a town of idol worshippers and calls upon them to turn to the living God.

> Then Jews from Antioch and Iconium came there; and having persuaded the multitudes, they stoned Paul and dragged him out of the city, supposing him to be dead. However, when the disciples gathered around him, he rose up and went into the city. And the next day he departed with Barnabas to Derbe (verses 19-20).

This kind of reaction is not caused by preaching a "pie in the sky," "in the sweet by and by" kind of gospel. It happens because the gospel of the kingdom demands a lifestyle change and a full commitment to Jesus as Lord and King here and now.

After ministering successfully in Derbe, Paul boldly returns to Lystra, Iconium, and Antioch (Acts 14:21), exhorting the new converts to continue in the faith no matter what, and he says, "We must through many tribulations enter the kingdom of God" (verse 22).

In like manner, the apostle Peter writes to scattered Jewish believers about the current blessings and future inheritance gained through Jesus's death, resurrection, and exaltation (1 Peter 1:1-12). He exhorts them to holy living and tells them to expect suffering (1:13–3:17).

> For Christ also suffered once for sins, the just for the unjust, that He might bring us to God, being put to death in the flesh but made alive by the Spirit...[Jesus] has gone into heaven and is at the right hand of God, angels and authorities and powers having been made subject to Him (1 Peter 3:18,22).

Summary

When we think of King Jesus and his kingdom, we must avoid the mistake of separating his death and resurrection from his exaltation. They are all key elements of God's end-time plan to restore creation. To preach Christ's death and resurrection apart from his present reign is a truncated and faulty gospel. There can be no crown without a cross and no throne without a resurrection.

13

I Pledge Allegiance to the Lamb

Baptism...the pledge of a clear conscience toward God.

1 PETER 3:21 NIV

Last year, Evelyn, a member of my adult Sunday school class, became a citizen of the United States. She was born in Ghana, Africa, and came to America to attend seminary. She fell in love with our country and its freedoms. After much contemplation and counting the cost, Evelyn applied for United States citizenship. Eligibility was rigorous. She had to reside in the United States for five years, study United States history and government, read our Constitution, and pass a comprehensive naturalization test. After meeting these qualifications, she was entitled to take the following oath of citizenship:

> I hereby declare, on oath, that I absolutely and entirely renounce and abjure all allegiance and fidelity to any foreign prince, potentate, state, or sovereignty of whom or which I have heretofore been a subject or citizen; that I will support and defend the Constitution and laws of the United States of America against all enemies, foreign and domestic; that I will bear true faith and allegiance to the same; that I will bear arms on behalf of the United States when required by the law; that I will perform noncombatant service in

the armed forces of the United States when required by
the law; that I will perform work of national importance
under civilian direction when required by the law; and that
I take this obligation freely without any mental reservation
or purpose of evasion; so help me God.

Before witnesses, Evelyn, along with several other candidates, raised
her right hand and pledged her allegiance to the United States of America. She did so of her own free choice. The oath of American citizenship
first of all requires an absolute and complete renunciation of all
allegiance and fidelity to one's former country and government. If Evelyn was not willing to break with the past, she was not fit to be an
American. She also pledged her complete and unreserved loyalty and
fidelity to the United States even if things get difficult. This commitment
involves a continuous and lifelong faithfulness to her new land. To
make an initial promise of fidelity but later withdraw it or spy for the
enemy would turn her into an infidel.

Citizenship involves both blessings and responsibilities. Freedom of
speech, freedom to vote, freedom to own property, freedom of religion,
and the host of other freedoms are balanced by our duty to support
and defend America's Constitution and laws. We are called upon to be
law-abiding citizens.

Citizenship in the Kingdom of God

We become citizens in God's kingdom in a similar way as Evelyn
became an American citizen. We must first meet the requirements.
These include repentance and faith, both of which are expressed
through the act of baptism, which is our oath or pledge of allegiance.

Repentance includes renouncing our former loyalties and allegiances. The word carries the idea of making an about-face or reorienting our lives. When we repent, we turn our backs on the kingdom
of darkness, to which we have belonged since our birth. We choose
to cease and desist from operating according to the principles of this
world. The apostle Paul instructs his protégé, Timothy, to faithfully
teach the Word to those opposing him in hope that "God perhaps will
grant them repentance, so that they may know the truth, and that they

I PLEDGE ALLEGIANCE TO THE LAMB 227

may come to their senses and escape the snare of the devil, having been taken captive by him to do his will" (2 Timothy 2:25-26).

Faith is a positive action. It includes pledging our fidelity and service to King Jesus and his kingdom. We take this oath and enter into a covenant agreement that requires complete and unreserved loyalty on our part when faced with danger and even death. We should think of our commitment to Christ as being akin to a recruit who joins the Marines and swears by an oath to remain steadfast to the Corps no matter what!

Repentance and faith are the two sides of Christian conversion. Genuine repentance includes the act of faith. In denouncing the one kingdom, we wholeheartedly embrace another. Likewise, genuine faith includes the act of repentance. To pledge our total commitment to one kingdom includes forsaking the other.

Baptism as Initiation into the Kingdom

In the book of Acts, those desiring to follow Jesus demonstrate their repentance and faith by submitting to public baptism. Baptism is the act of initiation into the kingdom of God, whereby the candidate pledges his or her allegiance to King Jesus as Lord. You can imagine the consequences when a Roman citizen converted to the Jesus movement. The cost of discipleship was high because baptism implied that Caesar was no longer one's Lord. Such a denunciation might result in a death sentence.

An Eschatological Event

In the New Testament, baptism is associated with entrance into the kingdom of God before it becomes a requirement for church membership. John the Baptist is the first to declare, "Repent, for the kingdom of heaven is at hand," and his hearers responded by being baptized. Jesus himself submits to John's baptism, at which time God anoints Jesus as King and inaugurates or launches his kingdom.

When Jesus's first followers repent and submit to baptism, they acknowledge him not only as their Savior but also as the exalted King of the universe, and thus they state their desire to affiliate with his messianic movement even to the point of death. In baptism the new believer participates in a graphic representation of the resurrection that will occur at the end of the age, when all God's enemies are destroyed, his faithful people are raised from the dead, and his ultimate kingdom arrives on earth.

Lutheran theologian and professor of New Testament Ernst Käsemann identifies baptism as "the seal of membership in the eschatological people of God."[1] Through the death and resurrection of his Son, God establishes a new eschatological people that populate a kingdom under his rule. Through baptism, people from all walks of life enter into a new relationship that transcends social, ethnic, economic, gender, and age barriers.

The apostle Peter likens baptism to the flood of Noah's day.

> A few, that is, eight souls, were saved through water. There is also an antitype which now saves us—*baptism* (not the removal of the filth of the flesh, but the answer [pledge] of a good conscience toward God), through the resurrection of Jesus Christ, who has gone into heaven and is at the right hand of God, angels and authorities and powers having been made subject to Him (1 Peter 3:20-22).

Three things make Peter's reference to the flood important for our discussion. First, Noah and his family were saved, or delivered from an evil world. "Saved" does not mean going to heaven in this instance, but living in a new world under the rule of God.

Second, we too are delivered by baptism, which Peter calls an antitype to the flood. Saved from what? In this context, it is not from hell, but from the authorities and powers who rule the world by usurpation. What saves us? It is not the liquid H_2O. Rather, we are delivered "through the resurrection of Jesus Christ [the Messiah], who has gone into heaven and is at the right hand of God." The one executed by Rome has emerged from the tomb victorious over his enemies and has received his lawful seat of authority. In baptism we reenact that event and claim it as our own. At the end of the age, we too will be raised to reign with Jesus.

Third, this passage is important because Peter tells us that baptism is "not the removal of the filth of the flesh, but the answer of a good conscience toward God." The Greek word translated "answer" (*eperōtēma*) comes from the business community of first-century Rome. It referred to a verbal promise at the end of a contract. It was a pledge to fulfill the agreement and was legally binding. The word was also used to describe the oath unto death a Roman soldier took when he entered Caesar's service. The early church borrowed *eperōtēma* and applied it to baptism. Thus baptism is the pledge toward God. So often we think of baptism as a profession of faith toward others. But Peter says that by baptism, the candidate pledges his or her loyalty to King Jesus and his kingdom.

New Testament scholar Günther Bornkamm says in baptism the candidate portrays graphically "the turning away from the old godless past and the turning towards God and his coming reign."[2] It is "the drama of decision."[3] As such, baptism is the act of repentance and faith.

Peter adds that this pledge is offered in "good conscience" without coercion or mental reserve. In baptism we pledge to live and die for Christ, knowing we will be raised at the eschaton to reign with Christ.

A Political Event

The apostle Paul compares baptism to the crossing of the Red Sea, when Jews escaped the political tyranny under Pharaoh and began afresh as a free people (1 Corinthians 10:1-2,11). The crossing of the Jordan River into the promised land is another picture of baptism and connotes entering a new kingdom, one that operates under the rule of God. Likewise, baptism has political significance. It speaks of the believer being delivered out from under an evil empire and into a new political reality, the kingdom of God.

In his Great Commission (Matthew 28:18-20), Jesus commands his followers, "Make disciples of *all the nations*," or members of nations subject to Rome. He prefaces his statement by claiming, "All authority has been given to Me in heaven and on earth," which implies his power surpasses Caesar's. Few statements can be more subversive than this. For the apostles to carry out their mission and call on multinational subjects of Rome to transfer their allegiance from Caesar to

Christ as Lord is traitorous and seditious. It will result in some being arrested, tried, and put to death as adversaries of the established government. Remember, Rome did not execute Peter and Paul for preaching about heaven or exile John to Patmos for preaching about forgiveness of individual sins.

Jesus's followers were to make disciples by baptizing them and teaching them to observe Christ's commandments. If baptism is a pledge of allegiance, as we have already established, and is followed by obedience to Jesus and not to a Roman caesar or a collaborating Jewish high priest, this entire project is politically motivated. With his concluding words, "I am with you always, even to the end of the age," Jesus additionally implies that his kingdom will outlive all others, including the Roman Empire.

In the first century, baptism was as much a political as a spiritual action. For believers to be baptized and declare Jesus as Lord in the very waters that Caesar, "Master of the Sea," owns and controls is audacious and politically seditious. Baptism is the vehicle of renunciation of Caesar as Lord. The believer's submersion in water vividly depicts death to the old life, effectively ending lifelong loyalty to Caesar. Rising from the watery grave represents a new life with new commitments to a different Lord and King. Baptism is the act of conversion, through which the candidate for citizenship publically renounces (repentance) and pledges allegiance (faith) to a new kingdom—the government, or empire, of God. When Paul writes, "There is...one Lord, one faith, one baptism" (Ephesians 4:4-5), he is denying that Caesar has any claims to a believer's loyalty. All of the convert's allegiance is pledged to the one Lord through baptism.

> How does the way we practice baptism compare with the way the early church did it? We relate baptism more to the church than the kingdom. We view it as the entrance point of church membership rather than the act of initiation into the kingdom of God.

Examples of Baptism as an Eschatological and Political Act

In the book of Acts, those who hear the gospel of the kingdom are commanded to be baptized. For instance, Peter exhorts the crowd gathered in Jerusalem on the Day of Pentecost, "Repent, and be baptized every one of you in the name of Jesus Christ so that your sins may be forgiven; and you will receive the gift of the Holy Spirit" (Acts 2:38 NRSV). Those expressing their repentance toward God through baptism are assured of two things—forgiveness of sins and the gift of the Holy Spirit.

Old Testament prophets speak of God entering into a new covenant with his people, through which he will offer eschatological forgiveness and the eschatological Spirit to the faithful (Jeremiah 31:31-34; Ezekiel 36:26-27; Joel 2:28). The new covenant marks the restoration of God's kingdom. Peter says that day has now arrived. He commands the people, "Save [deliver] yourselves from this corrupt generation" (Acts 2:40 NRSV), which implies most of their cohorts who support or tolerate corrupt religious and/or governmental practices will be judged. Luke gives us the outcome: "So those who welcomed his message were baptized, and that day about three thousand persons were added" (verse 41 NRSV).

Luke gives an account of Philip's stopover at Samaria, an entire city under the sway of a sorcerer (Acts 8:4-25). But "when they believed Philip, who was proclaiming the good news about the kingdom of God and the name of Jesus Christ, they were baptized, both men and women." Again, notice the gospel is about the kingdom of God, and the expected response is baptism.

We next find Philip in Gaza encountering an Ethiopian eunuch, who is described as "a court official of the Candace, queen of the Ethiopians, in charge of her entire treasury" (Acts 8:27 NRSV). To this confidante of a queen, Philip proclaims the good news about Jesus from the Suffering Servant section of Isaiah 53. Are we safe to assume that Philip preaches the same gospel at Gaza that he preached at Samaria? If so, the good news about Jesus is the same as the gospel of the kingdom and includes information about Jesus's role as Messiah, his death, and his exaltation as King.

"As they were going along the road, they came to some water; and the eunuch said, 'Look, here is water! What is to prevent me from being baptized?' Then Philip said, 'If you believe with all your heart, you may.' And he replied, 'I believe that Jesus Christ is the Son of God'" (verses 36-37 nrsv). The titles Christ and Son of God speak of Jesus as Messiah and King.

"He commanded the chariot to stop, and both of them, Philip and the eunuch, went down into the water, and Philip baptized him." An ambassador of Christ helps a seeker become a citizen in the kingdom of God. In a desert oasis, the eunuch pledges his allegiance to King Jesus before the wondering eyes of his entire entourage. Wouldn't you like to know how the queen responds when hearing of his new loyalty to another commander in chief?

Or how about Cornelius, the faithful Roman centurion, whose allegiance for years has been to Caesar as Lord? He hears Peter announce, "You know the message he [God] sent to the people of Israel, preaching peace by Jesus Christ—he is Lord of all" (Acts 10:36 nrsv). What a treasonous message! Caesar's *Pax Romana* is supplanted by God's peace plan, which comes through a Jewish Messiah, whom Peter declares to be Lord. The one Rome put to death as a criminal was raised back to life and will one day judge the world (verses 39-42). But then Peter announces that "everyone who believes in him receives forgiveness of sins through his name."

Can you imagine what price Cornelius might pay should he switch allegiance to Jesus as Lord and denounce Rome, its gods, and Caesar as demonic oppressors? God helps him to make the right decision. To the amazement of Peter's companions, "while Peter was still speaking, the Holy Spirit fell upon all who heard the word" (verse 44 nrsv). This leads Peter to inquire, "'Can anyone withhold the water for *baptizing* these people who have received the Holy Spirit just as we have?' So he ordered them to be *baptized* in the name of Jesus Christ. Then they invited him to stay for several days." Jewish and Gentile believers eat together as citizens of the same kingdom.

In each case history, baptism has eschatological and political implications.

The Making of the Apostle Paul

The story of Saul of Tarsus begins in Acts 9, where we find him receiving authority from the Sanhedrin, the Jewish ruling body, to hunt down messianic Jews and bring them back to Jerusalem for trial. But on the road to Damascus, the exalted Lord Jesus appears to him as a blinding bright light, knocking him off his horse, and instructs him to proceed into the city, where he will be told what to do. In the meantime, King Jesus appears in a vision to his disciple Ananias and instructs him to search out Saul and baptize him.

In a parallel account, Ananias inquires of Saul, "And now why are you waiting? Arise and *be baptized*, and wash away your sins, calling on the name of the Lord" (Acts 22:16). Paul responds positively and shifts his allegiance from the Jewish high authorities to Jesus the Messiah. This turning point will mark the beginning of his efforts as an ambassador for Jesus. In yet a third account, Paul is standing trial before King Agrippa, and he tells of a heavenly Voice at his conversion.

> I am Jesus, whom you are persecuting. But rise and stand on your feet; for I have appeared to you for this purpose, to make you a minister and a witness both of the things which you have seen and of the things which I will yet reveal to you. I will deliver you from the Jewish people, as well as from the Gentiles, to whom I now send you, to open their eyes, in order to turn them from darkness to light, and from the power of Satan to God, that they may receive forgiveness of sins and an inheritance among those who are sanctified by faith in Me (Acts 26:15-18).

Saul receives a mission that includes offering Gentiles—those living in darkness and under the power of Satan, or Roman authority—an inheritance that was previously offered mainly to Jews who pledge loyalty to King Jesus. Paul will spend the remainder of his earthly life preaching the gospel and announcing that God's kingdom is inclusive, not exclusive.

After being diverted from preaching the gospel in Asia Minor, Paul and his team cross the Mediterranean and land in Philippi, described as the foremost city in that part of Macedonia and a colony (Acts 16:6-12). The city does not have enough Jews to support a synagogue, so on the Sabbath they move to the outskirts of the city and find a place to pray on a riverbank. There they meet Lydia, a businesswoman with whom they share the gospel. "The Lord opened her heart to heed the things spoken by Paul." "To heed" means to obey, so "she and her household were baptized." This means that Paul includes in his gospel presentation a call to be baptized. Lydia's home likely serves as the location of the first messianic *ekklesia* in Philippi and becomes the home base for Paul's outreach (verse 40).

> Certain cities throughout the Roman Empire received favored status and were designated as colonies. Their inhabitants held prestigious Roman citizenship, spoke Latin, adopted Roman culture and customs, paid no taxes, and were exempt from military conscription. Each colony operated its governmental affairs according to the Roman constitution. A colony was an outpost or settlement situated in strategic locations, which represented Rome to its part of the Empire. To visit a colony was like visiting Rome itself, only on a smaller scale.

When Paul and Silas go into the marketplace to preach, they confront a demon-possessed fortune-teller who attempts to hinder their efforts. After they cast out the demon, they are arrested and brought before the magistrate with this accusation: "These men, being Jews, exceedingly trouble our city; and they teach customs which are not lawful for us, being Romans, to receive or observe" (Acts 16:20-21). Notice that the charge has nothing to do with preaching about going to heaven or salvation as we typically conceive it. The indictment is *political*. They have asked Roman citizens to do something unlawful— pledge their allegiance to Jesus as Lord. This causes a near riot in the courtroom.

> Then the multitude rose up together against them; and the
> magistrates tore off their clothes and commanded them to
> be beaten with rods. And when they had laid many stripes
> on them, they threw them into prison, commanding the
> jailer to keep them securely. Having received such a charge,
> he put them into the inner prison and fastened their feet
> in the stocks (verses 22-24).

Of course, this presents an opportunity for one of the well-known and miraculous conversion stories in the Bible. As Paul and Silas sit in their cell singing praises to God, an earthquake strikes, shaking the prison and opening the cell doors. The jailer thinks that his prisoners have escaped and that he will be held responsible, so he pulls out his sword to take his own life. Death by his own hand is preferable to what he will face at the hands of his superiors. When Paul reveals he is still present and accounted for, the shaking jailer cries out, "What must I do to be saved?" It is important that we don't assume the jailer is asking about spiritual salvation or deliverance. This man is not asking how to go to heaven. He's probably asking how he will escape the punishment of the Roman authorities.

Paul and Silas answer, "Believe on the Lord Jesus Christ, and you will be saved, you and your household" (Acts 16:31). Paul cannot guarantee the jailer will not be put to death, but he can assure him that he can be raised from the dead at the eschaton. "Then they spoke the word of the Lord to him and to all who were in his house. And he took them the same hour of the night and washed their stripes. And immediately he and all his family were baptized" (verses 32-34).

Based on what we know from our study thus far, we can draw some conclusions. First, we can be confident that "the word of the Lord" Paul preached included information that the crucified Jesus is Lord of all. Second, Paul's message also included a call for baptism. This is the response that the gospel demands. Third, by being baptized, the jailer and his family pledge their allegiance to King Jesus. Fourth, baptism is a pledge toward God. After all, the jailer's baptism takes place at midnight. Who is up to witness it? Finally, baptism is the jailer's and his family's expression of their faith. Paul says, "Believe" (verse 31), and they "were baptized" (verse 33), "having believed" (verse 34).

We can find no example under the new covenant of a person giving his or her life to Christ apart from baptism.

The jailer, a Roman citizen and government employee, transfers his allegiance to another Lord and a new kingdom. We are talking here about much more than making a spiritual commitment. This decision affects economics, ethics, politics, and more. The jailer becomes a citizen of a new kingdom.

At Corinth, Paul is ordered to leave the synagogue for preaching that Jesus is the Messiah-King (Acts 18:4-6). Paul warns as he departs, "Your blood be upon your own heads; I am clean. From now on I will go to the Gentiles." From there he moves next door to the house of Justus, a Gentile God-fearer. We are not told all that happens next or how long it takes, just that "Crispus, the ruler of the synagogue, believed on the Lord with all his household. And many of the Corinthians, hearing, believed and were *baptized*."

Despite threats of attack and being hauled into Roman court on at least one occasion (verses 9-17), Paul stays in the city. His converts will meet together as an *ekklesia*, or messianic association, and continue his work upon his departure.

Baptism is mentioned on only two other occasions in the book of Acts. On the first, Priscilla and Aquila meet Apollos, who knows only John's baptism. They bring him up to date and inform him that Jesus is the Messiah (Acts 18:24-28).

On the second occasion, Paul happens upon some disciples. Recognizing that something is missing in their lives, he asks, "Did you receive the Holy Spirit when you believed?" (Acts 19:1-2). When they plead ignorance about the Holy Spirit, he inquires into the nature of their baptism. This shows that Paul, like Peter before him, connects baptism with the receiving of the eschatological Spirit. When he discovers they are baptized disciples of John the Baptist, Paul reminds them that John's intention was that they "should believe on Him," the Messiah (verses 4-5). When they hear this, they are baptized in the name of the Lord Jesus. Again we have a connection between belief and baptism.

They are called to believe, and they respond by being baptized. They are no longer waiting for the arrival of the kingdom of God, but are now citizens of it. Then through the laying on of Paul's hands, they receive the Spirit.

John's Baptism and Christian Baptism

Baptism has its origin with John the Baptist. God sent John to prepare Israel for the arrival of God's kingdom. Described as a voice crying in the wilderness, John invited his hearers, "Repent, for the kingdom of heaven is at hand!" (Matthew 3:2). Those responding to his message "were baptized by him...confessing their sins." Mark writes in his Gospel, "John came baptizing in the wilderness and preaching a baptism of repentance for the remission of sins" (Mark 1:4; see also Luke 3:3). Three key concepts appear in these verses: baptism, repentance, and forgiveness of sins. All three were necessary to prepare one for the arrival of God's kingly rule. In this way John's baptism and Christian baptism are similar.

John's baptism of repentance was a call for Jews to escape the final judgment and become part of God's kingdom people. That John's baptism was characterized by repentance connotes that those submitting willfully to baptism desired to change their ways and claimed no special privilege or exemptions. They responded to God's message through his prophet on God's terms.

When some, having no inclination to change their moral lifestyle, come to the Jordan, John calls them vipers and challenges them, "Bear fruits worthy of repentance" (Luke 3:7-8). When they ascribe for themselves favored status with God because of their ancestry to Abraham, he pronounces judgment on them. For John, repentance bears fruit.

> "Whoever has two coats must share with anyone who has none; and whoever has food must do likewise." Even tax collectors came to be baptized, and they asked him, "Teacher, what should we do?" He said to them, "Collect no more than the amount prescribed for you." Soldiers also asked him, "And we, what should we do?" He said to them, "Do not extort money from anyone by threats or

false accusation, and be satisfied with your wages" (verses 11-14 NRSV).

John's baptism is eschatological, but it is only preparatory to Christian baptism, which incorporates people into the kingdom. The latter is called the baptism "with the Holy Spirit" (Mark 1:8; Acts 1:5; 11:16).

John's Baptism	Christian Baptism
repentance	repentance
baptism in water	baptism in water
forgiveness (Luke 3:3)	forgiveness
	the Holy Spirit
	(Acts 2:38)

Conclusion

When we view baptism only as a rite of the church or as a public confession, we miss the more important eschatological significance as the act of initiation into the kingdom. The New Testament writers mention baptism more than 100 times, so we should view it as a core component of the gospel of the kingdom.

Just as the end-time Spirit indwells Jesus after his baptism, this same Spirit takes up residence in all kingdom citizens.

14

The Church as a Colony and Embassy

Our citizenship is in heaven.

PHILIPPIANS 3:20

The New Testament uses several metaphors to describe the church, including a household, a body, a temple, and a bride. Many authors have examined these more traditional images. In this chapter we will look at two different images—the church as a colony and the church as an embassy.

The Church as a Colony of Heaven

After the apostle Paul encourages believers at Philippi to live according to kingdom standards, he gives the reason: "For our citizenship is in heaven, from which we also eagerly wait for the Savior, the Lord Jesus Christ, who will transform our lowly body that it may be conformed to His glorious body, according to the working by which He is able even to subdue all things to Himself" (Philippians 3:20-21).

This statement says more than meets the eye. First, it identifies us as citizens of heaven, yet we live on earth. This unusual arrangement makes us resident aliens. Imagine a Russian family moves to the United States. They are citizens of Russia but resident aliens in America.

Although they reside and work in the United States, their loyalties are to their own government back home.

Likewise, we are citizens of the kingdom of God, but we each have an earthly address. In whatever city, state, or country you live, your devotion should be primarily to King Jesus and his kingdom. The pure kingdom or reign of God exists in heaven, where all beings enjoy God's blessings and live in perfect obedience to their King.

Second, the phrase "our citizenship is in heaven" is difficult to translate. Moffatt translates it this way: "We are a colony of heaven," which implies that while citizens of heaven, believers in Philippi comprise a colony. The Greek word translated "colony" or "citizenship" (*políteuma*) carries the idea of a commonwealth of citizens who conduct the affairs of their government although far from home.

The concept of a colony was familiar to the inhabitants of Philippi because their city was a designated colony of Rome. As Roman citizens, the people of this Greek city held privileged status, spoke Latin, embraced Roman culture and law, and served Rome even though they lived more than 600 miles from the capital of the Empire. A colony was an outpost filled with people of one culture living in the midst of another. Roman colonists never forgot they were first and foremost Roman citizens. Philippi was like a miniature Rome planted in northeastern Greece, and it represented the will of Rome to all living in the region.

I have noticed that in my neck of the woods in north Texas, many resident aliens move into sections of town where others from their home country also live, thus forming ethnic enclaves or neighborhoods. We have a vibrant Greek community. They belong to the same Orthodox churches, eat at the same restaurants, observe the same customs, and have their own councils and community leaders. These resident aliens are in the United States but not of it. (By the way, if you want a taste of the Greek culture, you don't have to cross the Mediterranean to experience it. The annual Greek food festival will have you hoping your children or grandkids marry into a Greek family!)

In like manner, believers in each locale form a colony of the King. These local churches or *ekklesiai* represent the kingdom to their neighborhoods and towns. We embrace a social alternative to the culture and society in which we find ourselves, whether America, Canada, Cuba, Russia, Egypt, or any of the more than 190 countries of the world. We conduct our personal and corporate affairs according to standards set by our King.

Our citizenship is in heaven, but we live it out on earth. Like the Philippian believers, we live according to kingdom principles while "we also eagerly wait for the Savior, the Lord Jesus Christ" (Philippians 3:20). Our King currently rules over us from heaven, but we hope for his arrival on earth to establish his kingdom worldwide and "subdue all things to Himself" (verse 21). Right now Jesus is like a king in exile who plans to return and take back what rightfully is his.

When fascist Italian dictator Benito Mussolini invaded and conquered Ethiopia, Emperor Haile Selassie moved to Bath, England, where he lived in exile from 1936–1941. At no time did he cease to be Ethiopia's rightful ruler. He had a large group of loyalists in Ethiopia who served him and kept alive the hope of his triumphal return to claim his kingdom.

Jesus is earth's legitimate King, but he rules in exile from heaven. A usurper gained control of the landscape, but his days are numbered. The church is a colony of heaven, loyal to King Jesus and charged with recruiting others to become citizens of the kingdom of God, a government in exile that will one day envelop the world when its King returns. In the meantime we stay busy in his service.

The Church as an Embassy

The church is also like a foreign embassy, such as the British embassy in Washington, DC. I attended seminary in Washington and lived there for three years. Whenever I had out-of-town guests, I took them to Embassy Row on Massachusetts Avenue NW, only blocks from my seminary. The first embassy is the impressive British embassy compound, located next to the US Naval Observatory, which houses the atomic clock and serves as the home of the vice president of the United States. Situated on some of the most expensive real estate in America, valued at $30,000,000, the British embassy compound includes chanceries for the 200-member diplomatic corps and 250 staff. It also includes the ambassador's colonial-style mansion, with a larger-than-life statue of Winston Churchill on the front lawn.

The British embassy is located within the geographical boundaries of America, but the property is owned by the United Kingdom. Each morning the ambassador and his people arrive at work in fine British fashion. Women may be spotted wearing tweed and herringbone suits, and men wear bowler hats and shirts with Prince of Wales collars. A worker raises the red, white, and blue Union Flag with its combined Saint Andrew and Saint Patrick crosses with a Saint George cross overlay. All official functions open with a rousing rendition of "God Save the Queen."

The people in the embassy speak differently than the average American does. They have a distinguishable accent and idiomatic vocabulary that is often unfamiliar to the American ear. They show little interest in American sports but closely watch cricket and rugby scores. They ignore American holidays, but on the evening of November 5, they build a bonfire to celebrate Guy Fawkes Day. They might eat fish and chips served with mushy peas for lunch and enjoy beef and Yorkshire pudding for supper. At eleven each morning and four each afternoon, things come to a sudden halt. It is time for a spot of tea and a biscuit or scone served on Royal Doulton china.

Most importantly, the ambassador and his diplomats are British citizens who faithfully serve their government on foreign soil 3000 miles from home. Their main responsibility is to represent England in the United States. Americans do not have to travel to England in order to know what the country and culture are like. They can visit the embassy. Occasionally Americans seek British citizenship. They are directed to a British consulate in their region or the embassy in the nation's capital.

Churches are like embassies. They are located in most countries around the world. Christians are like ambassadors. Although living on foreign soil, we are citizens of God's kingdom and follow his laws and standards of ethical behavior. We are in the world but not of it. We give our attention to kingdom affairs, use kingdom language, eat a kingdom meal in honor of our Sovereign, sing distinctive kingdom songs, observe certain kingdom holidays and customs, and engage in many kingdom activities that most people consider strange. Regardless of our location on the planet, we are loyal subjects of God's government. As emissaries, we represent the kingdom of God to the world. When people want to know what the kingdom of God is like, we invite them to come and see. When they visit, they get a taste of the kingdom.

Although the church is not the kingdom of God per se, the Spirit of the kingdom permeates it. The church serves the kingdom and points people toward the kingdom. On the occasions when outsiders visit the church and seek kingdom citizenship, we explain the process. The process includes repentance, faith, and baptism.

Kingdom Focused and Kingdom Driven

The church is a signpost pointing to the kingdom. It does not expect to transform society into a paragon of Christian virtue any more than the British embassy in Moscow expects to persuade Russians to give up vodka and start drinking Earl Grey tea! When the church sees its mission as changing the culture of the country in which it resides, it will be disappointed.

In democratic countries, we should use our constitutional freedoms to influence our elected officials to do good or to vote them out of office. But many Christians around the world don't have this luxury. They are located in Communist, Fascist, Muslim, and Jewish states where church officials have little or no influence on governmental policies and Christians are forbidden to protest governmental policies or even share their faith in public. In tribal lands, petty dictators set the social agenda, and their military strongmen enforce it. What makes us think that governments run by godless thugs will adopt Christian virtues? Do we actually believe that Satan, the invisible power behind human governments, wants his earthly leaders to live by the Golden Rule?

Christians in the Western world make a mistake when they blindly assume that fighting culture wars is the normal thing to do. This philosophy doesn't work in Yemen, Somalia, or Zimbabwe.

The Scriptures are clear that the moral progression of human governments is downward and not upward. Think about nations and empires that ruled the world in the past. Did they become morally better or worse? Remember, Edward Gibbon entitled his monumental work *The History of the Decline and Fall of the Roman Empire*. Is America more moral today than at its founding? When followers of Christ in America devote so much of their time, energy, and money to rescuing America rather than being the church—a colony or embassy of Christ in America—they may one day look back and regret wasting so many human resources on a failed project.

In the 1800s and early 1900s, many believers in the West tied the arrival of the kingdom to the spread of democracy throughout the world. Such Christian leaders as Walter Rauschenbusch, a Baptist professor of theology at Rochester Theological Seminary in New York, equated Christianity with democracy and believed they could usher in the kingdom of God by democratizing the world. Needless to say, however noble the mission, they failed. The democratization or even the Christianization of a government is not our main mission as kingdom citizens.

We know from history what a Christianized government looks like and what it produces. For 900 years the Holy Roman Empire held sway over human affairs under the banner of Christendom. It was not a happy story.

A similar experiment took place in England when Protestants deposed King Charles II and on December 16, 1653, named Oliver Cromwell "Lord Protector" for life. Puritans gained control of Parliament and required that all MPs give evidence of a strong Christian faith. Cromwell had two objectives: eliminate the monarchy and Christianize the nation. Rather than solving England's problems, the Protestant leaders bickered and debated among themselves until the government ended in deadlock and Parliament was dissolved. The people cried, "Give us back King Charles II." The exiled king returned to England and regained his throne. A Christianized government is not the solution. A kingdom-driven church is.

Democracy and the kingdom of God are two different types of government. Democracy is a government of the people, by the people, and for the people. The will of the majority prevails, and the minority dissent. The kingdom of God is a government of God, by God, and for God. The perfect and righteous King has absolute authority. Period!

Our role as believers wherever we live is to demonstrate to the watching world what it looks like to live under the reign of a perfect King and invite others to do so.

Supporting and Exhorting the Government

So what is our responsibility toward government? First, we must be subject to its laws unless they require us to do something immoral or ethically reprehensible. For example, the ambassador of England and his embassy staff will make an attempt to obey the laws of their host country, but they will go only so far. There are limits. At times and under certain circumstances, a host government will become angry with an uncooperative ambassador, close down the embassy, and send the diplomats packing. Within 24 hours he and his team will be on a plane home. We too must be willing to pay a price when our commitment to Christ will not allow us to obey a law.

Second, if we happen to live in a country with individual freedoms—voting rights, lobbying rights, freedom of speech and assembly, and the like—we should use those freedoms to the fullest extent for good. In the West, we have the right to vote out immoral or corrupt leaders, run for office, and demand to be heard. The apostle Paul used his rights as a Roman citizen to legally defend himself.

Third, we should support the government when it enacts policies that promote civil rights, engages in compassionate care for the poor and disenfranchised, upholds civility, protects its citizenry from economic exploitation, stands for justice, and keeps its citizens safe.

Fourth, the church must prophetically call local, state, and national leaders to account for their unethical and immoral actions, warning them that one day they will stand before God to be judged. We must exhort them to submit to King Jesus as Lord and rightful ruler of the universe. The prophet speaks on behalf of God and his kingdom to presidents, kings, potentates, mayors, and judges, whether elected, appointed, or self-appointed. The ambassador of England is responsible to clearly and boldly represent the will of his homeland to the host government. He cannot do otherwise. We must do the same. Let's not forget, John the Baptist pronounced judgment on King Herod, and it cost him his head!

Drawing or Blurring the Lines

We must remember that the church is not a colony and embassy of America, Canada, Russia, or any other country. It only resides in these places. It is a colony and embassy of the kingdom of God. There is always a danger, especially in the West, to blur the lines. Such erroneous thinking leads to nationalism. We start equating the church with a particular country instead of the kingdom of God, or we act as if the church is dually aligned with both its host country and the kingdom of God. Once nationalism is ensconced in the Christian psyche, it is hard to jettison because it attaches itself to human emotions. In America, for instance, "God and country" is almost as sacred a doctrine to some believers as the virgin birth.

But those embracing a kingdom-focused theology know that nationalism is potentially dangerous. Let's look at two practices that most Christians in the West accept without a second thought but that actually promote nationalism rather than the kingdom of God.

Displaying an American Flag in the Church

When churches display the American flag in their worship center, what message do they convey? You might say, "It speaks of our love for country." That may be true, but what does that have to do with the gospel or the kingdom of God? A pulpit flag is more likely to send a message to the average person in the pew that we all have a dual allegiance to God and country. But we are not called to that commitment any more than a believer in North Korea is called to support the national agenda of the Communist government. Jesus calls us to pledge our allegiance to the kingdom of God.

We must remember that America is a kingdom of this world and that the church is independent of all earthly kingdoms. Churches are colonies and embassies of God's kingdom located in every country, representing God's will to those nations.

During Jesus's temptation in the wilderness, Satan shows and offers him the kingdoms of the world. Jesus doesn't take the bait. America is a present-day kingdom of the world. We make a mistake when we perceive it to be something else. In our mind's eye, many of us see Jesus as an American who, if he walked the earth today, would salute the flag.

Can you imagine Christians in the first century placing the flag of the Roman Empire in their place of worship? When King Herod raised the standard of the Roman Eagle over the temple entrance, a riot ensued. How would you feel if you visited a church in Beijing and saw the flag of the Republic of China displayed in the pulpit? Or what about a Russian or Cuban flag in the pulpits of their respective countries?

How do you think brothers and sisters in Christ from Pakistan, Iraq, China, or Syria feel when they visit a church in America and see a flag standing behind the pulpit? God is the God of all peoples, regardless of nationality. The flag is a symbol of national sovereignty and does nothing to unite the body of Christ. Instead it divides.

Nationalism should not be confused with patriotism. We can be patriotic without being nationalistic. Patriotism speaks of a love of country. None of us get to choose where we will be born. We grow up in a nation learning and loving its customs, culture, language, and laws. This is our country whether we are male or female, child or adult, rich or poor, or politically left, right, or center. Nationalism is an aspiration for our nation to be more important and more powerful than others, and it includes a sanctimonious belief that our way of doing things is superior to that of all other nations and should be adopted by them all.

By calling upon national pride, Hitler convinced the church hierarchy of Germany to support his cause. The Nazi flag stood near the altar of most Christian churches in Germany during World War II.[1] Believing Hitler to be God's man to revive Germany to its original greatness, more than 14,000 German pastors threw their support behind him and believed their Christian duty was to encourage their parishioners to do the same. An entire nation was deceived into believing that their plan for the world was in the best interest of all, when in fact, God's kingdom plan is best for all.

Sinclair Lewis (1885–1951), the first American novelist to win the Nobel Prize in Literature, recognized the potential danger ahead for the United States. He allegedly warned, "When fascism comes to America, it will be wrapped in a flag and carrying a cross."

Supporting a Government Going to War

Should the church of Jesus Christ ever support a nation going to war? This controversial question has led to heated debate among faithful believers. Most discussions center on the issue of whether a war is just. For example, does a nation enter a war because it has been attacked and must defend itself? Or because it is trying to stop the progression of evil, such as Hitler and Nazism's march across Europe? Because it wants to spread its ideology? Because it desires the spoils of battle, such as gold, territory, or oil?

But in my mind, these concerns are peripheral. The dispute is not over the nature or purpose of war, but the nature and purpose of the church as an outpost of God's kingdom.

The universal church is larger than any one nation. Its members live in every country of the world. Churches represent the kingdom of God to their respective nations. Like an embassy that supports only the agenda of its homeland, so the church supports God's agenda alone and not the nationalistic agenda of the country where it happens to be located.

When one nation declares war against another nation, the church should not blindly support the decision. War involves not only wreaking havoc on the enemy, killing and maiming enemy combatants, but also slaughtering thousands of innocents, including women and children, and the destruction of hospitals, schools, homes, and other institutions. This is what military strategists antiseptically label "collateral damage."

Additionally, there is another factor churches must consider. Imagine that two countries—Egypt and Chile—declare war on each other.

Churches are located in each country, which means their members live in both places. What if the churches in Egypt support that government's war efforts and the Chilean churches do the same? Will not Christ's church be divided, resulting in Christians from one nation killing Christians from the opposing nation? In doing so, they diminish the number of kingdom citizens on earth and thus lessen the church's own influence. Does this sound like a strategy that originates from the throne of God?

If Christians are forbidden to take each other to court (1 Corinthians 6:1-7), why do we think we are permitted to kill or mutilate each other? Our allegiance is to God and his kingdom alone. We must stand with other believers wherever they may reside.

So the issue is not whether one nation or another is justified in defending itself through violent means, but whether the church is justified in supporting death as a solution to international affairs.

Many will argue that God's people in the Old Testament fought wars. That is true, but the church is not Israel. It does not have national borders to defend. Our citizenship is in heaven, although we find ourselves spread throughout the countries of the world. As a result, we owe no allegiance to any one country.

Churches and the nations belong to separate domains that happen to be antithetical to each other. They operate according to different principles. One operates by faith, the other by force. This can be demonstrated by examining the difference between Caesar's and Jesus's methods of establishing peace on earth.

Two Divergent Paths to Peace

When Jesus was born, Augustus Caesar reigned over the Roman Empire, proclaiming that the gods gave Rome the divine right or "manifest destiny" to rule the world. Caesar launched a worldwide peace initiative known as *Pax Romana*, which was to spread Roman peace to the far-flung corners of the Empire and beyond. Hailed as one of the most remarkable accomplishments in history and considered a blessing from the gods, it motivated the Roman senate to declare Augustus to be the savior of the world.[2]

To accomplish the goal of universal peace, Caesar sent troops to neighboring countries with the offer that if they aligned with Rome and submitted to his leadership, Rome would be their protector. When a nation refused to acquiesce, they were swiftly and mercilessly conquered. The way to universal peace was by means of threats, coercion, and force.

The path to peace employed by Caesar is still practiced centuries later. Nations continue to claim divine justification for spreading their way of life to the world as they chant, "Peace through strength." Those nations following in Rome's footsteps need to realize, however, that such an effort is doomed from the start. As John Dominic Crossan insightfully reminds us, a forced peace that comes through war and violence is not peace at all but only "a lull—until the next and always more violent round of war."[3] It is only a matter of time before subjugated and oppressed peoples seek to defy their captors and drive out the occupation troops.

Jesus and the apostles offer an alternative universal peace plan, which is called good news (Luke 2:10) and is accomplished through nonviolent means. The good news of the kingdom is counterintuitive. Instead of using armed conflict to overthrow Rome, Jesus topples the Empire by becoming a victim of violence. When threatened with torture and death, Jesus does not respond in kind. Nor does he cower and cry out for his life to be spared. Rather, he stands face-to-face with Pontius Pilate and declares, "My kingdom is not of this world. If My kingdom were of this world, My servants would fight, so that I should not be delivered to the Jews; but now My kingdom is not from here" (John 18:36). When Jesus uses the phrase "not of this world," he is not implying that it is not on the earth, but that it does not originate from here. It is not part of the world system.

Jesus chooses a different path to establish his kingdom of peace. Rather than depending on worldly means, Jesus depends on his heavenly Father. Pilate is so confused by what he hears that he asks Jesus, "Are You a king then?" Jesus responds, "You say rightly that I am a king. For this cause I was born, and for this cause I have come into the world, that I should bear witness to the truth." Most likely the truth is about his role as King and about the kingdom of God, which leads Pilate to smugly reply, "What is truth?"

By rejecting violence as a means of bringing about his kingdom on earth, Jesus humbly faces death and trusts his heavenly Father to use it to usher in his kingdom. When Joseph and Nicodemus remove his lifeless body from the cross and place it in the tomb, they assume the Jesus movement is kaput. But on Sunday morning, God raises Jesus back to life. He emerges from the tomb victorious over death, and the world forever changes.

So here is the question: Who wins, Rome or Christ? Jesus is forever alive in a resurrected body, so Rome cannot crucify him again. To his disciples he announces, "All authority has been given to Me in heaven and on earth" (Matthew 28:18). He claims rule over much more than a nebulous ethereal or spiritual realm. He regains control of the world that the first Adam lost and Satan acquired. Rome is stripped of power, and the wily usurper is defeated. This means Jesus reigns and can never be overthrown. He is earth's rightful Ruler regardless of whether anyone acknowledges him. He is establishing a kingdom on earth that can never be defeated.

This shows that faith triumphs over force. Rome uses its ultimate weapon—death—to defeat Jesus, and it fails. Jesus defeats Rome without lifting a hand. His nonviolent peace plan based on faith in God alone proves more than adequate to conquer the most powerful empire in human history up until that time. In the end, every nation in the world will submit to King Jesus, and world peace will arrive at last.

Responding to War

So this brings us back to our discussion of war. When nations go to war, how should the church within participating nations respond? Here are six considerations.

First, it must state publicly and unequivocally that it opposes the war. The church does not support the use of death as a means for bringing peace. The end does not justify the means. The Bible identifies death as our enemy and Satan as a murderer from the beginning of time. Hitler employed the gas chamber as his ultimate solution to the so-called "Jewish problem." Because death ends all opportunity for a fallen soldier to gain eternal life through Christ, we stand opposed to war.

Second, the churches in a country must call on its governmental leaders to seek nonviolent means, such as diplomacy, to avert war. Just as an ambassador of an embassy urges the leaders in the host country to seek a peaceful solution rather than go to war, so the church must take a similar stand.

Third, the church must remind its members that when they sign up for combat duty, they will be called on to kill soldiers on the other side who are citizens of God's kingdom. They will be killing brothers and sisters in Christ.

A host of second- and third-century church leaders understood their responsibility to speak out against war, including Justin Martyr, Irenaeus, Clement, Athenagoras, Tertullian, and Origen. Justin Martyr included this in chapter 110 of his *Dialogue with Trypho*:

> We who were filled with war, and mutual slaughter, and every wickedness, have each through the whole earth changed our warlike weapons—our swords into ploughshares, and our spears into implements of tillage—and we cultivate piety, righteousness, philanthropy, faith, and hope, which we have from the Father Himself through Him who was crucified.

Fourth, the church must remind its members who volunteer to fight in war that their bullets will seal the fate of unbelievers for eternity who are fighting for the other side. Certainly no Christian wants to carry such a heavy burden.

Fifth, the church must dedicate itself to minister compassionately to the victims of war and their families. This includes providing friendship, grief counseling, relief, transportation, and services aimed at helping widowed spouses and orphaned children.

Sixth, the church must call on national leaders to repent, come under the reign of King Jesus, and obey his voice. Churches located in countries on both sides of the conflict must fulfill this responsibility.

Over the centuries churches have been lured into supporting war under the guise of duty to country. What about the churches in Iran or the Sudan, avowed enemies of America? Would you be comfortable with these believers supporting their country's war efforts? Why not? They likely love their homeland as much as we do ours.

The modern-day practice of churches supporting war is partially the result of Martin Luther's theory that two kingdoms exist side by side—one secular and one sacred—and that believers owe allegiance to both. Luther was right that there are two kingdoms, but he wrongly identified them. They are the kingdom of darkness and the kingdom of light. All nations are included in the first; only the kingdom of God comprises the second. Citizens of God's kingdom are in the world but not of the world. The writer of Hebrews calls us "strangers and pilgrims on the earth" (Hebrews 11:13). Peter likewise calls us "sojourners and pilgrims" (1 Peter 2:11). Therefore we owe our allegiance to no earthly kingdom.

When the church fails to live by the ethics of God's kingdom and embraces the ethics of a host country, it loses its prophetic voice and is no longer identifiable as an embassy of the kingdom. It becomes just another organization that supports nationalistic causes rather than an *ekklesia* standing for the good news of peace.

Conclusion

When government leaders listen to the great deluder rather than God, they advocate nationalism and its various expressions. Therefore, I don't expect to see national flags removed from pulpits or wars to cease anytime soon. By the world's standards they seem normal, but by kingdom standards they are misdirected. The Christian alternative to nationalism is allegiance to God's kingdom. The alternative to force is faith. Read Hebrews 11 and ponder how God rescued Noah from the flood, gave Abraham and Sarah a son beyond their childbearing years, opened the Red Sea for Israel's escape, and knocked down the walls of Jericho. If faith was important to the Old Testament saints, what about us? We must be the faith bearers of our time. At the consummation of the age, we will be vindicated for our stance against violence. The entire world will see that the meek indeed inherit the earth. The church, as a colony of heaven and an embassy of God's kingdom, must serve exclusively as God's representatives to the world.

Every local church and individual believer must make a choice. We can't serve two masters.

15

The Kingdom-Focused Church

*When He ascended on high, He led captivity
captive, and gave gifts to men.*

EPHESIANS 4:8

In the interim period between King Jesus's resurrection and his return, the kingdom of God finds expression in the local church. Churches in every locale are the *new* temples of God, where his glory resides and is experienced. Or at least they should be!

God's ultimate kingdom will one day envelop the earth. Creation will be renovated entirely to its pristine condition prior to the rebellion. Paradise lost will become paradise regained, perfect in every way. The problems we face today—recession, climate change, disease, pollution, drought, starvation, divorce, AIDS, human rights violations, sex trafficking, addictions, abortion, war, PTSD, terrorism, death, fraud, occultism, and every other disorder found in a fallen world—will be eliminated once for all. In the kingdom we will live in an unspoiled and peaceful environment, worship God without restraint or reservation, experience full and wholesome relationships with each other, and inhabit flawless bodies free of sin and guilt.

The most amazing thing about God's future kingdom is that his glory will reside there (Revelation 21:10-11,23). In Isaiah's prophetic vision, the seraphim cry out in antiphonal response, "Holy, holy, holy is the LORD of hosts; the whole earth is full of His glory!" (Isaiah 6:3).

The heavens declare his glory now (Psalm 19:1), but can you imagine his glory invading all space with no more shadows or shades of gray? His divine effulgence will brighten the entire earth!

God's Glory on Earth

God has always dwelt among his people in a temple or tabernacle (a "tent of meeting"). But his presence has never been limited to the temple alone. He surprisingly shows up in some strange places and to the most unsuspecting of people: in Ur of the Chaldeans (modern-day Iraq) to a pagan, in a burning bush to a wealthy murderer, and on a Damascus road to a religious persecutor. But despite these exceptional circumstances, God lives mainly among his people.

As we noted previously, Eden serves as the first temple. Here God walks and talks with the first humans. Likewise, God orders Moses to erect a tabernacle where his presence will reside among his people. David decides to build a permanent abode for God, a temple, which his son King Solomon completes and then dedicates.

> When Solomon had finished praying, fire came down from heaven and consumed the burnt offering and the sacrifices; and the glory of the LORD filled the temple. And the priests could not enter the house of the LORD, because the glory of the LORD had filled the LORD's house. When all the children of Israel saw how the fire came down, and the glory of the LORD on the temple, they bowed their faces to the ground on the pavement, and worshiped and praised the LORD (2 Chronicles 7:1-3; also see Ezekiel 8:4).

The temple becomes the house of God, his dwelling place. Here he lives and manifests his glory for Israel to see. When Israel eventually falls into disobedience and begins worshipping idols, God sends judgment on the land, and his glory departs (Ezekiel 10:4,18-19; 11:22-23). There is no evidence that God's presence ever returns to the temple after Israel's exile to Babylon.

At the time of Jesus, a bigger and better temple, the cornerstone of Jewish religious life, stands in Jerusalem. Despite its grandeur, the temple represents Rome's interests more than God's, and its priests are corrupt to the core. Jesus weeps over the city and cries, "See! Your house is left to you desolate" (Matthew 23:38). God has abandoned the temple, and Jesus identifies himself as the one who comes in the name of the Lord (verse 39). His cleansing of the temple is God's judgment on the nation.

God will now manifest his glory in Jesus, his Son. The apostle John writes of him, "The Word became flesh and dwelt among us, and we beheld His glory, the glory as of the only begotten of the Father, full of grace and truth" (John 1:14). Or as Young's Literal Translation renders it, "And the Word became flesh, and did *tabernacle* among us."

God's glory resides with Jesus. He is Immanuel, God with us. As the apostle Paul says, "God was in Christ" (2 Corinthians 5:19). "It pleased the Father that in Him all the fullness should dwell," and "in Him dwells all the fullness of the Godhead bodily" (Colossians 1:19; 2:9). Jesus becomes the new dwelling place of God. His body is God's tabernacle or house. When Jesus's life is threatened and he responds, "Destroy this temple, and in three days I will raise it up" (John 2:19), he is not speaking of the temple on Mount Zion. "He was speaking of the temple of His body" (verse 21).

But Jesus promises that after his ascension to the Father's right hand, he will send the Spirit of God to us.

> If you love Me, keep My commandments. And I will pray the Father, and He will give you another Helper, that He may abide with you forever—the Spirit of truth, whom the world cannot receive, because it neither sees Him nor knows Him; but you know Him, for He dwells with you and will be in you. I will not leave you orphans; I will come to you (John 14:15-18).

Paul writes, "You are...a holy temple in the Lord, in whom you also are being built together for a dwelling place of God in the Spirit" (Ephesians 2:19-22). "You are God's building...Do you not know that

you are the temple of God and that the Spirit of God dwells in you?"
(1 Corinthians 3:9,16).

Today the church is the dwelling place of God's end-time Spirit.
Therefore, shouldn't we experience his manifest presence in our midst?
Certainly we should experience it more than Israel of old did and more
like Jesus did when he walked the hills of Galilee. After all, the same
eschatological Spirit given to Jesus at his baptism was given to the church
at Pentecost. The Spirit indwelt Jesus's earthly body, and the Spirit
inhabits his new earthly body, the church.

If the assessment is correct that where the Spirit is, there is the
kingdom, then the reign of God on earth is presently displayed in
the church—not just any church, but in churches where the Spirit is
indeed present in a demonstrable way when the congregation comes
together. The kingdom is present to the degree that the Spirit moves
among his people. Simply believing in the presence of the Spirit in theory or as a doctrine is not enough. Let's face it—more than a few local
churches are devoid of the Spirit.

Kingdom-Focused Worship

From the book of Acts and the New Testament epistles we glean
bits and pieces of information that enable us to construct a composite
picture of how the first-century church might have worshipped. Some
texts provide us with specifics; others give only clues or hints. Worship services were not homogenous. For instance, the worship styles at
Corinth and Thessalonica were as different as night and day.

But we can say definitively that all *ekklesiai* participated in a full-
course banquet and symposium, a model that I believe can serve as a
dynamic pattern for modern-day worship as well.[1]

A Kingdom-Focused Feast

First, worship will be oriented around a full meal. That's what happened in the first churches. A church should be more like a dinner
club than a lecture hall with theater seating. God's people should come
together to eat. I find no evidence of a New Testament church ever
meeting without eating a meal. The early churches met weekly and

most likely in the evening. We may not recline on our left elbow in Greco-Roman style, but the table is still central to worship. It is where fellowship takes place and relationships develop and grow.

The meal can be held in a church hall or, in the case of a mega-church, in homes of members spread throughout the community, allowing for more relaxed and intimate gatherings. The meal can take the form of potluck, a dinner prepared in the church kitchen, or even a catered event.

A pastor, elder, or host opens the meal by breaking bread and distributing it to all present. Each person takes a piece. He then proclaims the words of Jesus: "This is my body which is given for you." He may offer an explanatory word and then invite all to eat. This officially begins the meal.

For the next hour or so a full meal is consumed. This is a joyous time.

When the meal is winding down, the leader pours a glass of wine or grape juice. The people do the same at their table. The leader then stands and lifts his cup, offering a toast or tribute to Jesus, and proclaims the words of Jesus, "This is my blood of the new covenant." He enjoins all to drink in honor of King Jesus, who is present at the meal (Revelation 3:20). This officially closes the meal proper and serves as a transition into the symposium or ministry portion of the meeting, which will last for another hour or so.

By eating together, all members get a foretaste of the kingdom banquet to come. They participate in a genuine kingdom activity.

Symposium Activities

The symposium or ministry time is an opportunity to experience God's presence and be used by him. If the church is the new temple of God, shouldn't we expect him to manifest his glory? Shouldn't we expect things out of the ordinary to occur?

The church at Corinth was the most carnal of all churches, but it was a kingdom church nevertheless. Its members, despite their fleshly excesses, experienced God's presence. God's Spirit moved throughout the congregation, ministering to and through them. As the apostle

Paul writes, "There are diversities of gifts, but the same Spirit. There are differences of ministries, but the same Lord. And there are diversities of activities, but it is the same God who works all in all. But the manifestation of the Spirit is given to each one for the profit of all" (1 Corinthians 12:4-7).

Here Paul speaks of three realities during worship:

- diversities of gifts, such as prophecy, healing, wisdom, and teaching
- differences of ministries, or service opportunities to use the gifts
- diversities of activities (Greek, *enérgema*), or levels of effectiveness

Each reality is related to a different divine personality: the same Spirit, same Lord, and same God, respectively. The fullness of the Godhead is involved in every aspect of ministry. Paul not only explains the workings of the Spirit in our midst but also provides a reason: "But the manifestation of the Spirit is given to each one *for the profit of all.*" It's for our benefit. Notice what it is exactly that profits us: "the manifestation of the Spirit." This refers to a demonstration or public display of the Spirit. When the Spirit moves and ministers in an unmistakable way, everyone notices and benefits.

What does this look like? How does the Spirit move in a congregation during the symposium hour?

When a kingdom-focused *ekklesia* draws together in a home or auditorium, it experiences a foretaste of glory divine, albeit a small taste in comparison to the fullness of God's glory to come. We have discussed in previous chapters the importance of preaching the gospel of the kingdom, the value of hearing God's voice, the availability of healing, and the necessity of discerning and expelling spirits. I won't repeat myself except to say we should expect ministries like these to occur. Add to this list the full range of gifts mentioned in Romans 12:6-8; 1 Corinthians 12–14; Ephesians 4:11; and 1 Peter 4:11, which include words of wisdom, words of knowledge, faith, miracles, tongues, interpretation of tongues, serving, teaching, exhortation, giving, leadership, mercy, helps, administration, and the offices of apostle, prophet, evangelist, and pastor-teacher.

This is not an exhaustive list, but it's representative of some of the ways the Spirit ministered to the saints in the first century. My point is simply this: We should expect the Spirit to use us in similar fashion when we come together.

Each gift reflects some aspect of the future kingdom. These are the benefits, the blessings God has for us. Does God speak in the future kingdom? You can hear him speak now! Will you be healthy and whole in the kingdom to come? You can experience the same now! Will you stand in awe of God's majesty? He wants you to worship his majesty now! Will your hunger be satisfied when the new age arrives? You are invited to eat at his table now! Will evil spirits abide in God's future kingdom? Get rid of them now! Will you harbor doubt in God's ability in the ultimate kingdom? Let faith reign in your heart now!

Will sin be present when the kingdom comes to earth? Exhort and discipline those who sin now! Will you enter God's final kingdom as a recipient of grace and mercy? Extend grace and mercy to others now! Will you be deprived of any need when the fullness of the kingdom arrives? Give generously to others in need now! Will anyone be treated as a second-class citizen in God's future kingdom? Treat everyone as an equal now! Will God's kingdom be rife with racism? Embrace peoples of all kindred, tribes, and tongues now! Will order abound then? Make sure things are done decently and in order now!

Whenever the church meets, its members should experience a little bit of heaven on earth.

This is a call to transform your congregation into a kingdom-focused church, where the kingdom of God sets the agenda for all church affairs. When we live as a community of the King and for the King, the way we do ministry changes. We will all know the blessings of the kingdom because we all serve the King. In ministering to one another, all receive the benefits.

But what if we invite and even expect God to manifest himself in our meetings, and nothing happens? What if we pray for a healing or ask God to break the bondage of drug addiction, and heaven is silent? What then?

If you believe in God, you believe in miracles! To believe otherwise is an oxymoron. Yet God is not a genie in a bottle who serves at our beck and call. We don't use his name as a magic incantation or expect him to show up at our command. He is the King, whom we worship. We gather, pray, and invite him to manifest himself because this is what he instructs us to do. The Scripture attests to his desire to live and move among his people now as he has throughout history. In fact, he desires to do so more now than before he gave us his end-time Spirit.

When we do not sense his presence and our prayers are not answered, we should continue to engage in all the other kingdom-related ministries. We should also persist in asking God to demonstrate his power in our midst. He will answer in due season.

No special formula or recipe can guarantee a healing or miracle, but some components are present whenever the supernatural occurs in Old Testament or New Testament times. I will mention briefly three necessary ingredients. The first is faith. We must believe God can and will heal or intervene on our behalf.

Second, we must be obedient. Under the old covenant, miracles are part of the "blessings and curses" contract between God and his people: "If you diligently heed the voice of the LORD your God and do what is right in His sight, give ear to His commandments and keep all His statutes, I will put none of the diseases on you which I have brought on the Egyptians. For I am the LORD who heals you" (Exodus 15:26). Obedience is a key to healing as well as other blessings under the old covenant (see Deuteronomy 28:1-14), and it is just as relevant under the new covenant. The person who lives according to Christ's kingdom standards is the blessed one (Matthew 5:3-11).

Third, we must listen for the Voice. When I speak of the Voice, I refer to God communicating with us through the Spirit at the level of subconscious thoughts or impressions gleaned from the Scripture. These communications are then conveyed aloud for the benefit of the congregation. We are often afraid to speak out in this way, assuming we are expressing the thoughts of our own mind. And we are, but they are thoughts that God gives us. Paul advises, "Let two or three prophets speak, and let the others judge" (1 Corinthians 14:29).

This is how ministry was done in the first century, and it will work today, especially in countries that don't allow people to minister outside the walls of the church.

When the church functions variously as a voluntary association of the King, a colony of heaven, and an embassy of the kingdom of God, it represents God's government and operates as an alternative to the government of the state where it is found. People will quickly see a difference between the way God and his people act and the way their own government and people act.

Other Symposium Ministries

Loving Outsiders

Let's wrap our arms of love around orphans, widows, prostitutes, alcoholics, drug addicts, the poor, resident aliens...all those who are marginalized and disenfranchised. Let's help them get on their feet, invite them to our meal, and allow them to be touched by the glory of God, which shows up when we gather. Let's bring them into the kingdom of God, where their lives can be transformed and their needs can be met.

Reaching the Lost

Like embassies, our churches should be places where desperate citizens of this world can seek refuge and asylum.

In explaining the advantage of speaking God's Word in the language of the people and not in tongues, Paul writes, "If...an unbeliever or an uninformed person comes in, he is convinced by all, he is convicted by all. And thus the secrets of his heart are revealed; and so, falling down on his face, he will worship God and report that God is truly among you" (1 Corinthians 14:24-25). Here Paul speaks of the potential power of an intelligible word to produce conversion.

Notice the progression. An unbeliever (one who is uninformed about kingdom things) attends the banquet and symposium. A Spirit-empowered utterance is given, and it pricks his heart. His heart is laid open like a book. Finally, he prostrates himself, worships God, and declares, "God is truly among you."

What could be more dramatic and exciting than this? Is this how unbelievers who visit our churches respond? Why not? Paul seems to expect things like this to happen in kingdom-focused churches. When was the last time you saw a sinner on his face, crying out for forgiveness, raising holy hands to the Lord, having experienced a manifestation of God?

The Ministry of Gifted Men

Christ gives one or more spiritual gifts to every believer to use when the church gathers, and he endows some with abilities to perform special ministries. We read about this in Paul's letter to the church at Ephesus.

> But to each one of us grace was given according to the measure of Christ's gift. Therefore He says:
>
> "When He ascended on high,
> He led captivity captive,
> And gave gifts to men" (Ephesians 4:7-8).

A few verses later Paul adds, "And He Himself gave some to be apostles, some prophets, some evangelists, and some pastors and teachers." The Greek text doesn't indicate whether the people themselves are the gifts or if they are the recipients of the gifts. Either way, God places certain gifted people in the church for special ministry purposes.

In verses 7-8 Paul is quoting Psalm 68:18, which describes a king winning a battle, bringing the captives home, and distributing the spoils of battle to the citizens of his kingdom. The apostle applies this imagery to Jesus, casting him as a King who defeats God's enemies, rescues the prisoners of war, and ascends his throne, from whence he distributes gifts. Thus the gifts flow from the throne of the exalted King Jesus. They are kingdom gifts and are depicted as the Victor's spoils, which Christ won in the battle of the ages on the cross. When we use our gifts, we share in the victory.

Now let's look at the five gifted persons. The first are apostles, but these are not apostles in the same sense as the original Twelve, who have a unique place in the foundation of the church and the restoration of Israel. These are *post-ascension* apostles, sent out by the local church as pioneer missionaries and church planters. Their office did not come into existence prior to the giving of the Spirit on Pentecost.

Likewise, the prophets mentioned here are not Old Testament prophets like Ezekiel and Jeremiah, who wrote Scripture and spoke on behalf of God to the entire nation of Israel. These are *post-ascension* prophets who minister in the local churches and speak for God to their congregations. Their ministry is limited in scope and design. Their words are fallible and need to be judged for authenticity.

The evangelists are heralds of the good news of the kingdom. Philip, a deacon in the Jerusalem church, is called an evangelist. An evangelist knows how to reach people for Christ and lead them into the local church.

Pastors and teachers pour their lives into local congregations, shepherding and instructing the people.

Paul then explains that the exalted Lord empowers these individuals and gives them to the church...

> for the equipping of the saints for the work of ministry, for
> the edifying of the body of Christ, till we all come to the
> unity of the faith and of the knowledge of the Son of God,
> to a perfect man, to the measure of the stature of the full-
> ness of Christ (Ephesians 4:12-13).

They are tasked with equipping or training the believers and with edifying them, or building them up. The offices are meant to exist until believers attain complete unity, a well-developed understanding of Jesus as God's Messiah, and a full maturity as a body of believers.

Finally, Paul gives a purpose statement: "that we should no longer be children" (verse 14), or vulnerable to deception and living like unregenerate Gentiles who lie, lust, covet, steal, and hate. Rather we must live by the principles of holiness and love one another (verses 15-32).

The people who function in these five ways are responsible to the exalted King to fulfill their assigned tasks of transforming the *ekklesia* into a well-functioning kingdom society.

Reading the Scriptures

Another weekly symposium practice was the reading aloud from the Hebrew Bible, the apostles' letters, and the Gospels. Nearly all the epistles are addressed to a local *ekklesia* or group of *ekklesiai* and are to be read openly in front of the entire church.[2] For instance, Paul writes this to the church at Colossae:

> Greet the brethren who are in Laodicea, and Nymphas and the church that is in his house. Now when this epistle is read among you, see that it is read also in the church of the Laodiceans, and that you likewise read the epistle from Laodicea (Colossians 4:15-16).

Likewise, he exhorts the believers at Thessalonica, "Greet all the brethren with a holy kiss. I charge you by the Lord that this epistle be read to all the holy brethren" (1 Thessalonians 5:26-27).

Some circular letters were intended to be distributed and read in several churches. These writings address various issues churches face as they attempt to represent the kingdom of God in an empire that claims the right of manifest destiny as its own. When analyzing these letters, we discover them to be as political as they are spiritual because they challenge Caesar's title as Lord, they speak of Jesus as a King, and they look forward to a kingdom that will spell the demise of all other kingdoms, including Rome.

Paul admonishes Timothy, the leader at Ephesus, "Till I come, give attention to reading" (1 Timothy 4:13). Certain portions of the Old Testament, which carry messianic overtones, were of particular interest to the churches. Isaiah 2, 7, 11, 53–55, 61–66; Psalms 2, 8, 24, 45, 72, 110; Ezekiel 36–40; and similar passages were likely read more than others.

Lest we forget, Jesus's first act of ministry was a public reading from the scroll of Isaiah 61:1-2. Jesus, our King, read the Scriptures aloud and then explained their meaning from the perspective of the kingdom of God, so this should be a part of every kingdom-focused church service today.

Praying

Luke tells us the 3000 converts on Pentecost "continued steadfastly in the apostles' doctrine [teaching] and fellowship, in the breaking of bread, and in prayers" (Acts 2:42). This verse is descriptive of a typical Christian-style banquet, with prayer as one of the symposium components.

When one of Jesus's disciples asks, "Lord teach us to pray," Jesus provides a model that is kingdom centered, opposes Roman ideology, and asks heaven's blessings to come on earth. When we analyze the words carefully, we notice how political it is.

> So He said to them, "When you pray, say:
>
>> Our Father in heaven,
>> Hallowed be Your name.
>> Your kingdom come.
>> Your will be done
>> On earth as it is in heaven.
>> Give us day by day our daily bread.
>> And forgive us our sins,
>> For we also forgive everyone who is indebted to us.
>> And do not lead us into temptation,
>> But deliver us from the evil one" (Luke 11:2-4).

The prayer is addressed to the God of Israel as Father. The Romans prayed to Jupiter, whom they conceived to be their heavenly father. To ask the living God that his will be done on earth is a request that supplants Jupiter's reign and Rome's right to rule on his behalf. If the Christian God's will is done, Rome falls.

The call for God to provide daily bread is a direct rejection of the Roman system of patronage. The mention of debt forgiveness challenges the entire economic structure of Rome, which seeks to keep everyone in debt and thus control them. The cry to be delivered from the evil one may refer to Caesar or to Satan, the power behind Caesar's throne. In either case, it is a call for political deliverance.

The point is clear: Genuine prayer is kingdom-oriented prayer. Kingdom citizens look to God alone as their patron and to his kingdom alone to sustain them.

As God answers our requests, we experience here and now a foretaste of the kingdom to come. Heaven's blessings are God's response to our prayers.

Quite frankly, many of our churches lack heaven's blessings because they no longer devote the time necessary to prayer. Many churches have abandoned congregational prayer and even the pastoral prayer. When was the last time your pastor and the congregation spent a sustained amount of time in corporate prayer? As a youngster, I watched the pastor of my Methodist church get down on his knees each Sunday and pour his heart out to God on behalf of his people. Reverend Willard Sylvester was not a great preacher, but he was a mighty pray-er. Even as a 12-year-old, I knew he was a man of God.

The prayer life of the typical church in the West is anemic at best. The weekly evening prayer meeting has gone the way of the dinosaur or has been replaced by programs for children and youth. And when we finally get around to praying, we focus on everything but the things of the kingdom. We are more concerned about Jack's back, Jane's pain, and Joe's toe rather than about the kingdom coming to earth.

Now is the time for pastors and the laity alike to transform their congregations into kingdom-driven churches. A good place to start is with prayer.

Church Discipline

The church will also use the symposium to handle matters of church discipline. When baptized citizens of the kingdom-focused church consistently choose to live according to the principles of the world rather than ethics of the kingdom, they must be confronted, encouraged, and helped to submit to the authority of King Jesus. If they refuse all advice and assistance and still wish to persist in their ungodly ways, the church officers must take disciplinary action. Just as in any colony, citizens must live within certain standard moral boundaries, or they are separated from society. An ambassador who breaks the laws of his nation or embarrasses his government is removed from office. In all voluntary associations, rules must be obeyed and dues paid. Members who refuse to abide by the rules are expelled.

The church is the community of the King. It is a holy nation set amid other nations, demonstrating an alternative way to live. When its citizens choose to ignore or defiantly disobey their kingdom's constitution, they harm the cause of Christ. In such cases church leaders must follow the protocol established by King Jesus in Matthew 18:15-17.

> Moreover if your brother sins against you, go and tell him his fault between you and him alone. If he hears you, you have gained your brother. But if he will not hear, take with you one or two more, that "by the mouth of two or three witnesses every word may be established." And if he refuses to hear them, tell it to the church. But if he refuses even to hear the church, let him be to you like a heathen and a tax collector.

Every reasonable effort must be made to restore sinners (Galatians 6:1), but if they continually refuse correction, the only action left is to send them out from the presence of God (see Deuteronomy 17:7; 19:19; 22:21,24; 24:7). They must not be allowed admittance to the community meal, where believers participate in kingdom life.

> I wrote to you in my epistle *not to keep company* with sexually immoral people. Yet I certainly did not mean with the sexually immoral people of this world, or with the covetous, or extortioners, or idolaters, since then you would need to go out of the world. But now I have written to you *not to keep company* with anyone named a brother, who is sexually immoral, or covetous, or an idolater, or a reviler, or a drunkard, or an extortioner—*not even to eat with such a person.*
>
> For what have I to do with judging those also who are outside? Do you not judge those who are inside? But those

who are outside God judges. Therefore *"put away from yourselves the evil person"* (1 Corinthians 5:9-13).

After spending a chapter and a half exhorting another church to live righteously and in unity of the faith, Paul instructs, "Reject a divisive man after the first and second admonition, knowing that such a person is warped and sinning, being self-condemned" (Titus 3:10-11).

To the Thessalonians Paul exhorts, "We command you, brethren, in the name of our Lord Jesus Christ, that you withdraw from every brother who walks disorderly and not according to the tradition which he received from us" (2 Thessalonians 3:6). He then speaks specifically about the person who shirks employment but desires to join in the congregational meal.

> Even when we were with you, we commanded you this: If anyone will not work, neither shall he eat. For we hear that there are some who walk among you in a disorderly manner, not working at all, but are busybodies. Now those who are such we command and exhort through our Lord Jesus Christ that they work in quietness and eat their own bread.
>
> But as for you, brethren, do not grow weary in doing good. And if anyone does not obey our word in this epistle, note that person and *do not keep company with him*, that he may be ashamed. Yet do not count him as an enemy, but admonish him as a brother (2 Thessalonians 3:10-15).

Notice that even after the separation is effectuated, we must still admonish the sinning brother to come to his senses.

Why does a kingdom-focused church engage in church discipline? Among other reasons, discipline is a testimony that God's kingdom consists of citizens who are obedient to their King and serve each other. It is a kingdom worthy to investigate and to join.

Like all kingdom undertakings, church discipline is political. After all, it is a kingdom act. Imagine the impact we could have on the world if all churches lived in accordance with the rules of God's government. Stanley Hauerwas, named "America's Best Theologian" by

Time Magazine in 2001, gives a vivid example of the potential power of church discipline. He asks what would have happened had former President Bill Clinton's church in Arkansas started church discipline proceedings, pointing out that although the federal government might not care about his affair with Monica Lewinsky, the government of God operates differently.[3] Had such occurred, President Clinton would have been summoned to stand before the church, hear the charges, and either repent or not. Without doubt, within a short time it would be evident whether he wanted to follow the Voice or continue to obey another voice. I can imagine him humbling himself before the Lord. If so, this might have sparked a nationwide revival!

To be fair, we can substitute Bill Clinton's name with that of any other public or private figure who takes the name of Christ but chooses to live outside the will of God.

When the local church practices church discipline, it not only points to the purity that will be found in God's future kingdom but also demonstrates what it is like to live under the reign of God now. In doing so it offers an alternative way of life that will attract the attention of others and eventually bring them into the kingdom of God.

I don't mean to paint a picture of local churches as severe and unforgiving. I doubt that discipline will be a weekly event. People who want to live like the devil but call themselves Christians are not likely to join a kingdom-focused church. And of those sincere believers who happen to fall into a pattern of sin, most will likely receive a rebuke and stop or be eventually restored and forgiven. The problem is not with congregations that take seriously church discipline, but the vast majority that do not—those that allow sin to run rampant and yet boast in their numerical growth. Paul addresses a church like this.

> Your glorying is not good. Do you not know that a little leaven leavens the whole lump? Therefore purge out the old leaven, that you may be a new lump, since you truly are unleavened. For indeed Christ, our Passover, was sacrificed for us (1 Corinthians 5:6-7).

Worship

All Roman associational meetings featured singing during the symposium portion of a formal supper. The first-century church followed suit, singing hymns, psalms, spiritual songs, and praises to the Lord (1 Corinthians 14:26; Ephesians 5:19; James 5:13). Some of the more famous are found in Philippians 2:6-11, Colossians 1:15-20, and 1 Timothy 3:16. If you turn to those songs in your New Testament, you will discover they are all kingdom centered. Worship is the ultimate in our participation in the kingdom here and now. In the Lord's Prayer, Jesus asks, "Your kingdom come. Your will be done on earth as it is in heaven." The book of Revelation discloses that in heaven, people and angels worship God in all his majesty. This is their occupation. When we worship, we are doing God's will on earth as it is in heaven.

Worship is an intricate component of a kingdom-focused church. Does most worship in the average church reflect heavenly worship? Robert Coleman's book *Songs of Heaven* offers us a glimpse into heavenly worship and calls us to follow suit on earth.[4]

God is not so much interested in the volume of worship, or its style (contemporary rock, praise and worship, or hymns), or whether it's led by a song leader or a praise team, or whether it's accompanied by instruments or sung a cappella. He is concerned about our motivation for worshipping him. He desires worship that comes from hearts filled with love and gratitude toward him for rescuing us out the present evil age and transferring us into the kingdom of his Son. He also desires worship that is singularly focused on him.

Let's be honest. If you look around the sanctuary this Sunday, many churchgoers will not be worshipping at all. Their minds are on the things of the world. Have you ever wondered why? We all know what God requires, so why is our worship so meager? Suppose what might happen if God suddenly and unexpectedly showed up and his glory moved across the auditorium like a fog sweeping in from the ocean, a presence so real that it could be felt. If everyone was touched by God's holiness and sensed his majesty, do you think their response might be different?

Here's the point. People in heaven worship God because they are in his presence. Their worship is not forced. They worship in response to his majesty. In a kingdom-focused church where God is allowed to move freely, worship will follow naturally. This is a little taste of heaven on earth.

Conclusion

As a Christianized voluntary association, the church participated in a full meal and symposium. But instead of honoring Caesar and the Roman gods with libations and upholding Rome's agenda of *Pax Romana*, believers lifted a cup to Jesus as Lord and to Yahweh, the God of Israel, proclaiming that true peace comes to earth only with the arrival of God's kingdom. Therefore, in the first century all worship was political, and by the Empire's standards, subversive!

Because Christians met behind closed doors, their pro-kingdom-of-God and anti-imperial activities flew for the most part under the Roman radar. However, if a Roman official or native Jewish retainer ever found out what Christians were actually doing and teaching, the full wrath of the law might fall on them.

Imagine the following scene. A first-century pagan on her way to the market passes by the open window of a home where followers of Jesus are gathered. She happens to look inside and sees people reclining and enjoying what looks like a typical Roman meal. The diners are having a good time as they eat, drink mixed wine, sing, and engage in lively discussions. Nothing seems out of the ordinary.

However, what if she decides to hide in the bushes and eavesdrop? She quickly discovers the participants are involved in subversive activities. They do not pour out a libation to a Roman deity or acknowledge Jupiter and Caesar as their patrons. She also notices that the banqueters cross all socioeconomic lines, with peasants and landowners sitting around the same table in defiance of the accepted social structure of the Empire. Listening to their hymns, she is shocked to find them singing of their allegiance to another kingdom and a different Lord. And when their teacher stands up and renounces Rome, her jaw drops open and her heart skips a beat.

But if she should linger a bit longer, she might witness an extraordinary manifestation of God's glory as members utter prophecies, sing
Spirit-inspired songs, pray for the sick, exhort sinners, encourage the
suffering, read letters and Scriptures, and proclaim the good news of
the kingdom. As she watches, an alcoholic neighbor falls to his knees
begging for help and is raised a new man praising God. A crippled
woman whom she recognizes is healed and stands to her feet. Witnessing firsthand the supernatural move of the Spirit, she decides not to
report the group to the authorities, but knocks on the door and seeks
entrance for herself.

This is what a kingdom-focused church looked like in the first century. This is what God wants the church to be today. Wherever believers are found—in Russia, Egypt, Nigeria, Cuba, Iran, or the United
States—they can experience heavenly blessings *now* as they gather as a
community of the kingdom.

16

Heaven on Earth—
the Ultimate Kingdom

*The kingdom of the world has become the kingdom of our
Lord and of his Messiah, and he will reign forever and ever.*

REVELATION 11:15

In 1516 Sir Thomas More, the Lord Chancellor of England under
Henry VIII and later named a saint by the Catholic Church, wrote
a book called *Utopia* about a mythical island paradise where society is
perfectly ordered, nature is totally balanced, and everyone shares equal
status and communal ownership of property. *Utopia* was More's literary attempt to contrast the oppressive sociopolitical environment of
his day to the ideal civilization for which he longed.

With its civil liberties and freedom of religion, America has served
as a venue for many utopian communities. One of the best known
was the Shakers, led by the eccentric Ann Lee, known as the "Mother
of the new creation," who settled the group in Albany County, New
York, in 1774. The Shakers spread their doctrine of pure egalitarianism, regardless of gender, social class, or education throughout New
England, eventually forming 20 utopian societies comprised of disciples who committed themselves to a life of celibacy and simplicity.
Unable to sustain their idealism, the communities eventually dwindled,

and today there are fewer than a dozen persons who claim the name Shakers.

Utopian religious communities have come and gone, yet the concept of utopia still captures the human imagination. From President Lyndon Johnson's Great Society to libertarian Ayn Rand's "perfect man," John Galt, a desire for something that transcends the ordinary remains an ever-present hope. One day this hope will become a reality.

The Bible teaches that God's goal for the world and his people is to locate the kingdom of God on earth. In the book of Revelation, the apostle John writes about this vision for the future. You can feel the emotion in his words.

> Then the seventh angel blew his trumpet, and there were loud voices in heaven, saying,
>
> > "The kingdom of the world has become the kingdom of
> > our Lord
> > and of his Messiah,
> > and he will reign forever and ever."
>
> Then the twenty-four elders who sit on their thrones before God fell on their faces and worshiped God, singing,
>
> > "We give you thanks, Lord God Almighty,
> > who are and who were,
> > for you have taken your great power
> > and begun to reign.
> > The nations raged,
> > but your wrath has come,
> > and the time for judging the dead,
> > for rewarding your servants, the prophets
> > and saints and all who fear your name,
> > both small and great,
> > and for destroying those who destroy the earth"
> > (Revelation 11:15-18).

A few chapters later, John portrays in picturesque language the beauty of the kingdom and the blessings that will be ours.

> Then I saw a new heaven and a new earth; for the first
> heaven and the first earth had passed away, and the sea was
> no more. And I saw the holy city, the new Jerusalem, com-
> ing down out of heaven from God, prepared as a bride
> adorned for her husband (Revelation 21:1-2).

Here we see utopia becoming a reality. But unlike man-made utopian communities that fail when they succumb to human nature, the
kingdom of God will last forever because it is divinely crafted and
maintained. It will not and cannot fail.

When examining the text above, we notice several things. First, we
see that the original creation ("the first heaven and the first earth") will
cease to exist. "Heaven" in this passage refers to the stratosphere and
includes the sun, moon, and stars, whereas "earth" refers to the terra
firma with its various life-forms and human structures and inventions.
We commonly use the words "passed away" to speak of death. John
forecasts the demise of creation as we know it.

Second, we discover that this present world is replaced by a new,
reconfigured world. Just as you might toss out or exchange an old tat-
tered garment for a new one, so God replaces the old world—no longer
fit for habitation—with the new. The present world, which is soiled by
the vestiges of sin, groans in agony as it waits the future day of redemption (Romans 8:22-24).

Third, we discover that the sea also disappears and is not replaced.
In Bible times the sea was a dangerous place. Throughout Scriptures,
it represents chaos (Genesis 1). Chaos will have no place in God's new
kingdom. Orderliness will rule the day. The sea can also represent separation. John was exiled on the isle of Patmos, so the sea separated him
from his friends and loved ones. On the new earth there will be no
separation.

Fourth, our attention is drawn to a city identified as the new Jerusalem, which replaces Jerusalem of old. The entirety of Revelation 21
and a portion of Revelation 22 focus on the new Jerusalem. Since this
will be our home for eternity, we should learn as much about it as we
can. Let's take a closer look at this city.

A new city. We all like new things. Have you ever visited a city whose downtown has been completely renovated? There are dazzling fountains with reflecting pools, lots of green spaces with plenty of shade trees and seating, curio shops and unique eateries, and even strolling musicians or bandstand entertainers. Music fills the air, and everything feels bright and fresh. People are carefree as they take in the sights or sip a latte at a sidewalk café.

I imagine the new Jerusalem will be such a place. It will be a city that remains eternally new and never grows old or tiresome. Imagine yourself strolling down the streets of the city, praising God for its beauty and never getting bored. What an exciting place to live! Within a few seconds of entering the new Jerusalem, you'll forget how the old world looked before the divine renovation. Its gloom and despair will be things of the past.

A consecrated city. John uses the word "holy," which means hallowed or sacred. It is a city consecrated for God. During New Testament times, Jerusalem was not a very nice place to live. The Roman Empire oppressed God's people, and the Jewish leaders entered into an unholy alliance with Rome and did its bidding by collecting tribute and taxes for Caesar. In Revelation 11:8 the apostle John likens old Jerusalem to "Sodom and Egypt, where also their Lord was crucified." Not a very positive description! Sodom was the center of the worst kinds of sin and rebellion against God. Egypt was a tyrannical kingdom that enslaved God's people. The old Jerusalem that once served Caesar and Rome will be replaced by a holy city where everyone honors and serves God. The Jerusalem of the future will be unlike any other place on earth—at least anyplace built by human hands. It will be pure and will reflect God's glory.

A beautiful city. John also describes the new Jerusalem as "a bride adorned for her husband." We've all attended weddings. What could be more beautiful than a bride? As the bridal march begins, all eyes are on the bride, followed by "oohs" and "aahs" and comments like "She looks so lovely" and "Isn't she beautiful?" Very few guests look at the father of the bride or the preacher. The bride is the center of attention.

The new Jerusalem will be the crown jewel of God's new creation. Its beauty will be unsurpassed.

A heavenly city. The old Jerusalem was occupied originally by Canaanites and tainted by idolatry. Israel had to drive out the heathen and destroy their idols. Not so with the heavenly city, which originates with God. It has never been tainted. The apostle Paul calls it the Jerusalem above (Galatians 4:26). It has been God's dwelling place and a home for the angels and for spirits of those made righteous. The author of Hebrews tells us that Abraham and his descendants actually yearned to see it for themselves. "He looked forward to the city that has foundations, whose architect and builder is God" (Hebrews 11:10). If you are one of God's children, you will be a citizen of the new Jerusalem.

A descending city. People often take trips to distant cities for business or pleasure, but I have never heard of a distant city coming to them! John sees "the new Jerusalem, coming down out of heaven from God." The writer of Hebrews speaks in similar language. "For here we have no lasting city, but we are looking for the city that is to come" (13:14). One day, heaven will come down to us. Wow!

So often, when people grow old or face a terminal illness, they express a desire to go to heaven. We all understand their attitude. They are tired of living in broken or diseased bodies and a run-down world. But these sentiments are shortsighted at best. God has so much more in store for believers than going to heaven as disembodied spirits. Heaven is not your destiny. Life after death is only transitory. It is an intermediate state, a temporary stop on your way to your ultimate destination. It would be like flying from Dallas to New York City but having a layover in Little Rock, Arkansas. Little Rock is a nice place, but it is not New York City! You want to see the bright lights of Broadway and Times Square, take in a show, visit the Statue of Liberty and the Empire State Building, and maybe dine at Delmonico's or shop at Saks Fifth Avenue. With such expectations, I doubt the port of Little Rock would rattle your cage.

God's ultimate goal is not for us to go to heaven but for heaven to come down to us on earth! In our new resurrected bodies, we will experience the fullness of God's blessings. The mere anticipation of such an exciting place makes me want to shout for joy. How about you?

You Ain't Seen Nothin' Yet

Next, the apostle John hears a heavenly announcement that must have unsettled him.

And I heard a loud voice from the throne saying,

"See, the home ["tabernacle," NKJV] of God is among mortals.
He will dwell with them;
they will be his peoples,
and God himself will be with them" (Revelation 21:3).

What an amazing declaration! Not only does the new Jerusalem descend to earth, but God himself comes down as well. This is God's ultimate goal. He wants to live permanently with us on earth. By the way, this has always been his desire. In the garden of Eden, for example, God walked and talked with Adam and Eve. He manifested his presence. They knew him in a real and literal way. Even after he expelled them from paradise, he didn't abandon them or their offspring.

God continually expressed his desire to live among his people. God instructed Moses to build a tabernacle where he could dwell. As the 12 tribes trekked across the wilderness, they encamped around the tabernacle—three tribes to the north, three to the east, three to the south, and three to the west—and God was in their midst.

Likewise, when David planned a house for God and Solomon built and dedicated it, God came down from heaven and made it his abode, again living among his people.

The New Testament tells how God came to earth in the form of a man. Christ was "Emmanuel, (which means 'God with us')." The apostle John writes, "And the Word became flesh and lived [literally, "tabernacled"] among us, and we have seen his glory" (John 1:14).

After his death and resurrection, Jesus poured out the Spirit of God, and the church became the new temple, where God lives. Whenever the church gathers, God is in the center of the activities. Unfortunately, many congregations do not recognize or welcome his presence.

And finally, God lives in the body of each believer. The apostle Paul says our bodies are temples or homes of the Holy Spirit.

The testimony is clear and conclusive. God has always lived among his people but only in a temporary way. The prophets, however, foretold of a day when God would descend from heaven to live permanently on earth (Ezekiel 37; Zechariah 2:10). The ultimate fulfillment of this takes place in Revelation. The kingdom of heaven will be on earth!

The Kingdom Defined Negatively

In order to describe one thing we must sometimes contrast it to another. The voice emanating from the throne does this very thing when it tells John what the kingdom of God on earth will be like.

> He will wipe every tear from their eyes.
> Death will be no more;
> mourning and crying and pain will be no more,
> for the first things have passed away (Revelation 21:4).

Sometimes negatives are good. This is a case in point. To start with, there will be no more crying. In our present world, tears are a fact of life. We cry when we are injured, sad, frightened, and emotionally vulnerable. Medical research has shown that tears help us cope in these distressful situations. Tears are both a psychological response and a chemical reaction to stress. They remove toxins that our bodies produce when we experience anxiety and trauma. But when heaven comes to earth, we won't need tears because we will never again experience stress or suffering.

Best of all, there will be no more dying. Death will take flight along with the things that accompany it, including mourning and pain. Funerals and grief will be things of the past. You'll never again stand before an open grave as the casket of your best friend, spouse, or child is lowered into the cold earth. I will never have to deliver a eulogy or comfort a heartbroken saint in the new Jerusalem.

What a drastic change from the world in which we now live! No more ambulances, hospitals, AIDS wards, or ICUs. No more canes or walkers, pacemakers, or defibrillators. No more throbbing migraines, agonizing labor pangs, or nausea from chemotherapy. No more artificial hips or knees, and no more war heroes having to use prostheses. Cancer, heart disease, lupus, diabetes, and blindness will be eliminated. We will bask in the continual presence of the eternal God, whose life will permeate the universe. We will be whole persons, just as God intended before sin entered the world. I look forward to the day when heaven comes to earth and utopia begins. I hope you do too.

God's Guarantee

When a Men's Wearhouse commercial comes on TV, I usually watch it until the end because I want to hear George Zimmer say, "I guarantee it!" There is something about a guarantee. When a man's word becomes his bond, you have certainty about the matter at hand. To assure us that the kingdom of heaven will come to earth and be as great as described in the book of Revelation, the apostle John records these words from the exalted Lord: "See, I am making all things new… Write this, for these words are trustworthy and true" (Revelation 21:5).

George Zimmer's guarantee is good up to a point, but God offers an even better surety. Unlike a suit of clothes, which eventually grows old and wears out, the world God has in store for us remains perpetually new. It will surpass our greatest expectations and wildest imaginations. We have God's word on it! Then God adds, "It is done! I am the Alpha and the Omega, the beginning and the end" (verse 6).

The victorious shout translated "It is done!" is found only in two other places in the New Testament. The first falls from the lips of Jesus on the cross when he pronounces pardon for sinners (John 19:30). The second occurs when an angel announces punishment on the wicked world (Revelation 16:17). The third time comes here, when God declares that paradise will arrive on earth.

Interestingly, all three exclamations are made in advance of the reality. These are prophetic flash-forwards that speak of future events as if they had already occurred. For example, Jesus declares pardon is done before he actually dies on the cross for sins. Likewise, the last two pronouncements, the angelic and the divine respectively, are made before the fact. John received his visions more than 1900 years ago. Final judgment is still being held in abeyance, and heaven has not yet come to earth. But God, "the Alpha and the Omega, the beginning and the end," not only conceives the plan but will bring it to completion. The future is as good as if it already happened. You can count on it!

Before moving on, John includes these words from Jesus: "To the thirsty I will give water as a gift from the spring of the water of life. Those who conquer will inherit these things, and I will be their God and they will be my children" (Revelation 21:6-7). He not only promises a new world but also provides the eternal sustenance needed to live in such an amazing environment. This elixir of life—the water of life—emanates from an eternal spring and is given to us as a gift. Do you remember when Jesus said to the woman at the well, "If you knew the gift of God, and who it is that is saying to you, 'Give me a drink,' you would have asked him, and he would have given you living water" (John 4:10)? She may not have completely understood his offer, but she said, "Sir, give me this water" (verse 15). That was the start of her journey on the road to the kingdom.

Jesus adds, "Those who conquer will inherit these things" (Revelation 21:7). We are inheritors of God's kingdom because we are God's children. My wife, along with her brothers and sisters, recently received a small inheritance from her father's estate. He didn't leave our next-door neighbors anything because they were not related to him. Only those who have a relationship with God through Christ will inherit the kingdom. This is why it is so important that each of us is certain we have a personal relationship with God.

Here Comes the Bride

In the next section of Revelation, John offers more exciting details about the kingdom of God. He writes, "Then one of the seven angels who had the seven bowls full of the seven last plagues came and said to me, 'Come, I will show you the bride, the wife of the Lamb'" (Revelation 21:9). In this visionary scene, John has an encounter with an angel whom he has met once before. This same angel had taken him to a wilderness to view another woman, a harlot who enticed the masses in the

Roman Empire to commit spiritual fornication by practicing idolatry (Revelation 17:1-6). Everyone throughout the Empire was expected to offer sacrifices and libations to the Roman gods and to the divine Caesar, and refusal to do so was considered unpatriotic at least and subversive at worst.

In this vision the angel promises to show John another woman who is identified as a bride and a wife. We are not told the significance of this imagery. Possibly the angel is contrasting her with the harlot of Revelation 17. A bride is pure and beautiful, and a wife is intimate and faithful to her spouse, but a harlot is faithless and filthy and diseased. The angel also reveals the identity of the bride's husband—the Lamb, an image of the crucified and risen Messiah.

Expecting to see a bride, John must be surprised by what he sees next.

> And in the spirit he carried me away to a great, high mountain and showed me the holy city Jerusalem coming down out of heaven from God. It has the glory of God and a radiance like a very rare jewel, like jasper, clear as crystal (Revelation 21:10-11).

The promised and expected bride is actually a city, the heavenly Jerusalem! This is not the first woman to represent a city in John's visions. The harlot mentioned above is identified as Babylon (a cryptic title for Rome), the capital city of the Roman Empire, which metes out violence and oppresses God's people. In contrast, the holy city of Jerusalem sent to earth from God will serve as the capital of God's kingdom, from which he will govern the world. It is described as a glorious city because it reflects the glory of God and as a radiant city because it sparkles like a precious jewel. John likens it to jasper, a stone with the brilliance of a many-faceted blue-white diamond, in order to illustrate the city's splendor. The new Jerusalem is actually composed of God's people, which means we will reflect the glory of God. We will shine like the stars!

Additional Symbols and Specifics

What must John have thought as he saw the holy city descending?

How did he interpret the meaning of the visionary symbols? Did he have to meditate on them before he wrote them down on paper? How did he go about choosing the right words to describe the new Jerusalem? Many people read Revelation as if it contains ordinary prose. This is a mistake. As a result they interpret it as you would a recipe in a cookbook—"three ounces of milk and a cup of sugar" means exactly what it says. But the book of Revelation is apocalyptic literature, a genre that we must approach differently than we would most other genres. Among other things, apocalyptic literature contains signs and symbols with meanings that are not always clear. As we read the next few paragraphs, you will see what I mean. They challenge us to be careful and judicious in our interpretation. Speaking of the new Jerusalem, John writes this:

> It has a great, high wall with twelve gates, and at the gates twelve angels, and on the gates are inscribed the names of the twelve tribes of the Israelites; on the east three gates, on the north three gates, on the south three gates, and on the west three gates. And the wall of the city has twelve foundations, and on them are the twelve names of the twelve apostles of the Lamb (Revelation 21:12-14).

In John's day, a large city was usually surrounded by a high wall to protect it from enemy invasion and to keep out undesirables. But the walls were not invincible. In AD 70, Roman soldiers stormed and penetrated the walls of the earthly Jerusalem, destroying the city and scattering the people. In time, Rome itself fell. This will not happen in the new Jerusalem because its walls are made in heaven.

The point of this section of the vision is that the city will be a safe place to live. God will protect you. You will never have to worry about who may be lurking behind a bush, waiting to attack you. Nor will you need to lock the doors of your house. Just think of the relief some people will experience who now live in bad neighborhoods and fear for their lives.

The new Jerusalem has 12 gates upon which are written the names of the 12 tribes. In most ancient cities, gates were labeled according to their function, such as Fish Gate, Dung Gate, Sheep Gate, Horse Gate,

and Water Gate (Nehemiah 3:1-8). These gates, however, are designated as tribal entrances: one for the tribe of Judah, another for Benjamin, another for Reuben, and so on. What does this imagery mean? It
likely indicates that Old Testament saints who lived faithfully in covenant relationship with God will be part of the new Jerusalem.

The vision doesn't stop there. Others will inhabit the city as well.
John notices the city rests on 12 foundations, inscribed with the names
of the apostles of the Lamb, most likely representing new-covenant
believers who have given their allegiance to the crucified and glorified
Messiah. That the city has a foundation speaks of stability. In the modern world, cities are leveled by earthquakes, hurricanes, and tornadoes.
The new Jerusalem, however, will not only be safe, it will be secure.
There will be a permanency to it, unlike Israel's portable tent city in
the wilderness or any other tent city occupied by protesters or nomads.

After establishing that old- and new-covenant believers comprise
the city's residents, John gives the parameters of the city.

> The angel who talked to me had a measuring rod of gold to
> measure the city and its gates and walls. The city lies four-
> square, its length the same as its width; and he measured
> the city with his rod, fifteen hundred miles; its length and
> width and height are equal. He also measured its wall, one
> hundred forty-four cubits by human measurement, which
> the angel was using (Revelation 21:15-17).

Once again, it's important that we do not approach the text too literally. Rather than focusing on the precise dimensions of the city, let's
look for their meaning. In other words, what is John trying to convey
through this imagery? As Wes Howard-Brook notes, "The cube was a
symbol of perfection par excellence."[1] It mirrored the Holy of Holies,
a cubed enclosure within the temple where God resided (1 Kings 6:20).
Those commentators and teachers who interpret apocalyptic literature
according to a stiff literalism will often miss this point. This passage is
not about geographical boundaries or square mileage, but about perfection and moral uprightness.[2] The new Jerusalem will be the dwelling place of God, the home of the righteous made perfect, and a place

where justice prevails. There will be nothing in it that compromises or impairs its perfection.

The City of a Thousand Points of Light

> The wall is built of jasper, while the city is pure gold, clear as glass. The foundations of the wall of the city are adorned with every jewel; the first was jasper, the second sapphire, the third agate, the fourth emerald, the fifth onyx, the sixth carnelian, the seventh chrysolite, the eighth beryl, the ninth topaz, the tenth chrysoprase, the eleventh jacinth, the twelfth amethyst (Revelation 21:18-20).

As a young man I worked for a jewelry manufacturer. My lowly job involved machine-stamping 10-karat gold high-school and college rings. The skilled jewelers, however, designed and handcrafted some of the most beautiful rings and necklaces you could imagine. They worked mainly with the much more valuable 18-karat gold. Each piece was an original with many unique features. The most precious stones were chosen and placed in settings. Filigree and beautiful etchings were carved into the gold to accent the pieces. Each day I stopped by the row of jewelers' benches to watch these masters at work. I always came away amazed at the magnificence of their creations.

John the Revelator speaks of heaven on earth in terms of pure gold, which he depicts as clear as glass. Pure gold is 24-karat gold! It is the highest quality gold available. The only time I ever saw pure gold was at an exhibit at a museum of art, where the treasures of the ancient Etruscan Empire were on display. It was fantastic! The royal jewelry—earrings, headdresses, necklaces, bracelets, and signets—and the sacred vessels were made with pure gold. The depth and magnificence of the sheen was unbelievable.

By choosing the most precious metal known in his day, John conveys the sense that the new Jerusalem is beautiful beyond compare, like a highly buffed piece of pure gold. It dazzles like the finest jewels made exclusively for the richest people in the world. In other words, it is first-class all the way. You might be facing financial difficulty and living on a shoestring now, but one day in the new Jerusalem, you will be treated like royalty.

Next, John lists the construction materials of the new Jerusalem. Most major cities are made of brick and mortar, but John twice mentions jasper (to which he referred in verse 11) in addition to 11 other stones of various colors as the building blocks of this holy metropolis. The new Jerusalem comes out of heaven, so these are not jewels mined from the ground. Rather, John uses the most cherished earthly materials he knows to approximate the heavenly reality. John chooses these particular stones for their brilliance and variety of colors in a feeble effort to describe the most beautiful city eyes have ever beheld. The task was virtually impossible. Regardless of what you imagine the new Jerusalem to be like, it is far more stunning.

When God instructed Moses to build a tabernacle, a place where God could dwell temporarily among his people on earth, he told him to use certain earthly items in the construction that came relatively close to representing their heavenly counterpart. The tabernacle was exquisite and priceless, but it could not compare to God's heavenly home.

So when the apostle John gets a glimpse of God's heavenly home as it descends to earth, he is forced to use analogous human language to depict its majesty.

As he moves on to describe the gates and streets of the city, he resorts again to comparative language. "And the twelve gates are twelve pearls, each of the gates is a single pearl, and the street of the city is pure gold, transparent as glass" (Revelation 21:21). What else can John add to accentuate the city's beauty? He says that each gate is made of a single pearl. Now, that's a big pearl! It certainly is not a man-made pearl or one produced by an oyster. In order to describe what he sees in his vision, John chooses the image of a gigantic pearl. How else do you describe an enormous gem that is out of this world?

John adds that the streets are made of pure gold and are translucent. Even the surfaces where you will place your feet will be beautiful. Having been to Disney World, I have walked on some of the cleanest streets in America, but nothing like this! Again, we are dealing with symbolic language. As you know, pure gold (24-karat gold) is opaque, not transparent. Yet that's what comes to John's mind when he sees the streets in the vision. The streets must have a golden hue, and when you look down they are crystal clear.

The Sonburst

John proceeds to reveal even more details about the future capital of the kingdom. He adds, "I saw no temple in the city, for its temple is the Lord God the Almighty and the Lamb" (Revelation 21:22). We will not have to go to a local temple to worship God because God will be everywhere. We will have direct access to him. Remember the woman at the well, the one who asked Jesus whether people should worship God on Mount Gerizim or on Mount Zion? Jesus told of a day when true worship would be held in neither place, and he urged her even then to worship God in spirit and truth (John 4:24). Just as there was no temple in the garden of Eden and people freely walked and talked to God, so it will be when paradise is restored.

John continues in his account. "And the city has no need of sun or moon to shine on it, for the glory of God is its light, and its lamp is the Lamb" (Revelation 21:23). Until the late nineteenth century, nature alone provided humans with light. Sun, moon, stars, lightning, and fire were the sources of all light. When Thomas Edison, the Wizard of Menlo Park, invented the electric lightbulb, artificial light became a reality. The lighting system for the new Jerusalem will be totally different. Notice the unusual language. God is identified as being the light, but the crucified Jesus is called the lamp. That means the radiance or light of God will emanate through Christ and spread to the entire city. Therefore, the city will be lighted supernaturally by a divine power source.

I cannot fathom living in a city bathed in Sonlight. Can you? Will we be able to feel the rays of God's warmth on our bodies just as we feel the warmth of the sun?

Next we discover, "The nations will walk by its light, and the kings of the earth will bring their glory into it. Its gates will never be shut by day—and there will be no night there" (Revelation 21:24-25). For John in the first century, the nations and kings were those who were conquered and controlled by the Roman Empire and who gave their allegiance to Caesar. John now sees them living freely under the reign of God. The practice of a king bringing his glory to the capital was well known. Often client kings in the Empire brought their wealth and gifts to lay at the feet of Nero to acknowledge their loyalty to him.

When John mentions that the gates will never be shut, he is reiterating that God's kingdom will be a safe place. There will be no need to close the gates. His comment that there will be no night is intended to make the same point. The absence of darkness is meant to be a contrast to ancient Rome, where darkness meant danger. At night, gangs roamed the streets, prostitutes came out, people got drunk, and robbers broke into houses.

John completes his thought on this matter when he writes, "People will bring into it the glory and the honor of the nations. But nothing unclean will enter it, nor anyone who practices abomination or falsehood, but only those who are written in the Lamb's book of life" (Revelation 21:26-27). Here we see that all the nations of the world will align with the kingdom. There will be no discord or resistance. Universal peace will reign over the earth. There will be no terrorist attacks, assassinations, or wars. Those practicing abominations, which according to Revelation 21:7-8 include the "cowardly, the faithless, the polluted, the murderers, the fornicators, the sorcerers, the idolaters, and all liars," will have no place in the kingdom of God. Their lot is the lake of fire. These abominable persons consist of those who pledge faith to Christ but then declare Caesar to be Lord in order to keep their jobs or save their lives, those who encourage others to do likewise, and those who persecute the faithful. Only those found in the book of life will inherit the kingdom of God.

In John's day, faithfulness to the Empire and its gods was a prerequisite for steady employment. Tradespeople, for example, belonged to guilds that held monthly meetings where libations were poured out to Caesar and offerings were made to the guild's deities. Many church members participated in these activities in order to keep their jobs or escape persecution from the Roman government (Revelation 2–3). They likely reasoned, "I accept Jesus as my Lord, but I have to make a living. So I'll go through the motions of sacrificing to Caesar, but deep within my heart, my allegiance is to Christ." According to Christ, such a practice is not acceptable and amounts to denying the faith.

Some church members around the globe in our day face similar challenges. The apostle Paul affirmed, "If we endure, we will also reign with him; if we deny him, he will also deny us" (2 Timothy 2:12). Unfortunately, many professing Christians view faith as a one-time event that takes place at the start of the Christian walk. This mistaken understanding has led them to deny Christ while still claiming to believe in him. It is a contradiction in terms. Faith is by nature a life-long commitment. It carries the idea of faithfulness, allegiance, loyalty, fidelity, steadfastness.

What would you think of a soldier who took an oath of allegiance to the United States but ten years later sold secrets to Russia? Is he exhibiting faithfulness? Would we proclaim him a citizen of the United States in good standing, or would we consider him a traitor? To ask the question is to answer it. The mark of a believer is perseverance regardless of the cost, even if it means death. We do not persevere in order to get saved. Nor do we persevere in order to stay saved. We persevere because we are saved. The real believer is an overcomer. He does not bow the knee, but boldly proclaims allegiance to Jesus as reigning Lord.

The new Jerusalem will be populated with faithful believers. All others, regardless of whether they are church members, will not be allowed to enter.

The Resources of Life at Our Disposal

As John concludes his guided tour throughout the new Jerusalem, he offers a few more interesting details and then gives a concluding summary.

> Then the angel showed me the river of the water of life, bright as crystal, flowing from the throne of God and of the Lamb through the middle of the street of the city. On either side of the river is the tree of life with its twelve kinds of fruit, producing its fruit each month; and the leaves of the tree are for the healing of the nations (Revelation 22:1-2).

Several things warrant mention. The water of life, referenced already in Revelation 21:6, is now characterized as a streaming river that traces its source to the reigning God and to the Lamb, who is emblematic of the crucified and risen Messiah. From there the sparkling waters are dispersed and run through the center of town. What does this picture imply? In the garden of Eden, a similar river watered the ground and sustained life (Genesis 2:6-14). Located in the heart of the city, the water of life is readily available to all. The foliage of the new Jerusalem will be lush and green because of the life-giving properties of its water.

A tree of life that produces a monthly crop stands on each side of the river in the middle of the city. Notice that both the water and the tree are associated with life-giving properties. The tree of life is described in the book of Genesis as growing in the middle of the garden of Eden (Genesis 2:9; 3:22-24). God planted it to nourish Adam and Eve. As long as they ate of its fruit they possessed life. After their disobedience, God expelled them from the garden and stationed an angel with a flaming sword in front of the tree to keep Adam and Eve away. Paradise was lost. In the new Jerusalem, paradise is regained. All occupants will have access to the tree of life.

John adds, "The leaves of the tree are for the healing of the nations." The word translated "healing" comes from the Greek term *therapeitan*. Our words "therapy" and "therapeutic" are cognates and carry the varied meanings of curative, restorative, and calming.

In the late nineteenth and early twentieth centuries, the wealthy flocked to healing resorts, where they bathed in therapeutic hot springs and ate specially formulated diets. Many satisfied customers claimed a new vitality. Over time, however, these grand and opulent health resorts died out because of criticism and investigation by medical professionals.

Within the human heart resides a desire for health and life. Scientists work day and night as they race the clock to discover cures for deadly diseases and secrets to prolonging life. Despite our deepest yearnings and efforts, death still takes its toll. But in John's vision, the leaves of the tree of life possess curative powers, bringing healing for the nations. The prophet Ezekiel has a similar vision of the kingdom that includes healing leaves (Ezekiel 47:12).

In John's vision, the nations receive the healing. If ever the nations needed to be healed, they need it now. The world is in bad shape economically, ecologically, and especially morally. When John sees this vision, the nations are following the beast, the ruler of the Roman Empire. All the nations' resources and wealth flow from Rome. In Revelation 18, the nations fall into a great depression when the Empire comes under God's judgment. In God's kingdom the nations will be healed as they give their allegiance to Christ.

Under the reign of a compassionate God, creation will be restored. This is supported by the next words of John's vision.

> Nothing accursed will be found there any more. But the throne of God and of the Lamb will be in it, and his servants will worship him; they will see his face, and his name will be on their foreheads. And there will be no more night; they need no light of lamp or sun, for the Lord God will be their light, and they will reign forever and ever (Revelation 22:3-5).

The curse that began in the garden of Eden will be reversed. All creation will be redeemed. The environment will be perfect. Work will be a blessing and not toil.

If you are like I am, some workdays are more difficult than others. As a college professor, I may find myself teaching classes, working on a book or article, completing a committee assignment, advising students, attending a faculty meeting, and navigating rush-hour traffic in a city with three million cars—all in one day. On such occasions, I come home exhausted with my nerves on edge. I might even have a stress headache above my eye. I can't wait to put on something more comfortable, flop back in my recliner, and just "veg out." My batteries need recharging.

All the negative symptoms associated with work—pressure, anxiety, tension, nervousness and the like—are the result of living in a world that is out of kilter with the Lord's will. I can't wait for the arrival of the new Jerusalem, where nothing accursed will be found. The new world will be a place of total refreshment.

We are told that the throne of God and of the Lamb will be there. God will be the sovereign ruler over his kingdom. We will serve and worship him with pure motives and wholehearted devotion. Best of all, we will see his face. Now we see him through the eyes of faith, but then we will see him face to face. This means he will be looking at us as well.

In the Old Testament, the high priest related God's face with the blessing of his people: "The LORD bless you and keep you; the LORD make his face to shine upon you, and be gracious to you; the LORD lift up his countenance upon you, and give you peace" (Numbers 6:24-26). No greater comfort can be found than to know God watches over us. His face represents blessing, grace, and peace for his people.

John next mentions, "His name will be on their foreheads." This is his way of saying that we belong to God. We are his people. Our allegiance belongs to him.

In a concluding statement, John reiterates that in the new Jerusalem, there will be no more night and no need for natural or artificial light because "the Lord God will be their light." And then he adds, "They will reign forever and ever." We will be coheirs and corulers in the kingdom of God on earth.

The Trip of a Lifetime

Have you ever glanced at a colorful travel brochure or a vacation website? Each picture makes the destination look like paradise. Of course, the photographs are digitally enhanced to make the grass greener, the water bluer, the sand finer and whiter, and the rooms larger and more luxurious than they are in real life. The pictures of food look delectable and delicious. Everyone in the brochure appears to be happy and carefree. But graphics can be deceptive. They are intended to get you to book a trip. When you actually take the trip, you might be disappointed.

I'll never forget my first discouraging travel experience many years ago. My wife and I were on our honeymoon. We had planned our trip with great detail. After spending the first night on the road in a motel, we drove to our destination, Colonial Williamsburg (Virginia). The hotel looked great in the brochure. When we arrived, we thought we were in the wrong place. It was starkly furnished, and the staff was not friendly. After a nice evening of dining and conversation and walking the grounds of old town Williamsburg, we returned to our room. Like all newlyweds, we had plans for the rest of the night. No sooner had we gotten into bed than the world's largest roach crawled out from under the covers! He stopped and looked up at me as if to say, "What are you doing here?" You've never seen anyone jump as high and fast as I did. I flailed and wailed and squealed. With no other rooms available at the hotel, Lynn and I spent the entire second night of our honeymoon sleeping in orange leatherette chairs. The next day, with Williamsburg in the rearview mirror, we headed for the ocean.

In Revelation 21:1–22:6, John gives us a travel brochure of sorts. But unlike slick publicity pieces, he does not exaggerate when he describes our destination. He relates as accurately as possible what we can expect to see and experience when we enter the kingdom of heaven on earth. John's only difficulty is that he does not have words that are adequate to communicate the splendor. After all, how do you paint a picture of a perfect world, a utopian paradise that is unmatched by anything on earth?

John sees in his divinely produced series of visions the new Jerusalem descending from heaven and coming to earth. These visions are transitory, so he must recreate them from memory and draw for us word pictures designed to inspire a longing for our real home.

We now live in an imperfect world. Even America, arguably the best country on earth, is no match for the kingdom to come.

You might live in the richest part of the city, drive a $100,000 luxury automobile with all the bells and whistles, lunch at the most exclusive country clubs, vacation in Monte Carlo, and stay at the Ritz (or wish you could!). Still, such lifestyles of the rich and famous come far short of life in the kingdom of God. Even the wealthiest people in the world yearn for transcendence, something more than they presently experience—a real-life utopia that truly satisfies.

One day the kingdom of God will become a reality, and when it arrives, you will not be disappointed. But even before it appears, you can enjoy many of its benefits. So I invite you to join the journey of a lifetime. Come under the reign of Christ and begin to experience the kingdom of God in the here and now.

Notes

Chapter 1: Discovering the Kingdom

1. See William J. Abraham, *The Logic of Evangelism* (Grand Rapids: Eerdmans, 1989).

2. Lesslie Newbigin, *The Open Secret* (Grand Rapids: Eerdmans, 1978), 44.

3. Carl F.H. Henry, "Reflections on the Kingdom of God," *Journal of the Evangelical Theological Society* 35 (1992): 44.

Chapter 2: In the Beginning Was the Kingdom

1. Craig G. Bartholomew and Michael W. Goheen, *The Drama of Scripture: Finding Our Place in the Biblical Story* (Grand Rapids: Baker, 2004), 34.

2. Gordon Wenham makes this observation:

   > The garden of Eden is not viewed by the author of Genesis simply as a piece of Mesopotamian farmland, but as an archetypal sanctuary, that is, a place where God dwells and where man should worship him. Many of the features of the garden may also be found in later sanctuaries, particularly the tabernacle or Jerusalem temple. These parallels suggest that the garden itself is understood as a sort of sanctuary (Gordon J. Wenham, "Sanctuary Symbolism in the Garden of Eden Story," *Proceedings of the World Congress of Jewish Studies* 9 [1986]: 19).

   Likewise, the Hebrew phrase that describes God walking in the garden (Genesis 3:8) is also used to describe God moving among his people in the tabernacle or temple (Leviticus 26:12; Deuteronomy 23:14; 2 Samuel 7:6-7). If Greg Beale (*The Temple and the Church's Mission* [Downers Grove, IL: IVP, 2004], 66-67) is correct, Adam was likely the first priest of the garden temple. He is told to "tend [cultivate] and keep [guard]" it (Genesis 2:15 NKJV). This

297

same language is used only three other times in the Old Testament, where it refers to the Levit-
ical priests serving in the temple (Numbers 3:7-8, 8:26, and 18:5-6). Priests cultivated and pro-
tected the temple grounds, which included gardens. Beale concludes that the garden of Eden
was God's earthly sanctuary and set the stage for a successive series of temples, concluding with
the church, the bride of Christ, God's final temple.

The book of Revelation bears out such an interpretation: "Then I, John, saw the holy city,
New Jerusalem, coming down out of heaven from God, prepared as a bride adorned for her husband. And I heard a loud voice from heaven saying, 'Behold, the tabernacle of God is with men,
and He will dwell with them, and they shall be His people. God Himself will be with them and
be their God'" (Revelation 21:2-3 NKJV).

3. Bruce C. Birch, Walter Brueggemann, et al., *A Theological Introduction to the Old Testament*
(Nashville: Abingdon, 2005), 45.

4. Ibid., 49.

5. Vaughan Roberts, *God's Big Picture: Tracing the Storyline of the Bible* (Downers Grove, IL: IVP,
2002), 42.

6. See John Driver, *Images of the Church in Mission* (Scottdale, PA: Herald, 1997), 25.

Chapter 3: The Kingdom in the Old Testament Era

1. Georgia Harkness, *Understanding the Kingdom of God* (Nashville: Abingdon, 1974), 69.

2. An alternative interpretation is that the king is forbidden to build his military forces. God wants
the king to trust him (and not the size of Israel's army) for victories.

3. See, for example, Isaiah 1:4-5,15-23,28-29; 5:1-7,24; 6:1-13; 26:21; 30:1-5; Jeremiah 7:1-7; Hosea
4:1; 6:8; 10:4; Amos 2:6-16; 3:9-10; 4:1-13; 5:22; 6:12; Micah 3:1-2.

4. Richard A. Horsley, *Jesus in Context: People, Power and Performance* (Minneapolis: Fortress,
2008), 25.

5. Geza Vermes, *Who's Who in the Age of Jesus* (New York: Penguin, 2005), 16.

Chapter 5: God's Appointed and Anointed King

1. Matthew usually uses the term "kingdom of heaven," but the other Gospel writers always use the
term "kingdom of God." Some first-century Jews avoided as much as possible a direct reference
to God, so Matthew uses "heaven," a more ambiguous word. The terms "kingdom of heaven"
and "kingdom of God" are used interchangeably in the New Testament and mean the same thing.

2. Cicero, *De Divinatione*, trans. by W.A. Falconer, Loeb Classical Library series, no. 154 (Cam-
bridge: Harvard University Press, 1923).

3. James D.G. Dunn, *The Christ and the Spirit*, vol. 2 (Grand Rapids: Eerdmans, 1998), 50.

Chapter 7: Kingdom Healings and Miracles

1. For the most comprehensive treatment of postapostolic miracles, see Craig S. Keener, *Miracles:
The Credibility of the New Testament Accounts*, 2 volumes (Grand Rapids: Baker Academic, 2011).

Chapter 9: AM and FM Christians

1. Helen H. Lemmel, "Turn Your Eyes upon Jesus," public domain.

Chapter 10: The Church and Its Worldwide Mission

1. R. Newton Flew, *Jesus and His Church: A Study of the Idea of the Ecclesia in the New Testament*, 2nd ed. (New York: Epworth, 1943), 127.

2. Kathleen E. Corley, *Maranatha: Women's Funerary Rituals and Christian Origins* (Minneapolis: Fortress, 2010), 12.

3. Ibid. Also see Simon B. Jones, *The World of the Early Church* (London: Lion, 2011), 113.

4. Oscar Cullmann, *Peter: Disciple, Apostle, Martyr* (London: SCM, 1953), 18-19. Joachim Jeremias, *Golgotha* (Leipzig: Pfeiffer, 1926), 73, notes a parallel in rabbinic literature, where Abraham is called the rock of the world: "When God looked upon Abraham, who was to appear, he said: Behold, I have found a rock on which I can build and base the world. Therefore, he called Abraham a rock."

5. George R. Beasley-Murray, *Jesus and the Kingdom of God* (Grand Rapids: Eerdmans, 1988), 183-84.

Chapter 11: The Final Week

1. Warren Carter, *Matthew and Empire* (Harrisburg, PA: Trinity International Press, 2001), 88.

2. N.T. Wright, *How God Became King* (New York: Harper One, 2012), 181-83.

Chapter 13: I Pledge Allegiance to the Lamb

1. Cited in David J. Bosch, *Transforming Mission* (New York: Orbis, 1991), 167.

2. Günter Bornkamm, *Jesus of Nazareth* (London: Hodder and Stoughton, 1960), 46.

3. Oscar S. Brooks, *The Drama of Decision: Baptism in the New Testament* (Peabody, MA: Hendrickson, 1987).

Chapter 14: The Church as a Colony and Embassy

1. C.K. Robertson, *A Dangerous Dozen: Twelve Christians Who Threatened the Status Quo but Taught Us to Live like Jesus* (Woodstock, VT: Skylight Paths, 2011), 109.

2. Chester G. Starr, *The Emergence of Rome* (Ithaca, NY: Cornell University Press, 1953), 90.

3. John D. Crossan, "The Challenge of Christmas," *The Huffington Post*, December 12, 2011. www.huffingtonpost.com/john-dominic-crossan/the-challenge-of-christma_b_1129931.html. See also Marcus J. Borg and John D. Crossan, *The First Christmas* (New York: HarperOne, 2009), 166.

Chapter 15: The Kingdom-Focused Church

1. R. Alan Streett, *Subversive Meals: Eating the Lord's Supper under Roman Domination During the First Century* (Eugene, OR: Wipf and Stock, 2013). This book provides the biblical, theological, and historical basis for Christian communal meals.

2. See Romans 1:7; 1 Corinthians 1:2; 2 Corinthians 1:2; Galatians 1:2; Ephesians 1:1; Philippians 1:1; Colossians 1:1; 1 Thessalonians 1:1; 2 Thessalonians 1:1; Philemon 2; 2 John 1; 3 John 9; Revelation 1:4.

3. Stanley Hauerwas, "Why Clinton Is Incapable of Lying: A Christian Analysis," in Gabriel J. Fackre, ed., *Judgment Day at the White House* (Grand Rapids: Eerdmans, 1999), 31.

4. Robert Coleman, *Songs of Heaven* (Old Tappan, NJ: Revell, 1982).

Chapter 16: Heaven on Earth—the Ultimate Kingdom

1. Wes Howard-Brook and Anthony Gwyther, *Unveiling Empire: Reading Revelation Then and Now* (Maryknoll, NY: Orbis, 2008), 187.

2. According to Herodotus (1:178), ancient Babylon was built as a perfect geometrical and geographical square, but it could not produce righteousness in the hearts of its citizens.